THE RECORDING ENGINEER'S HANDBOOK

Second Edition

Bobby Owsinski

Course Technology PTR

A part of Cengage Learning

COURSE TECHNOLOGY
CENGAGE Learning

Australia • Brazil • Japan • Korea • Mexico • Singapore • Spain • United Kingdom • United States

COURSE TECHNOLOGY
CENGAGE Learning

The Recording Engineer's Handbook, Second Edition

Bobby Owsinski

Publisher and General Manager, Course Technology PTR:
Stacy L. Hiquet

Associate Director of Marketing: Sarah Panella

Manager of Editorial Services: Heather Talbot

Marketing Manager: Mark Hughes

Executive Editor: Mark Garvey

Project Editor/Copy Editor: Cathleen D. Small

PTR Editorial Services Coordinator: Jen Blaney

Interior Layout : Jill Flores

Cover Designer: Mike Tanamachi

Indexer: Katherine Stimson

Proofreader: Heather Urschel

For product information and technology assistance, contact us at
Cengage Learning Customer & Sales Support, 1-800-354-9706

For permission to use material from this text or product,
submit all requests online at **cengage.com/permissions**
Further permissions questions can be emailed to
permissionrequest@cengage.com

Front and back cover photos were taken at Sonora Recorders in Los Feliz, California, by Edward Colver. Thanks to Richard Baron of Sonora.

All trademarks are the property of their respective owners.

Library of Congress Control Number: 2008935092

ISBN-13: 978-1-59863-867-7

ISBN-10: 1-59863-867-X

Course Technology, a Part of Cengage Learning
20 Channel Center Street
Boston, MA 02210
USA

Cengage Learning is a leading provider of customized learning solutions with office locations around the globe, including Singapore, the United Kingdom, Australia, Mexico, Brazil, and Japan. Locate your local office at: **international. cengage.com/region**

Cengage Learning products are represented in Canada by Nelson Education, Ltd.

For your lifelong learning solutions, visit **courseptr.com**

Visit our corporate website at **cengage.com**

Printed in Canada
4 5 6 7 11 10 09

About the Author

A longtime veteran of the music industry, **Bobby Owsinski** has worked with a wide variety of artists as a producer/engineer, guitar and keyboard player, and songwriter for records, DVDs, motion pictures, and television shows. One of the first to delve into surround-sound music mixing, Bobby has worked on more than 200 surround projects and DVD productions for such diverse acts as Elvis, Jimi Hendrix, The Who, Willie Nelson, Neil Young, The Ramones, and Chicago, among many, many others. Currently a principal in the music production house Surround Associates and content creator 2B Media, Bobby has also penned several hundred articles for many popular music and audio trade publications and has authored books that are now staples in audio recording programs in colleges around the world, including *The Mixing Engineer's Handbook* (Course Technology PTR, 2007), *How To Make Your Band Sound Great* (Hal Leonard, 2009), *The Mastering Engineer's Handbook: The Audio Mastering Handbook* (Course Technology PTR, 2007), and *The Drum Recording Handbook* (Hal Leonard, 2009). A frequent moderator, panelist, and program director for a variety of music and professional audio industry conferences, Bobby has served as the longtime producer of the annual Surround Music Awards and is currently an executive producer for the *Guitar Universe* and *Favorite Music of the Stars* television programs. Visit Bobby's website and blog at www.bobbyowsinski.com.

Contents

Introduction

When the first edition of this book was written back in 2002, the recording world was a different place. There were still quite a few real commercial studios around to record in, the old studio structure of master and apprentice engineer was still in place, and record labels were still where you wanted to be if you were an artist. Boy, everything has really changed seven years later. Anyone can have a pretty good-sounding personal studio for not much money, record labels have lost all of their power, and because there aren't a lot of commercial studios around anymore, there aren't many pro engineers to pass on the tricks of the trade—which makes this book all the more useful.

The idea behind my books is to preserve the techniques of the recording masters for history and pass those techniques on to you, the reader. That might not be as hands-on or efficient as the master/apprentice (engineer and assistant) system used in large facilities for 50 years, but at least there's something to refer to if you don't know how to record an instrument and there's no one around to ask.

In this new era of samples, loops, and modeling, there's a whole generation of engineers who have grown up with little working knowledge of microphone technique, and that's understandable when you can make great recordings without ever having to do much tracking. But sooner or later there will be a time when questions such as "What's the best way to mike the snare to really make it punchy?" and "How do I get a big guitar sound like [*name your favorite artist*] gets?" can cause a mild panic. That's where this book comes in.

While there are many books available that touch upon the basics of recording (especially stereo orchestral material), there aren't many books that feature multiple techniques in miking a wide variety of instruments in the detail needed to achieve a reasonable and consistent result. And there is no book that concentrates upon this basic, yet all-important facet of recording in quite the same way as it's presented here.

To that end, *The Recording Engineer's Handbook, Second Edition* is not meant to be a replacement for the many books that have long been the staple of microphone and recording background. It's meant to be a reference book. And that being said, I have provided a brief overview of the technical basics for those new to the subject.

As you'll see, there are many ways to get the same basic result. There's no right way to mike an instrument, but some ways are more accepted than others and therefore become standards. Whenever possible, I've tried to provide a high-resolution photo of a described miking technique taken during an actual session, as well as a written description of the theory behind and the variables of the technique.

Chapters 1 through 9 of this book take a look at microphone basics, as well as some classic models frequently used and the techniques used by the best tracking engineers in the business. Of special interest in Chapter 7 is the interview with Ross Garfield, "The Drum Doctor," who gives some tips and techniques for making the drum kit sound its best in the studio.

Chapters 10 and 11 give an overview of what tracking is about to become with the emergence of surround sound. Chapter 12 provides a final recording checklist you can refer to if things just don't sound right. Chapters 13 through 25 contain interviews with a number of engineers whom you'll meet in a moment. The book ends with a glossary of useful terms for your reference.

Meet the Engineers

Here's a list of the engineers who contributed to this book, along with some of their credits. You'll find that there are some industry legends here, as well as others who specialize in all different types of music. I'll be quoting them from time to time, so I wanted to introduce them early on so you have some idea of their background when they pop up.

▶ **Chuck Ainlay.** Chuck Ainlay is one of the new breed of Nashville engineers who brings a rock-and-roll approach to country music sensibility. With credits such as George Strait, Dixie Chicks, Vince Gill, Patty Loveless, Wynonna, and even such rock icons as Dire Straits and Mark Knopfler, Chuck's work is heard worldwide.

▶ **Steve Albini.** One of the most respected of the new breed of engineers, Steve Albini gained his considerable experience and reputation working primarily with underground and alternative bands. While his most famous credit remains Nirvana's *In Utero*, Steve has worked with a diverse lineup of artists such as PJ Harvey, The Pixies, The Breeders, Silkworm, The Jesus Lizard, Nina Nastasia, and even the mainstream Jimmy Page/Robert Plant *Walking into Clarksdale*.

▶ **Michael Bishop.** There are few more versatile engineers today than Michael Bishop, easily shifting between the classical, jazz, and pop worlds. Shunning the current recording method requiring massive overdubbing, Michael instead mostly utilizes the old-school method of mixing live on the fly, with spectacular results. Working exclusively for the audiophile Telarc label, Michael's highly regarded recordings have become reference points for the well done.

▶ **Bruce Botnick.** Few engineers have the perspective on recording that Bruce Botnick has. After starting his career in the thick of the L.A. rock scene recording hits for The Doors, The Beach Boys, Buffalo Springfield, The Turtles, and Marvin Gaye, Bruce became one of the most in-demand movie soundtrack recordists and mixers, with blockbuster credits including *Star Trek, Poltergeist, Air Force One, Aladdin, Mulan, ET,* and most recently *The Sum of All Fears, Scooby-Doo,* and *Star Trek: Nemesis.* Always on the cutting edge of technology, Bruce has elevated the art of orchestral recording to new heights.

▶ **Ed Cherney**. One of the most versatile and talented engineers of our time, Ed Cherney has recorded and mixed projects for The Rolling Stones, Iggy Pop, Bob Dylan, Was (Not Was), Elton John, Bob Seger, Roy Orbison, and the B-52s, along with many, many others. Ed has also recorded and mixed the multiple Grammy-winning *Nick of Time* and *Luck of the Draw* CDs for Bonnie Raitt, and he engineered the Grammy-winning "Tears in Heaven" track for the Eric Clapton–scored film, *Rush.*

▶ **Wyn Davis.** Best known for his work with the hard-rock bands Dio, Dokken, and Great White, Wyn Davis's style in that genre is as unmistakable as it is masterful. From his Total Access studios in Redondo Beach, California, Wyn's work typifies old-school engineering coupled with the best of modern techniques.

▶ **Frank Filipetti.** From Celine Dion, Carly Simon, James Taylor, Tony Bennett, and Elton John to Kiss, Korn, Fuel, Foreigner, and Hole, Frank Filipetti's credits run the entire musical spectrum. Known for his fearless ability to either extensively experiment or get instant sounds as the session dictates, Frank's old-school wisdom combined with his adventuresome and modern approach continues to push the cutting edge.

▶ **Eddie Kramer.** Unquestionably one of the most renowned and well-respected producer/engineers in all of rock history, Eddie Kramer's credits list is indeed staggering. From rock icons such as Jimi Hendrix, The Beatles, The Rolling Stones, Led Zeppelin, Kiss, Traffic, and The Kinks to pop stars Sammy Davis Jr. and Petula Clark, as well as the seminal rock movie, *Woodstock,* Eddie is clearly responsible for recording some of the most enjoyable and influential music ever made.

► **Mark Linett.** Mark Linett is a Sunset Sound alumnus who went on to a staff position at the famous Warner Bros.–owned Amigo Studios before subsequently putting a studio in his house. You've heard his work many times, with engineering credits for the likes of the Beach Boys, Brian Wilson, America, Rickie Lee Jones, Eric Clapton, Christopher Cross, Buckwheat Zydeco, Randy Newman, Michael McDonald, and many more.

► **Mack.** With a Who's Who list of credits such as Queen, Led Zeppelin, Deep Purple, The Rolling Stones, Black Sabbath, Electric Light Orchestra, Rory Gallagher, Sparks, Giorgio Moroder, Donna Summer, Billy Squier, and Extreme, the producer/engineer who goes simply by the name Mack has made his living making superstars sound great. Having recorded so many big hits that have become the fabric of our listening history, Mack's engineering approach is steeped in European Classical technique coupled with just the right amount of rock-and-roll attitude.

► **Al Schmitt.** After 11 Grammys for Best Engineering and work on more than 150 gold and platinum records, Al Schmitt needs no introduction to anyone even remotely familiar with the recording industry. Indeed, his credit list is way too long to print here (but Henry Mancini, Steely Dan, George Benson, Toto, Natalie Cole, Quincy Jones, and Diana Krall are some of them), but suffice it to say that Al's name is synonymous with the highest art that recording has to offer.

You'll also hear from these special non-engineer guests:

► **Ross Garfield, "The Drum Doctor."** Anyone recording in Los Angeles certainly knows about the Drum Doctors, the place in town to either rent a great-sounding kit or have your kit fine-tuned. Ross Garfield is the "Drum Doctor," and his knowledge of what it takes to make drums sound great under the microphones may be unlike anyone else's on the planet. Having made the drums sound great on platinum-selling recordings for the likes of Alanis Morissette, the Black Crowes, Bruce Springsteen, Rod Stewart, Metallica, Marilyn Manson, Dwight Yoakam, Jane's Addiction, Red Hot Chili Peppers, Foo Fighters, Lenny Kravitz, Michael Jackson, Rage Against the Machine, Sheryl Crow, Nirvana, and many more than can comfortably fit on this page, Ross agreed to share his insights on making drums sound special.

► **Jerry Hey, "Trumpeter Extraordinaire."** There may be no other trumpet player as respected and widely recorded as Jerry Hey. The first call for a Hollywood recording date for more than 25 years, Jerry has not only played on thousands of recordings by just about every major artist as well as movie soundtracks too numerous to mention, but he is also a widely sought-after arranger. So when it comes to what it takes to make brass sound great in the studio, it's best to get the facts straight from the master.

▶ **Michael Beinhorn.** With credits that include Aerosmith, Soundgarden, Soul Asylum, Red Hot Chili Peppers, Ozzy Osbourne, Fuel, Korn, and Marilyn Manson, producer Michael Beinhorn is no stranger to music that rocks. But unlike many others who work in that genre, Michael approaches the music with a care and concern usually associated with more traditional styles of acoustic music.

▶ **David Bock.** Not many people know as much about microphones as Soundelux Microphones co-founder and managing director David Bock. From repairing vintage mics of all kinds to building newer versions of the classics, David knows why and how they work and why they are made the way they are.

I'm sure you'll find these interviews as much fun to read as they were for me to conduct. I'm also sure that even if you're pretty good at recording, you'll find some interesting techniques in the book that you never thought of and might find useful along the way. I know I did.

CHAPTER 1

How Microphones Work

Microphones appear in an almost endless variety of shapes, sizes, and design types, but no matter what their physical attributes, their purpose is same—to convert acoustic vibrations (in the form of air pressure) to electrical energy so it can be amplified or recorded. Most achieve this by the action of the air vibrating a diaphragm connected to something that either creates or allows a small electron flow.

There are three basic mechanical techniques that are used in building microphones for professional audio purposes, but all three types have the same three major parts:

▶ **A diaphragm.** The sound waves strike the diaphragm, causing it to vibrate in sympathy with the sound wave. In order to accurately reproduce high-frequency sounds, it must be as light as possible.

▶ **A transducer.** The mechanical vibrations of the diaphragm are converted into an electronic signal by the transducer.

▶ **A casing.** As well as providing mechanical support and protection for the diaphragm and transducer, the casing can also be made to help control the directional response of the microphone.

Let's take a closer look at the three types of microphones—dynamic, ribbon, and condenser.

EDDIE KRAMER: *To me a microphone is like a color that a painter selects from his palette. You pick the colors that you want to use.*

The Dynamic Microphone

The dynamic microphone is the workhorse of the microphone breed. Ranging from really inexpensive to moderately expensive, there's a dynamic model to fit just about any application.

HOW IT WORKS

In a moving-coil (more commonly called *dynamic*) microphone, sound waves cause movement of a thin metallic diaphragm and an attached coil of wire that is located inside a permanent magnet. When sound waves make the diaphragm vibrate, the connected coils also vibrate in the magnetic field, causing current to flow. Since the current is produced by the motion of the diaphragm, and the amount of current is determined by the speed of that motion, this kind of microphone is known as *velocity sensitive* (see Figure 1.1).

Figure 1.1
Dynamic mic block diagram.

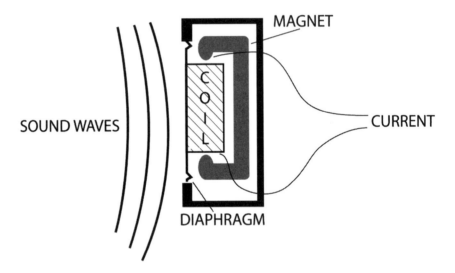

The ability of the microphone to respond to transients and higher frequency signals is dependent upon how heavy the moving parts are. In this type of microphone, both the diaphragm and the coil move, so that means it's relatively heavy. As a result, the frequency response falls off above about 10 kHz.

The microphone also has a resonant frequency (a frequency or group of frequencies that is emphasized) that is typically somewhere from about 1 to 4 kHz. This resonant response is sometimes called the *presence peak* because it occurs in the frequency region that directly affects voice intelligibility. Because of this natural effect, dynamic microphones are often preferred by vocalists, especially in sound reinforcement.

These microphones tend to be expensive because they're somewhat complex to manufacture, but they're generally very robust (you can actually hammer nails with some of them, and they'll still work!) and insensitive to changes in humidity.

▶ **Advantages:** Robust and durable, can be relatively inexpensive, insensitive to changes in humidity, needs no external or internal power to operate, can be made fairly small.

▶ **Disadvantages:** Resonant peak in the frequency response, typically weak high-frequency response beyond 10 kHz or so.

The Ribbon Microphone

The ribbon microphone operates almost the same as the moving-coil microphone. The major difference is that the transducer is a strip of extremely thin aluminum foil, wide enough and light enough to be vibrated directly by the moving molecules of air of the sound wave, so no separate diaphragm is necessary. However, the electrical signal generated is very small compared to that of a moving-coil microphone, so an output transformer is needed to boost the signal to a usable level (see Figures 1.2 and 1.3).

Figure 1.2
Ribbon mic block diagram.

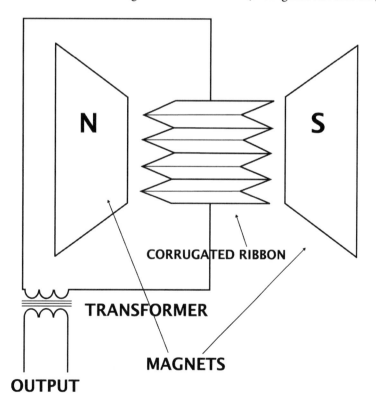

3

Figure 1.3
Ribbon mic transducer. Courtesy of
Royer Labs.

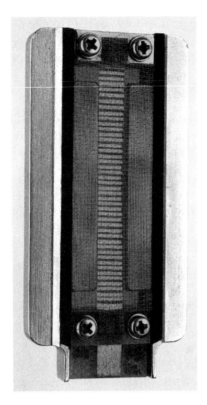

Like the dynamic microphone, the high-frequency response is governed by the mass of the moving parts. But because the diaphragm is also the transducer, the mass is usually a lot less than a dynamic type. As a result, the upper frequency response tends to reach slightly higher, to around 14 kHz. The frequency response is also generally flatter than for a moving-coil microphone.

All good studio ribbon mics provide more opportunity to EQ to taste because they "take" EQ well. Ribbon mics have their resonance peak at the bottom of their frequency range, which means that a ribbon just doesn't add any extra high-frequency hype like condenser mics do.

▶ **Advantages:** Relatively flat frequency response, extended high-frequency response as compared to dynamics, needs no external or internal power to operate.

▶ **Disadvantages:** Fragile—requires care during operation and handling, moderately expensive.

A Short History of Ribbon Microphones

You're going to read a lot about ribbon microphones in this book because they seem to have been rediscovered in recent years and therefore have recently returned to widespread use. So, a bit of history seems in order.

The ribbon-velocity microphone design first gained popularity in the early 1930s and remained the industry standard for many years, being widely used on recordings and broadcasts from the '30s through about the early '60s.

Ribbon-microphone development reached its pinnacle during this period. Though they were always popular with announcers and considered state of the art at the time, one of the major disadvantages of early ribbon mics was their large size, since magnetic structures and transformers of the time were bulky and inefficient. When television gained popularity in the late 1940s, their size made them intrusive on camera and difficult to maneuver, so broadcasters soon looked for a more suitable replacement.

About that time, newer breeds of condenser and dynamic microphones were developed that were a lot more compact and far more rugged. As a result, television and radio began to replace their ribbons with these new designs. Since ribbon mics were being used less and less, further development was considered unnecessary, and the ribbon soon suffered a fate similar to that of the vacuum tube when transistors hit the scene.

Although ribbon mics might have been out of favor in broadcast, recording engineers never quite gave up on the technology. While always fragile, ribbon mics still provided some of the sweetest sounds in recording, as most old-school engineers realized. As a result, vintage ribbon mics commanded extremely high prices in the used marketplace.

Recently, a few modern manufacturers began to not only revive the technology, but improve it as well. Companies like Coles, Beyer, Royer, and AEA now make ribbon microphones at least as good as or better than the originals, and they are a lot more robust as well. Thanks to recent developments in magnetics, electronics, and mechanical construction, modern ribbon microphones can be produced smaller and lighter, yet still maintain the sound of their vintage forbearers while achieving sensitivity levels matching those of other types of modern microphones. Their smooth frequency response and phase linearity make them ideally suited for the digital formats that dominate the industry today.

The Condenser Microphone

The condenser microphone has two electrically charged plates—one that can move, which acts as a diaphragm, and one that is fixed, called a *backplate*. This is, in effect, a capacitor (or *condenser*) with a positively and negatively charged electrode and an air space in between. Sound depresses the diaphragm, causing a change in the spacing between it and the backplate. This change in capacitance and distance between the diaphragm and the backplate causes a change in voltage potential that can be amplified to a usable level. To boost this small voltage, a vacuum tube or FET transistors are used as an amplifier. This is why a battery or phantom power is needed to charge the plates and also to run the preamp. Because the voltage requirements to power a vacuum tube are so high and therefore require some large and heavy components, some microphones have the power supply in a separate outboard box (see Figure 1.4).

Figure 1.4
Condenser mic block diagram.

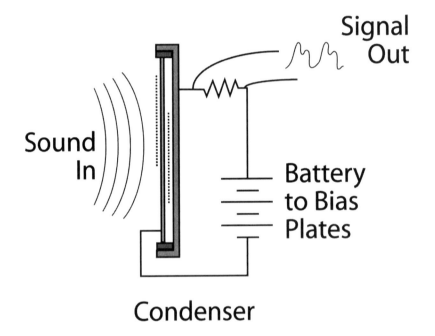

A condenser has an omnidirectional pickup pattern in its native state. In order to make it directional, little holes are punched in the backplate. The object of the holes is to delay the arrival of sound at the rear of the diaphragm to coincide with the same sound at the front, which then cancels the sound out. The size and position of the holes determines the frequencies that will be cancelled.

Most large-diaphragm condensers are multi-pattern microphones. This design consists of a single backplate placed between two diaphragms. By varying how much signal from each diaphragm is fed to the preamp, the microphone can have selectable patterns ranging from a tight cardioid, to a figure-eight, to full omnidirectional.

Condenser mics, however, always ring (resonate) a bit, typically in the 8- to 12-kHz range. A condenser mic's pattern of resonance is a major part of its character. Their built-in top-end response bump limits the EQ you might want to add, since a little bit of high-frequency boost can start to sound a bit "edgy" rather quickly.

The Electret Condenser

Another less expensive type of condenser microphone is the electret condenser. An electret microphone uses a permanently polarized electret material as a diaphragm, thus avoiding the necessity for the biasing DC voltage required in a conventional condenser. Electrets can be made very small and inexpensive and are the typical microphones on portable tape recorders. Better quality electret condensers incorporate a preamplifier to match their extremely high impedance and boost the signal. One of the problems with early electret condenser microphones, however, is that the electret material loses its charge over time.

▶ **Advantages:** Excellent high-frequency and upper harmonic response, can have excellent low-frequency response.

▶ **Disadvantages:** Moderate to very expensive, requires external powering, can be relatively bulky, low-cost (and some expensive) models can suffer from poor or inconsistent frequency response, two mics of the same model may sound quite different, humidity and temperature affect performance.

CONDENSER MIC FALLACIES

A large-diaphragm condenser has more low end than a small-diaphragm condenser.

This is not necessarily true. In many cases, small-diaphragm condensers reproduce the low end even better than their larger kin.

A cardioid condenser has a better low-end response than an omni.

Not true. In condenser mics with an omnidirectional polar response, the bass response is only limited by the electronics. So even a very small diaphragm can have a flat response down to DC.

A large-diaphragm condenser has a flatter response than a small-diaphragm condenser.

Not true. Large-format capsules are prone to low-frequency resonance, which means they can have trouble reproducing low frequencies at a high level. They "bottom out" by the diaphragm hitting the backplate, which is the popping that can occur when a singer is too close to an unfiltered microphone. In order to minimize this, some microphones over-damp the capsule, making the mic sound either thin or alternatively lumpy in response, while some address this by adding a low-frequency roll-off or EQ circuitry to try to put back frequencies suppressed in the capsule.

A small-diaphragm condenser is quieter than a large-diaphragm condenser.

Not true. The difference in the size of the diaphragm translates into a difference in signal-to-noise ratio. The bigger diaphragm gives you more signal for a certain electrical noise level and therefore can be quieter than the small diaphragm.

Condenser mics have consistent response from mic to mic.

They're not as close as you might think. Despite what the specs might say, there can be vast differences in the sound between two mics of the same model, especially in the less expensive categories. This particularly applies to tube-type mics, where there are not only differences between the capsules, but also matching of the tubes. This is usually the result of not enough attention being paid to small details during design and manufacture.

So unless two mics are specifically "matched," differences in response are inevitable. The exact value of precise matching of microphones is open to much debate, however. One school of thought says that you need closely matched response for a more precise stereo soundfield, while another school thinks that the difference can actually enhance the soundfield.

CONDENSER OPERATIONAL HINTS

While not particularly fragile, condenser microphones do require a bit more care than dynamic microphones. Here are some tips to keep your condenser mics sounding as good as new.

1. The most commonly seen problem with condenser microphones is dirt on the capsule, which causes the high-end response to fall off. Since a condenser is always carrying a static charge when operating, it will automatically attract small airborne particles. Add to this people singing and breathing into it, and you have your response slowly deteriorating. Because the metal film of the capsule is very thin, the layer of dirt can actually be much thicker than the original metal film and polymer support. Despite what is commonly believed, the mesh grill of the mic will not do much more than stop people or objects from touching the capsule, and the acoustic foam inside the grill has limited effect.

Cleaning a capsule is a very delicate and potentially damaging operation that is best left to a professional, so the next best thing is preventive maintenance.

- ▶ Always use a pop filter.

- ▶ Keep your condenser microphones cased when not in use.

- ▶ Cover the mic if it will be left set up overnight.

2. Humidity and temperature extremes can have undesirable effects on performance. When exposed to a warm or humid room after a period of very low temperature, condensation in the casing can cause unwanted noises or no signal until the unit has dried out.

3. Don't blow into the microphone. Some diaphragms can bottom out onto the plate and stick. (Switching off the microphone and disconnecting the power supply may unstick it, though.)

4. A condenser microphone can be overloaded, which can cause either distortion or harshness of tone. Usually this is not from the diaphragm overloading, but from the high output from the capsule overloading the built-in FET preamplifier. This is less likely in the case of a vacuum tube model since tubes naturally "soft clip" (overload in a sonically unobtrusive manner). Most internal mic preamps have a –10-dB pad switch to lower the output from the capsule. In the event that this is insufficient, the bottom-end roll-off will also reduce power from the capsule.

PHANTOM POWER

Unlike dynamic and ribbon microphones, all condenser microphones require power of some type. Older tube condensers require an outboard power supply, while electret condensers are sometimes powered with a battery. All other condenser microphones require power from an outside source, called *phantom power*. This is a 48-volt DC power source fed by a recording console, microphone preamp, or DAW interface over the same cable that carries the audio. On most recording consoles, phantom power is switchable, since it may cause a loud pop when disconnecting a cable connected to a dynamic mic.

Microphone Specifications

Although hardly anyone selects a microphone on specifications, it's good to know some of the issues. The following won't delve too much into the actual electronic specs as much as the considerations they imply for your application.

SENSITIVITY

This is a measure of how much electrical output is produced by a given sound pressure. In other words, this tells you how loud a microphone is. Generally speaking, for the same sound pressure, ribbon microphones are the quietest, while condensers, thanks to their built-in preamplifier, are the loudest.

Where this might be a concern is in how your signal chain is responding when recording loud signals. For instance, a condenser mic on a loud source might easily overload the console, outboard microphone preamp, or DAW interface because of its inherent high output.

On the other hand, the low output of a ribbon mic placed on a quiet source might cause you to turn up that same mic preamp to such a point that electronic noise becomes an issue.

Sensitivity ratings for microphones may not be exactly comparable, because different manufacturers use different rating systems. Typically, the microphone output (in a soundfield of specified intensity) is stated in dB (decibels) compared to a reference level. Most reference levels are well above the output level of the microphone, so the resulting number (in dB) will be negative. Thus, as in Table 1.1, a ribbon microphone with a sensitivity rating of −38 will provide a 16-dB hotter signal than a microphone with a sensitivity of −54 dB, which will in turn provide a 6-dB hotter signal than one rated at −60 dB. *Note that good sensitivity does not necessarily make a microphone "better" for an application.*

Table 1.1 Typical Microphone Sensitivities

Ribbon	Dynamic	Condenser
−60 (Beyer M160)	−54 (Shure SM57)	−38 (Neumann U 87 in omni)

OVERLOAD CHARACTERISTICS

Any microphone will produce distortion when it is overdriven by a loud sound level. This is caused by various factors. With a dynamic microphone, the coil may be pulled out of the magnetic field; in a condenser, the internal amplifier might clip. Sustained overdriving or extremely loud sounds can permanently distort the diaphragm, degrading performance at ordinary sound levels. In the case of a ribbon mic, the ribbon could be stretched out of shape, again causing the performance to seriously degrade. Loud sound levels are encountered more often than you might think, especially if you place the mic very close to loud instruments like a snare drum or the bell of a trumpet. In fact, in many large facilities, a microphone that has been used on a kick drum, for instance, is labeled as such and is not used on any other instrument afterward.

FREQUENCY RESPONSE

Although a flat frequency response has been the main goal of microphone companies for the last three or four decades, that doesn't necessarily mean that a mic is the right one for the job. In fact, a "colored" microphone can be more desirable in some applications where the source has either too much emphasis in a frequency range or not enough. Many mics have a deliberate emphasis at certain frequencies, which makes them useful for some applications (vocals in a live onstage situation, for example). In general, though, problems in frequency response are mostly encountered with sounds originating off-axis from the mic's principal directional pattern. (See the upcoming "Polar Patterns (Directional Response)" section.)

NOISE

Noise in a microphone comes in two varieties: self-noise generated by the mic itself (as in the case of condenser microphones) and handling noise.

Condenser microphones are most prone to self-noise because a pre-amplifier must be used to amplify the very small signals that are produced by the capsule. Indeed, the audio signal level must be amplified by a factor of more than a thousand, and any electrical noise produced by the microphone will also be amplified by that amount, making even slight amounts of noise intolerable. Dynamic and ribbon microphones are essentially noise-free but subject to handling noise.

Handling noise is the unwanted pickup of mechanical vibration through the body of the microphone. Many microphones intended for handheld use require very sophisticated shock mountings built inside the shell.

POLAR PATTERNS (DIRECTIONAL RESPONSE)

The directional response of a microphone is the way in which the microphone responds to sounds coming from different directions around it. The directional response is determined more by the casing surrounding the microphone than by the type of transducer it uses.

The directional response of a microphone is recorded on a polar diagram. This polar diagram shows the level of signal pickup (sometimes shown in decibels) from all angles and at different frequency ranges. It should be noted that all mics respond differently at different frequencies. For example, a mic can be very directional at one frequency (usually higher frequencies) but virtually omnidirectional at another.

A microphone's polar response pattern can determine its usefulness in different applications, particularly multi-microphone settings where proximity of sound sources makes microphone leakage a problem.

There are four typical patterns commonly found in microphone design: omnidirectional, figure-8, cardioid, and hypercardioid.

Omnidirectional

An omnidirectional microphone picks up sound equally from all directions. The ideal omnidirectional response is where equal pickup occurs from all directions at all frequencies. (See Figure 1.5.)

Figure 1.5
Omnidirectional polar pattern.

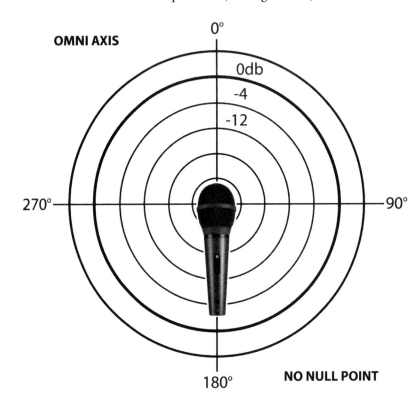

MICHAEL BISHOP: *I like to start with an omni before anything. Now, there are particular instances where I'll immediately go to something like a figure-8, but I'll use figure-8s and omnis more than anything.*

Figure of Eight

Figure of 8 (or *bidirectional* or *figure-8*) microphones pick up almost equally in the front and back, but nearly nothing on each side. It should be noted that the frequency response is usually a little better (as in brighter) on the front side of the microphone, although the level between front and rear will seem about the same.

Because the sensitivity on the sides is so low, figure-8s are often used when a high degree of rejection is required. (See Figure 1.6.)

Figure 1.6
Figure-8 polar pattern.

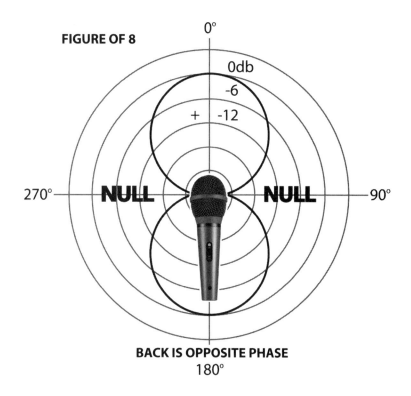

FIGURE OF 8

0°

0db

-6

+   -12

270°   90°

NULL   **NULL**

BACK IS OPPOSITE PHASE
180°

Cardioid

The cardioid microphone has strong pickup on the axis (in the front) of the microphone, but reduced pickup off-axis (to the side and to the back). This provides a more or less heart-shaped pattern, hence the name *cardioid*. (See Figure 1.7.)

Figure 1.7
Cardioid polar pattern.

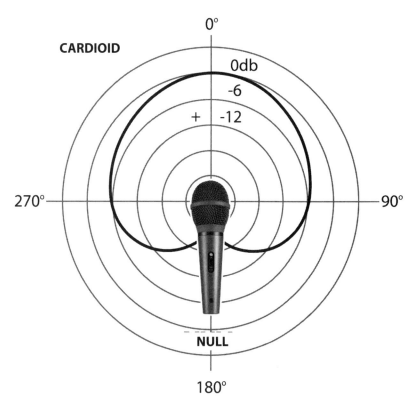

CARDIOID

0°

0db

-6

+   -12

270°   90°

NULL

180°

Hypercardioid Microphones

By changing the number and size of the ports (openings) on the case, it is possible to increase the directionality of a microphone so that there is even less sensitivity to sounds on the back and sides. (See Figure 1.8.)

Figure 1.8
Hypercardioid polar pattern.

PROXIMITY EFFECT

A peculiarity of the pressure-gradient microphone is that it has a different frequency response in the near and far field. Cardioid and hypercardioid microphones experience low-frequency buildup the closer you get to the mic, which is known as *proximity effect*. In many cases this can be used to good effect, adding warmth and fullness to the source, but it can also make the frequency response seem out of balance if it is not taken into account.

Specialty Microphones

Although not used much in music recording, there are several additional types of mics available for special situations.

SHOTGUN MICROPHONES

There are a number of applications that require an even more highly directional microphone, such as in news gathering, wildlife recording, or recording dialogue on movie and television sets. One such microphone is the shotgun (sometimes called *rifle* or *interference tube*) microphone. This consists of a long tube with slots cut in it connected to a cardioid microphone. (See Figure 1.9.)

Figure 1.9
Neumann KMR 82 shotgun mic.
Courtesy of Neumann USA.

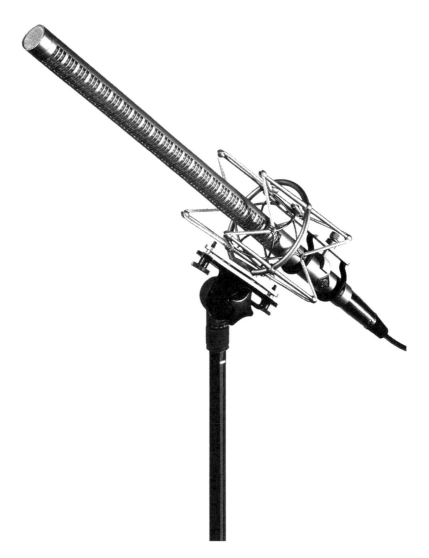

Sound arriving from the sides enters through a number of slots in the interference tube, and those frequencies tend to cancel at the microphone. Sound entering at the end of the tube goes directly to the microphone, providing large differentiation between the source and other background noise. The tube is normally covered with a furry windshield for outdoor use.

LAVALIERE

Extremely small "tie clip" microphones are known as *lavaliere* mics (sometimes just called *lavs*). They are usually electret condenser and omnidirectional and are generally designed to blend in with an article of clothing. One of the major problems with lavalieres is handling noise, which can be quite severe if an article of clothing (such as a jacket) is rubbing against it. Therefore, placement becomes crucial. (See Figure 1.10.)

Figure 1.10
DPA 4026 lavaliere mic. Courtesy
of DPA Microphones.

PZM

The *pressure-zone microphone*, or *PZM* or *boundary mic*, is designed to decrease the amount of echo or reverberation when recording in a large room. It accomplishes this by placing the microphone capsule very close to a flat surface. This flat surface is called the *boundary* and is why this type of microphone is also called a *boundary microphone*. Getting the microphone capsule close to the boundary cuts down on the large array of reflected sound waves hitting it from all angles. The waves that are reflected off of the closely positioned boundary are much stronger than waves that have bounced all around the room. This helps the microphone to become more sensitive, and as a result keeps the audio from sounding too reverberant.

PZM microphones, which are omnidirectional, are flat and designed to be mounted to a wall or placed on the floor or a tabletop. The bigger the boundary underneath the microphone, the better it will perform. The PZM is an omnidirectional microphone. (See Figure 1.11.)

Figure 1.11
Crown PZM6D microphone.
Courtesy of Crown Audio.

WIRELESS

It's long been the dream of many performers to increase their freedom by removing the connecting cable from the microphone, and guitarists in the studio have wanted to play in the control room ever since overdubs became possible. Until recently, wireless systems weren't of sufficient quality to use in the studio, but the latest generation has begun to rival the wired versions.

A wireless system consists of three main components: an input device, a transmitter, and a receiver. The input device provides the audio signal that will be sent out by the transmitter. It may be a microphone, such as a vocalist's handheld model, or a lavaliere "tie-clip" type. In wireless systems designed for use with electric guitars, the guitar itself is the input device.

The transmitter handles the conversion of the audio signal into a radio signal and broadcasts it through an antenna. The antenna may stick out from the bottom of the transmitter or it may be concealed inside. The strength of the radio signal is limited by government regulations. The distance that the signal can effectively travel ranges from 100 feet to more than 1,000 feet, depending on conditions.

Transmitters are available in two basic types. One type, called a *body-pack* or *belt-pack* transmitter, is a small box about the same size as a packet of cigarettes. The transmitter clips to the user's belt or may be worn on the body. For instrument applications, a body-pack transmitter is often clipped to a guitar strap or attached directly to an instrument, such as a trumpet or saxophone. In the case of a handheld wireless microphone, the transmitter is built into the handle of the microphone, resulting in a wireless mic that is only slightly larger than a standard wired microphone. Usually, a variety of microphone elements or *heads* are available for hand-held wireless microphones. All wireless transmitters require a battery (usually a 9-volt alkaline type) to operate. (See Figure 1.12.)

Figure 1.12
Shure UHF wireless transmitter and receiver. Courtesy of Shure Incorporated.

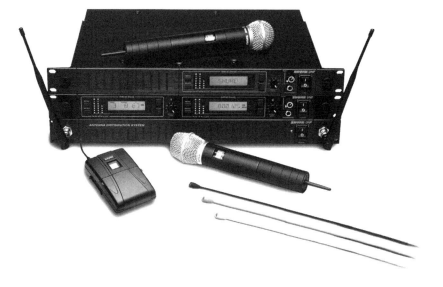

The job of the receiver is to pick up the radio signal broadcast by the transmitter and change it back into an audio signal. The output of the receiver is electrically identical to a standard microphone signal and can be connected to a typical microphone input in a sound system.

Wireless receivers are available in two different configurations. Single-antenna receivers utilize one receiving antenna and one tuner, similar to an FM radio. Single-antenna receivers work well in many applications but are sometimes subject to momentary interruptions or *dropouts* in the signal as the person holding or wearing the transmitter moves around the room.

Diversity receivers provide better wireless microphone performance. A diversity receiver utilizes two separate antennas spaced a short distance apart, utilizing (usually) two separate tuners. An "intelligent" circuit in the receiver automatically selects the better of the two signals, or in some cases a blend of both. Since one of the antennas will almost certainly be receiving a clean signal at any given moment, the chances of a dropout occurring are reduced.

Wireless systems operate in two different frequency spectrums: VHF and UHF. Audio performance for VHF and UHF is nearly identical, but some of the high-end (and much more expensive) UHF systems offer real improvements in audio bandwidth, transient response, and system noise floor. In terms of operational range or distance, UHF offers some advantages, especially in inhospitable RF environments. Another advantage is that broadband RF interference (compressors, elevator motors, computers, and so on) is often below UHF frequencies.

STEREO MICS

Stereo microphones are essentially two microphones in a single casing or body. These are designed primarily for ease of placement, since the body is considerably smaller than two separate microphones. An added advantage is that the capsules are normally closely matched in response. The capsules usually rotate in order to give some flexibility as to the recorded sound-field. Examples are the Royer SF-12, Neumann SM 69, Shure VP88, and AKG C 24. (See Figure 1.13.)

Figure 1.13
Neumann SM 69 stereo mic.
Courtesy of Neumann USA.

PARABOLIC

If you watch football on television, you've probably seen a parabolic microphone on the sidelines. This is usually a clear handheld dish that an operator will point out onto the field in an attempt to pick up some of the sounds of the games.

Similar to a radio telescope, a parabolic microphone is essentially an omni mic that is pointed toward the middle of a rounded (parabolic) dish. The dish provides acoustical amplification by focusing the sound on one place. If the dish itself acoustically amplifies a certain frequency range by 10 dB, it means that there's 10 dB less electronic amplification (and therefore 10 dB less noise) required within that range. The acoustical amplification increases with frequency, with the lowest frequency depending upon the diameter of the dish.

The problem with parabolic mics is that they will not respond to wavelengths longer than the diameter of the dish. This tends to make them sound unnatural for many sounds unless the dish is really huge.

Although widely used in sports broadcasting, it's not surprising that the parabolic microphone is one of the staples of the spying and espionage business as well. However, the most common use for parabolic mics in recording is to record birdcalls, since most bird chirps are only composed of high frequencies. (See Figure 1.14.)

Figure 1.14
Parabolic mic.

Microphone Accessories

A number of accessories have become indispensable in modern vocal recording.

POP FILTERS

Not to be confused with windscreens (see the following section), pop filters, either built into the mic (such as in a Shure SM58) or external, can work great or be of little value. All microphones are subject to plosives or pops. However, many engineers are fooled into thinking that a foam windscreen is all that's needed to control them when, in fact, positioning and vocal/microphone technique come more into play in the reduction of these pops. (See Figure 1.15.)

Figure 1.15
Pop filter (Pauly Superscreen
model 120-01). Courtesy Pauly
Superscreens.

The problem with pop screens built into mics is that they are simply too close to the capsule. Wherever high-speed air meets an obstacle, such as a pop screen, it will generate turbulence, which takes a few inches to dissipate. If the mic capsule is within that turbulence, it will pop. Another problem with acoustic foam used within microphones is that it becomes brittle over time, and eventually tiny bits of it break off and find their way inside the capsule (which is definitely not good for the sound quality).

Spitting on a valuable mic is a really big reason to use a pop screen. Condensation from breath can stop a vintage condenser microphone in its tracks in a very short time.

External pop screens are designed to be as acoustically benign as possible, especially in the areas of transients and frequency response. That being said, they are not acoustically transparent, especially at very high frequencies. A U 87–style windscreen will knock the response at 15 kHz down about 2 to 3 dB, for instance.

Although there are many models of pop filters available commercially, it's fairly easy to build your own. Buy an embroidery hoop and some pantyhose, cut a leg of hose until you have roughly a square sheet, clamp it in the embroidery hoop, then place it between the mic and the singer.

A lot of people affix pop filters to a gooseneck device that attaches to the boom stand that holds the mic. It's usually easier to mount to a pop filter on a second boom because it makes positioning less frustrating and more exact.

WIND SCREENS

Unlike pops, wind requires a completely different strategy. Wind isn't a nice, smooth flow, but rather turbulent and random. The noise that it causes is the change in air pressure physically moving the element or ribbon in the microphone. The vibrations of wind (which is low-frequency in nature) against the element are substantially stronger than the sound vibrations. Also, the more turbulent the wind, the less you will be able to find the null in a directional mic's response.

Although acoustic foam-only may be sufficient for omni mics in gentle breezes, directional mics require more elaborate two-stage windscreens. For any amount of wind, a "blimp," which is much more effective and will kill on the order of 20 to 30 dB, is required. Companies such as Lightwave and Rycote make a variety of blimps and windscreens that are frequently used for location recording. For windscreens in general, the larger it is, the more effective it be. A spherical shape is best because it's the least affected from wind in all directions. (See Figure 1.16.)

Figure 1.16
A blimp windscreen (Lightwave Superscreen). Courtesy of Lightwave Audio.

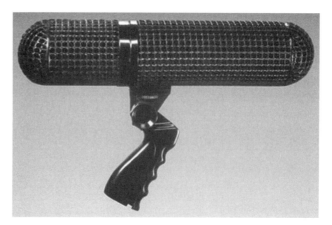

A trick that's been used on presidential outdoor speeches is to slip a condom (use the non-lubricated ones) over the microphone and then slip a foam windscreen over it to visually improve the arrangement. Although the frequency response will suffer, the wind noise will be attenuated.

SHOCK MOUNTS

Shock mounts are designed to shield the microphone from picking up transmission noises that occur through the mic stand. Shock mounting is largely dependent on the mass of the microphone. Large-diaphragm mics are much more massive, and therefore present a greater inertia to mechanical noise. Small-diaphragm mics, on the other hand, have far less mass and therefore do not present the inertia of their larger cousins. As a result, the shock mount has to be much "looser," therefore causing the mount to be "floppier" and sometimes more difficult to position. (See Figure 1.17.)

Figure 1.17
A shock mount.

CHAPTER 2

Common Microphones

It used to be that every studio had virtually the same mics in their microphone lockers. Not so much because that's all that was available, but because that's what every engineer used. Today, there's a wide variety of mics that will do the job well that range from the all-time classics, to new versions of the classics, to some new mics that are quickly becoming standards, to some very inexpensive mics that still do a great job. Let's take a look at each category.

Classic Microphones

One of the questions that I always got when I was teaching dealt with what the microphones that I frequently talked about actually looked like. It's one thing to speak abstractly about placing a 47 FET on the kick or C 12As as overheads, but unless you know what they look like, you're totally in the dark. Likewise, this book discusses the use of various "classic" microphones, so it seemed appropriate to include a section with not only some pictures, but a bit of history as well.

Classic mics refer to the tried and true. Although they may be old, they have proven over time to provide the sound that artists and engineers have found to be superior. Although one of the goals of this book is to promote the theory that good technique and placement alone are sufficient in getting good sounds, a set of microphones is an important set of tools. Certainly, these mics have proven to be successful tools over the long haul, and having one or more at your disposal will definitely help you in your quest for excellent-sounding recordings.

MICHAEL BEINHORN: *To me, if you are able to have access to them, you can't really have enough of them.*

RCA 44–STYLE RIBBON MICROPHONE

Developed in the late 1920s by the famous audio scientist Dr. Harry Olson, RCA's first permanent magnet bidirectional ribbon microphone, the 44, entered the market in 1931. The 44 had a relatively low cost, which helped propel it to its legendary success and vast market penetration of the time period.

The 44 series began with the 44A, which was a relatively large microphone mostly because it used a large horseshoe magnet around the ribbon. The slightly larger 44B was introduced in about 1938, with the 44BX model soon after. All were bidirectional with a frequency response extending from 30 cycles to 15,000 cycles. In contrast with the 44B, the 44BX had the ribbon mounted more toward the rear of the case, which gave it a smaller figure-8 lobe on the back side. The 44B was finished in a distinctive black with chrome ribbing on the lower portion, while the 44BX was an umber gray and stainless steel. All versions of the mic featured two jumper positions within the case—V (voice, which substantially attenuated the low-frequency response) or M (music).

The 44BX was manufactured up to around 1955. The 44B/BX has become one of the classic influences in microphone technology, is still in demand today, and has one of the most recognizable shapes in the world. (See Figure 2.1.)

Figure 2.1
RCA 44BX.

RCA 77 UNIDIRECTIONAL RIBBONS

Realizing the need for a directional mic, Dr. Olson developed the unidirectional 77A in the early 1930s. The 77A, B, and C models utilized double ribbons to achieve the unidirectional pattern. Improvements in magnet material allowed a significant reduction in size starting with the B model. The C and D models were capable of multiple patterns. The differences between the 77D and 77DX models are that the 77DX had an improved magnet and transformer that produced a little more output. A screwdriver-operated switch was provided at the bottom of the lower shell with positions marked M for music and V1 and V2 for voice. This switch inserted a hi-pass filter into the circuit that attenuated the low frequencies.

The 77 was discontinued around 1973, but its legacy continues because its shape remains the graphic icon for microphone that is recognized worldwide. This mic can still be seen today on *Larry King Live*. (See Figure 2.2.)

Figure 2.2
RCA 77DX.

NEUMANN U 47

The original U 47, which was first marketed in 1948, was actually distributed by Telefunken. It was the first switchable-pattern condenser microphone, capable of switching between cardioid and omnidirectional patterns. It uses the 12-micron-thick M7 capsule and VF-14 tube amplifier, which soon became the most popular of all U 47 capsule and amplifier combinations. (See Figure 2.3.)

The U 47 was updated in 1956 when the capsule finish was changed from chrome to matte and the body length was reduced by about 3 inches. Also, the U 48, a cardioid/bidirectional version, was introduced that year. Two years later, Neumann's distribution deal with Telefunken dissolved, enabling Neumann to distribute their own products under their own name.

Figure 2.3
Neumann U 47. Courtesy of
Neumann USA.

NEUMANN U 47 FET

Although now the *de facto* standard outside kick mic (if you can find one), the U 47 FET started its life in 1969 as Neumann's answer to Sony and AKG's FET-based microphones. (FET stands for *Field Effect Transistor*, which means it was solid state instead of tube.) While originally designed to take the place of the tube U 47, the 47 FET never found acceptance in that role. Thanks to its fixed hypercardioid pattern and its ability to take high SPL, the 47 FET eventually found a home in front of innumerable rock kick drums. (See Figure 2.4.)

Figure 2.4
Neumann U 47 FET. Courtesy of
Neumann USA.

NEUMANN U 67

With a streamlined, tapered body shape that has since become famous, Neumann introduced the U 67 in 1960. Thought of as an updated U 47, the U 67 featured a new Mylar film capsule, an internal 40-Hz hi-pass filter, and an amplifier pad switch to help overcome overload and proximity effect during close-up use. A three-way switch for selecting the directional pattern was added for extra versatility. The amplifier was based around the EF 86 tube. (See Figure 2.5.)

Figure 2.5
Neumann U 67. Courtesy of Neumann USA.

NEUMANN M 49/50

Designed in 1949, the M 49 was the first electronically remote-controlled variable-pattern condenser microphone. The M 50, a lookalike twin of the M 49, shares the same design shape and the AC701K tube, but it is strictly an omni designed for distant orchestral miking work. The mic features a high-frequency boost, and it becomes cardioid at high frequencies. The M 50 still reigns supreme as a Decca Tree microphone of choice for orchestral recording. (See Figure 2.6.)

Figure 2.6
Neumann M 49. Courtesy of Neumann USA.

NEUMANN KM 84 SERIES

First introduced in 1966, the KM 84 was the first 48-volt phantom-powered microphone and one of the earliest FET mics. One of Neumann's all-time bestselling mics, it was made in the tens of thousands between 1966 and 1988. The KM 84 has a cardioid pickup pattern, while the KM 83 is omni and the KM 85 is hypercardioid. (See Figure 2.7.)

Figure 2.7
Neumann KM 84. Courtesy of
Neumann USA.

In 1988, Neumann introduced the KM 100 series to replace the KM 80 series and incorporated several technical changes into the new series. In this series, the mics are modular with the FET amplifier in the capsule and not in the body of the mic itself. This enables the KM 100 series to have an extremely low profile (important for television work) since the mic body need not be directly attached to the capsule and can be located some distance away. The capsules are also interchangeable, with the AK 30 being omni and the AK 40 cardioid. Thus, the KM 140 is the cardioid mic from the KM 100 series and is the direct descendant of the KM 84.

This AK 40 capsule was retuned just slightly from the original KM 64/84 in that a bump in the upper mids (approximately +4 dB at 9 kHz) was added. The self-noise, output level, and maximum SPL specifications were all improved over the older 84 as well.

Since modularity is expensive, and engineers and musicians with project or home studios could not often afford the KM 140 as a result, the KM 184 was born. The same capsule was used from the KM 140, as well as the same FET, transformerless circuit, making the specs and performance the same. The KM 184 does not have a pad, and the capsules are not interchangeable.

NEUMANN KM 54/56

The KM 56 is a small-diaphragm tube condenser using an AC701 tube and featuring a dual-diaphragm nickel capsule with three polar patterns (omni, figure-8, and cardioid) selectable on the body. (See Figure 2.8.)

Figure 2.8
Neumann KM 54. Courtesy of Neumann USA.

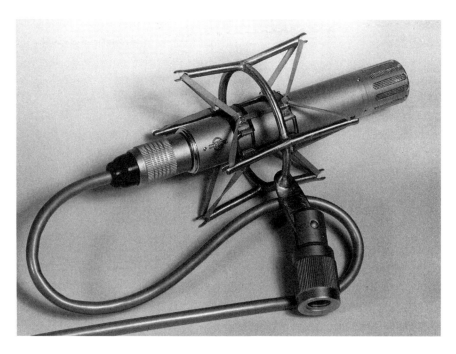

Despite its size, the sound character of the KM 56 is strikingly similar to a U 47 but with slightly less fullness in the bass and a more detailed top. The KM 54, which is cardioid only, is a brighter, slightly more aggressive-sounding mic, which works great for close-miking guitars and other acoustic instruments where you want to minimize the boominess resulting from the proximity effect when you get close. The KM 53 was the omni-directional member of the family.

Neumann stopped making the KM 54's all-metal diaphragms in 1969, in large part because their ultra-thin construction was so fragile. Since many thousands of KM 54 microphones had been sold, all of Neumann's stock of replacement capsules was then exhausted in attempting to keep those microphones functional.

By 1970, Neumann devised an adapter to let them use the Mylar capsules of the KM 60/70/80 series on the bodies of KM 53 or 54 microphones, along with a slight wiring change to correct the polarity of the output signal. This modification prevented a KM 53 or 54 with a broken capsule from becoming entirely useless. But the resulting microphone doesn't sound like a KM 53 or KM 54; instead, it sounds more like the model with the capsule being used with a more limited dynamic range.

NEUMANN U 87

The U 87 is probably the best known and most widely used Neumann studio microphone. First introduced in 1967, it's equipped with a large dual-diaphragm capsule with three directional patterns: omnidirectional, cardioid, and figure-8. These are selectable with a switch below the head grille. A 10-dB attenuation switch is located on the rear, which enables the microphone to handle sound pressure levels up to 127 dB without distortion. (See Figure 2.9.)

Figure 2.9
Neumann U 87. Courtesy of
Neumann USA.

The U 87 A has lower self-noise and higher sensitivity (in other words, for the same sound pressure level, it puts out a higher voltage) than the original U 87. The overall sound of the two models is generally quite similar. The U 87 could be powered by two internal photoflash batteries (22.5 V apiece). That option was removed in the U 87 A model.

The latest model, the U 87 AI, features a 6-dB hotter output and a slightly different frequency response in the midrange.

AKG D 12/112

Introduced in 1953, the D 12 was the first dynamic microphone with cardioid characteristics. Originally a standard choice for vocal applications for more than a decade, the mic's proximity effect and slightly scooped midrange eventually made it a favorite choice for rock kick drums. (See Figure 2.10.)

Figure 2.10
AKG D 12. Courtesy of AKG Acoustics.

The AKG Model D 112 is a descendent of AKG's earlier D 12 dynamic microphone, widely known for its ability to handle high-level signals from bass drums and bass guitars in the studio. The microphone was designed with a low-resonance frequency with the ability to handle very high transient signals with extremely low distortion. High-frequency response has been tailored to keep both bass drum and bass guitar clearly distinguishable in the mix. A built-in windscreen makes the D 112 also suitable for high SPL. (See Figure 2.11.)

Figure 2.11
AKG D 112. Courtesy of AKG Acoustics.

AKG C 12/TELEFUNKEN ELA M 250/251

AKG, which stands for Akustische und Kino-Gerate (Acoustic and Film Equipment), developed the original C 12 condenser microphone in 1953, and it remained in production until 1963. (See Figure 2.12.)

Figure 2.12
AKG C 12.

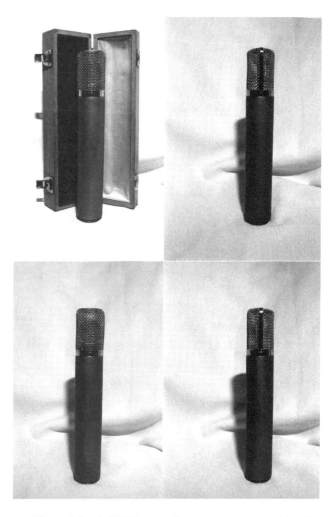

The original CK 12 capsule membrane was 10-micron-thick PVC but was later changed to 9-micron-thick Mylar. The amplifier design was based around a 6072 tube. The C 12 had a remotely controlled pattern selection from omni to bidirectional via the selector switch located in a box between the microphone and the power supply.

In 1965, AKG developed the C 12A, which shared the capsule design with the original C 12 (but not the electronics), but had a whole new body style—one that would foreshadow what was to become the 414 series.

In 1959, Telefunken commissioned AKG to develop a large-diaphragm condenser microphone, which soon became the Ela M 250 (which stands for *electroacoustic microphone*). This design incorporated the same CK 12 capsule but in a wider body with a thicker wire mesh grille, with a two-pattern selector switch (cardioid to omnidirectional) placed on the microphone. The Ela M 251 added a third bidirectional pattern to the switching arrangement. The 251E model indicates an export model and incorporates a 6072 tube amplifier. A plain 251 indicates the use of the standard German AC701K tube amplifier.

There were approximately 3,000 Elas (M and M251s) built between about 1964 and 1969, although Telefunken's original records were lost so no one knows for certain. Because of their full-bodied yet crisp sound, the C 12 and Ela M 250/251 microphones have since become some of the most expensive and highly prized vintage tube mics on the market today.

AKG C 451

With a styling reportedly based upon a large cigar smoked after a creative wine-tasting session, the 451 series was AKG's first FET amplifier featuring interchangeable capsules. Most 451s are usually found with CK-1 cardioid capsules, although some can be found with CK-2 omni capsules, CK-9 shotgun capsules, or the CK-5, which was a shock-mounted version with a large protective windscreen/ball end for handheld use. (See Figure 2.13.)

Figure 2.13
AKG C 451.

The 452 was identical to the 451 except it had an amplifier that required 48-volt phantom power, while the 451 could run on anything from 9 to 48 volts. As 48-volt phantom power became the standard, the 452 gradually replaced the 451.

Subsequent replacement versions of the 451 are the 460 and 480 series. These both feature flatter frequency response, quieter preamps, and more headroom, but never gained the same acceptance as the original 451. A reissue of the 451 with the popular CK-1 capsule, the C 451 B, is currently being produced.

AKG 414 SERIES

Basically the transistor version of the C 12A (see Figure 2.14), which used a Nuvistor miniature tube, the 414 has gone through many updates and changes through the years. Starting off as the model 412 in the early '70s, the mic was the first to use phantom power (12–48VDC) instead of an external supply. This version was susceptible to radio frequency interference if not modified, and since the grille housing was made out of plastic, it was prone to cracking.

Figure 2.14
AKG C 12A. Courtesy of AKG
Acoustics.

The C 414 EB (Extended Bass) was introduced in the late '70s and consisted of an all-metal silver housing. Early versions had the original brass CK-12 capsule, while the later ones had a plastic injected type. This mic was able to operate on phantom power of 9 to 48 volts. Of all 414 versions, this one seems to be the most desirable. (See Figure 2.15.)

The C 414 EB-P48 appeared sometime in the early '80s and is a 48V-only phantom-power version of the C 414 EB. The housing is black.

C 414 B-ULS stands for *Ultra Linear Series* and was introduced in the late '80s. This mic has a redesigned preamp that provides a flatter frequency response.

The C 414 B-TL is the exact same mic as the C 414 B-ULS except it uses a transformerless output stage, which gives the mic a slightly lower frequency response.

Figure 2.15
AKG C 414 B-TLII. Courtesy of
AKG Acoustics.

The C 414 B-TLII is the same mic as the C 414 B-TL except it uses the TLII version of the CK-12 plastic injected capsule, which was designed to give a high-end boost to emulate the sound of the original brass CK-12.

The C 414 B-XLS is the latest version in the 414 family, featuring a slightly larger grill and body, decreased handling noise, and higher sensitivity. It also incorporates an entirely new electronics section that does away with the old mechanical switches and replaces them with flush-mounted electronic pushbuttons for pattern, attenuation, and low-pass filter. The XLS has five pattern choices, including a new wide cardioid position; attenuation choices of 0, –6, –12, or –18 dB; and low-pass filter positions of flat, –12 dB at 40 Hz, –12 dB at 80 Hz, and –6 dB at 160 Hz.

The C 414B-XL II is the same as the XLS version except for a pronounced presence peak at 3 kHz.

All 414s feature a multi-pattern switch on the front and a 10-dB pad and hi-pass filter switch on the rear of the casing.

SONY C-37A

Introduced in 1955, the C-37A was Sony's answer to the Neumann U 47. In fact, the original C-37A was considered the finest general-purpose condenser mike available until Neumann answered it with the U 67, which incorporated many of its features (such as the high-frequency resonance filtered out, the shape of the windscreen, and the built-in low-cut filters). (See Figure 2.16.)

Figure 2.16
Sony C-37A.

The C-37A is a tube mic with a single diaphragm and pattern switching from omni to cardioid that is achieved by a mechanical vent, which is opened and closed with a screwdriver. This is very unique for a large-diaphragm mic (to get multiple patterns with only one diaphragm), and is what some feel is the secret to its sweet sonic character. The C-37A was first manufactured with the power supply model CP2, which used a tube for the main B+ voltage supply. This was later replaced with a completely solid-state power supply—the model CP3B.

The C-37P was introduced in 1970 and was mechanically identical to the tube C-37A except that it used an FET instead of a preamp with a 6AU6 tube. This version of the mic is far less desirable than the original A model.

SCHOEPS M 221B

The Schoeps M 221B is an interchangeable system in which 10 different capsules with different directional or frequency response characteristics can be attached to a tube amplifier body. Schoeps in general—and this mic in particular—is known for its sweet, smooth sound, especially off-axis. (See Figure 2.17.)

Figure 2.17
Schoeps M 221B. Courtesy of
Schoeps GmbH.

As with so many vintage mics, the condition of the capsule membranes is very important in this series because Schoeps no longer manufacturers the M 221 and can no longer replace the capsules. The model that replaces it, the M 222, uses the modern Colette series of capsules and has a different sound as a result.

STC/COLES 4038

The 4038 ribbon microphone was designed by the BBC in 1954 and was originally manufactured by STC and most recently by Coles. Long the favorite of British engineers and used on countless records in the '50s and '60s, the 4038 never found its way into many American studios. Somewhat on the fragile side, the 4038 excels on brass and as an overhead drum mic. (See Figure 2.18.)

Figure 2.18
STC/Coles 4038.

SHURE SM57

Over the years the Shure SM57 has established itself as the second-most popular microphone in the world (after the SM58). It is widely used in both live sound and recording applications, particularly on vocals, guitar amplifiers, and snare drums. It is used in such a large variety of situations that it often tops engineers' lists of "the one microphone to be stranded with on a desert island." (See Figure 2.19.)With a heritage dating back to the original Unidyne capsule used in the Shure Model 55 in 1939, the cardioid dynamic SM57 utilizes an updated Unidyne III capsule first used on the Model 545 in 1959.

Figure 2.19
Shure SM57. Courtesy of Shure
Incorporated.

Introduced in 1965, the SM57 was offered as a high-quality microphone for speech applications in broadcast, recording, and sound reinforcement. Though the microphone achieved some acceptance in the broadcast field, its ultimate success was with live sound applications and recording. By about 1968, the SM57 had been discovered by the fledgling concert sound industry. To engineers at that time (and now as well), the microphone provided a wide frequency response with an intelligibility-enhancing presence peak, a very uniform cardioid polar pattern to minimize feedback and other unwanted pickup, and an affordable price. (The original retail price was about $85 with cable.)

The SM57 has not undergone a major change to its basic design since its introduction and still remains widely available.

SENNHEISER MD421

Go to any tracking date, and chances are you'll find a 421 on either the toms or a guitar amp. There have been three basic 421 models: the original 421 in gray, the newer 421 in black (which sounds pretty much the same as the gray), and the new MK II version, which sounds different from the first two. The cardioid 421 has a very useful roll-off switch located near the XLR connector. The response ranges from the flat M (or "music") position to the rolled-off S (or "speech") position. Over the years the number of stops between S and M on the roll-off switch has changed, with five being the most common. (See Figure 2.20.)

Figure 2.20
Sennheiser 421II. Courtesy of Sennheiser.

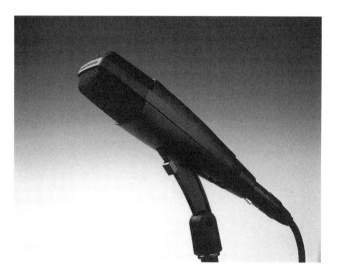

SENNHEISER MD441

The 441 was designed to have more upper midrange and less low-frequency response than the 421, as well as extremely directional response. When used in a live situation, the gain before feedback is indeed impressive. Because of its supercardioid pickup pattern, the 441 excels as a scratch vocal mic and both on top of and under a snare drum. (See Figure 2.21.)

Figure 2.21
Sennheiser 441. Courtesy of
Sennheiser.

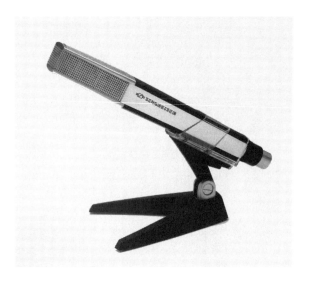

BEYER M160

The Beyer M160 is one of the so-called "modern" ribbon mics. Utilizing dual ribbons to attain a hypercardioid pickup pattern, the M160 is a lot more rugged than its ribbon predecessors. (You still have to be careful, though.) Although used primarily on acoustic instruments by most engineers, the M160 has nonetheless gained a sterling reputation for use on guitar amplifiers. There is also a figure-8 version of the M160 called the M130. (See Figure 2.22.)

Figure 2.22
Beyer M160. Courtesy of Beyer
Dynamic.

ELECTRO-VOICE RE20

A staple of any mic locker, the E/V RE20 is a large-diaphragm dynamic mic featuring an E/V innovation called *Variable D*. Thanks to the abundance of ports along the sides of the microphone, Variable D allowed the mic to reduce proximity effect while maintaining a flat frequency response. A favorite of broadcasters since its introduction, the RE20 has found its way into the studio as a kick drum mic, a vocal mic (a favorite of Stevie Wonder), a floor tom mic, and anywhere that a condenser mic would usually be used. (See Figure 2.23.)

Figure 2.23
E/V RE20. Courtesy of Electro-Voice.

New Versions of the Classics

While every engineer agrees that the classic mics sound great (which is why some of them are still in daily use even though they may be as many as 60 years old), there are just not enough of them to go around. This has driven up the prices to the point where only the most successful artists, studios, producers, and engineers can afford them. As a result, there are many new versions of the old classics currently made by small boutique manufacturers at a considerably lower cost than the originals. Although some manufacturers get closer to the original sound than others, all are sufficiently in the ballpark in a way that makes these mics a pretty safe purchase. After all, even the originals didn't sound the same from mic to mic, and if they were made exactly the same today, they wouldn't sound the same as the ones made 20 to 60 years ago due to the aging of the parts.

Even with the original specifications, new versions of the classics sound a bit different because many of the parts just aren't made any more. Capacitors and diaphragms are made differently, transformers and inductors cannot be made the same due to the latest OSHA safety laws, and VF14 vacuum tubes (for instance) haven't been made in at least 50 years. That being said, today's boutique microphone makers do an amazing job of getting close to the original sound with the parts available on the market today.

It should be noted that the AKG C 12/Ela M 251, Neumann U 47 and U 67, and RCA 77 are the most copied, since most of the others, such as the Shure SM57, the E/V RE20, the Beyer M160, and the Sennheiser 441, are still made exactly as they were when they were first introduced. Others, such as the Sennheiser 421 and the AKG 414 and 451 are currently manufactured but have changed their sound over the years (some for the better, contrary to popular belief) due to continual upgrades.

Let's take a look at some of the new classic microphone manufacturers and their offerings.

▶ Audio Engineering Associates' Wes Dooley has long been both a connoisseur and an expert on ribbon microphones, and his new microphones based loosely on the RCA microphones of old have been drawing rave reviews from recording luminaries around the world (see Figure 2.24). Wes also completes the line with a microphone preamp (the TRP) specially designed to complement ribbon mics.

Figure 2.24
AEA R84. Courtesy of Audio
Engineering Associates.

▶ Bock Audio Designs (formerly Soundelux), named after microphone maven David Bock, currently manufactures an Ela M 251 clone known appropriately as a 251 (see Figure 2.25) and a less expensive cardioid-only version called a 151. Bock Audio Designs is unique in that there's no attempt to make their mics look like the mics they emulate, nor is there an attempt to exactly copy the inner workings at the expense of better performance. For more information on modern microphone philosophy and manufacturing, see David Bock's interview at the end of this chapter. Also check out bockaudiodesigns.com.

Figure 2.25
Bock Audio Designs 251. Courtesy of Bock Audio Designs.

▶ Korby Audio Technologies takes a different approach to emulate the classics with its Korby Convertible, which comes with interchangeable capsules for U 47, U 67, Sony C-800, or C 12 and 251 flavors. Tracy Korby also manufactures several other mics that provide a different, more modern interpretation of the classics. For more information, go to korbyaudio.com. (See Figure 2.26.)

Figure 2.26
Korby Audio KAT Convertible
system. Courtesy of Korby Audio
Technologies.

▶ Mojave Audio is an offshoot of Royer Labs in that all their products are designed by David Royer but none are ribbons. The company has a number of mics that don't exactly physically resemble the classics, but they sure sound like them. The MA-200 is a large-diaphragm tube condenser that knowledgeable users say has a sound similar to the famed U 67 (see Figure 2.27), while the MA-100 is a small-diaphragm tube mic along the lines of the Schoeps M 221 or the Neumann KM 56.

Figure 2.27
Mojave Audio MA-200. Courtesy
of Mojave Audio.

▶ Pearlman Microphones makes a hand-built (as most boutique items are) version of the U 47 that comes in various flavors and prices. For more information, go to pearlmanmicrophones.com. (See Figure 2.28.)

Figure 2.28
Pearlman TM 1. Courtesy of
Pearlman Microphones.

▶ Peluso Microphone Lab is the brainchild of John Peluso, who, like most other boutique microphone designers, has been a longtime mic repairman. Like David Bock, John makes clones of not only the popular 251s and U 47s, but the RCA 77 and the Schoeps CMC line as well. Peluso mics differ from other boutique manufacturer mics in that they're fairly inexpensive. For more information, go to pelusomicrophonelab.com. (See Figure 2.29.)

Figure 2.29
Peluso Microphone Lab CEMC-6.
Courtesy of Peluso Microphone
Lab.

▶ Telefunken USA is the modern incarnation of the original Telefunken division that initially distributed the classic, sought-after Ela M 251 and U 47. Today, Telefunken USA builds extremely faithful reproductions of those mics (some at prices similar to their vintage forbearers) in several versions, as well as a reproduction of the RCA BK-5 ribbon mic. For more information, go to telefunkenusa.com. (See Figure 2.30.)

Figure 2.30
Telefunken USA U 47v. Courtesy of Telefunken USA.

▶ Wunder Audio makes not only microphones based on the classics, but a microphone preamp, an EQ, and even a console as well. The microphone line consists of the standard 251 and U 47, but also the revered M 49/M 50. For more information, go to wunderaudio.com. (See Figure 2.31.)

Figure 2.31
Wunder Audio CM49. Courtesy of Wunder Audio.

The New Classics

While many believe that microphone technology hasn't really improved in at least 30 years, a host of new mics have taken the technology to the next step. Some have even become classics in their own right and can be found as standard equipment in mic lockers the world over.

AUDIO-TECHNICA AT4050/4033

The AT4050 is a large-diaphragm multi-purpose, multi-pattern condenser mic that's found its way into mic lockers everywhere (see Figure 2.32). Its open and airy top end, low noise, and ability to take punishing SPL levels have made this a go-to mic when your usual favorite just isn't cutting it. It's also relatively inexpensive compared to the similarly featured German and Austrian favorites. The cardioid-only 4033 is a less expensive version of the same mic.

Figure 2.32
AT4050. Courtesy of
Audio–Technica.

HEIL PR 40

Another new mic that has caught on as a kick drum mic is the Heil PR 40 (see Figure 2.33). The PR 40 incorporates a large 1-1/8th dynamic element for an extended low-frequency response as well as a presence bump from 2.5 to 4.5 kHz. It's also capable of handling very high SPL levels, and its supercardioid pattern provides excellent back-side rejection. Many feel that the response of the PR 40 is sort of a "pre-EQ" built into the mic that makes EQing later either unnecessary or a lot more gentle than with other mics.

Figure 2.33
Heil PR 40. Courtesy of Heil
Sound.

ROYER R-121

Introduced in 1996, the R-121 is the first radically redesigned ribbon microphone in that it has a higher output than older ribbons, is a lot more rugged, and can take all the SPL you can hand it. You'll see it used where the old favorite ribbons are used (overheads, brass), but in some new places, too (such as kick drums and guitar amps). (See Figure 2.34.)

Figure 2.34
Royer R-121. Courtesy of Royer
Labs.

SHURE BETA 52

The Beta 52 (or B52, as some call it) is the first mic to give the revered AKG D 112 some competition as a kick mic. The mic is specially designed for kick and bass with an EQ curve built in to attenuate the 300- to 600-Hz "boxy" frequencies and boost around 4 kHz for presence. It can also handle extremely high SPL levels up to 178 dB. (See Figure 2.35.)

Figure 2.35
Shure Beta 52A. Courtesy of Shure.

SHURE SM81

Although not a truly recent mic (it was introduced in 1978), the small-diaphragm SM81 condenser has been building in favor through the years until it has now become a clear go-to mic whenever a small-diaphragm mic is called for. Known for its flat frequency response from 20 Hz to 20 kHz, low noise, and RF susceptibility, the SM81 is ruggedly constructed and operates over a wide variety of temperatures. It has a built-in 10-dB pad and a switchable flat, 6-, or 18-dB per octave hi-pass filter (see Figure 2.36).

Figure 2.36
Shure SM81. Courtesy of Shure.

YAMAHA SKRM-100 SUBKICK

The Yamaha SKRM-100 is an answer to the subkick phenomenon that started due to the burning desire to get more bottom end without having to crank up the EQ. The unit only captures 20 to 30 Hz, which is something that you feel more than you hear.

The trend started when a few engineers began to take the woofer from a Yamaha NS-10M, use the magnet to attach it to a mic stand about two inches in front of the bass drum, and plug it into a direct box. (This wasn't a new idea by any means, as engineer Geoff Emerick tried this on Beatles records in the '60s.) See Figure 2.37. The problem is that Yamaha no longer produces the NS-10, and the factory that made the woofer has been closed. So engineer Russ Miller took the idea to Yamaha, who manufactured a unit that contains a 10-inch speaker mounted inside a 7-ply maple shell with black mesh heads, so it's actually a speaker mounted inside a 10-inch drum (see Figure 2.38).

Figure 2.37
A homemade subkick.

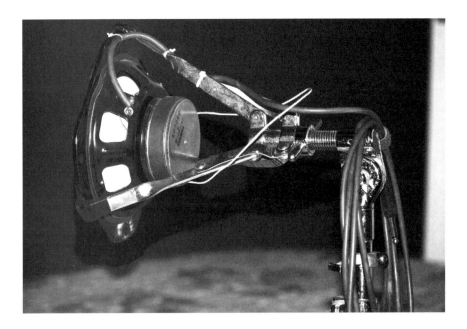

Unlike a homemade subkick, the Yamaha subkick is tunable, but some engineers argue that the sound still isn't as good as what you can get from just a raw NS-10 woofer.

Figure 2.38
Yamaha SKRM-100 subkick.
Courtesy of Yamaha.

Inexpensive Microphones

One of the more interesting recent developments in microphones is the availability of some extremely inexpensive condenser and ribbon microphones in the below-$500 category (in some cases, even less than $100). Although you'll never confuse these with a vintage U 47 or C 12, they do sometimes provide an astonishing level of performance at a price point that we could only dream about a few short years ago. But there are some things to be aware of before you make that purchase.

QUALITY CONTROL'S THE THING

Mics in this category have the same thing in common: They're all made in China, mostly in the same factory. Some are made to the specifications of the importer (and therefore cost more), and some are just plain off-the-shelf. Regardless of how they're made and to what specs, the biggest issue from that point is how much quality control (or QC—also sometimes known as *quality assurance*) is involved before the product finds its way into your studio.

Some mics are completely manufactured at the factory and receive a quick QC just to make sure they're working, and these are the least expensive mics on the shelf. Others receive another level of QC to get them within a rather wide quality tolerance level, so they cost a little more. Others are QC'd locally by the distributor, with only the best ones offered for sale, and these cost still more. And others have only their parts manufactured in China, with final assembly and QC done locally—and of course, these have the highest price in the category.

YOU CAN NEVER BE SURE OF THE SOUND

One of the byproducts of the rather loose tolerances due to the different levels of QC is the fact that the sound can vary greatly between mics of the same model and manufacturer. The more QC (and the higher the resulting price), the less difference you'll find, but you'll still have to go through a number of them to find one with some magic. This doesn't happen with the more traditional name brands that cost a lot more, but what you're buying (besides better components in most cases) is a high assurance that your mic is going to sound as good as any other of the same model from that manufacturer. In other words, the differences between mics are a lot smaller.

THE WEAKNESS

There are two points that contribute to the mic sounding good or bad (this can be said of all mics, really), and those are the capsule and the electronics. The tighter the tolerances and the better the QC on the capsule, the better the mic will sound and the closer each mic will sound to another of the same model.

The electronics is another point entirely in that a bad design can cause distortion at high SPL levels and limit the frequency response or change it to something less than desirable. The component tolerances are a lot closer, so that doesn't enter into the equation as much as having a bearing on the sound. In some cases, you can have what could be an inexpensive great mic that's limited by poorly designed electronics. You can find articles all over the Internet about how to modify some of these mics, some that make more of a difference than others. If you choose to try doing a mod on your mic yourself, be sure that your soldering chops are really good, since there's generally so little space inside the mic that even a small mistake can render your mic useless.

SOME GOOD CHOICES

While new inexpensive mics are coming on the market every day, here are a few that users have been generally pleased with.

Behringer B-1

While everything that Behringer makes is in the budget category, the large-diaphragm B-1 condenser seems to be an item that found some acceptance. It's a remarkable value in that you get a carrying case, shock mount, and windscreen along with the mic.

Cascade FAT HEAD

While other budget mic companies have concentrated on condenser mics, Cascade Microphones have gone a different direction into inexpensive ribbon mics. The FAT HEAD is just about the least expensive ribbon mic on the planet (complete with a wooden box), but it still has a host of very satisfied users.

MXL SP1/2001

Marshall Electronics were one of the first to bring out large-diaphragm condensers for an ultra-inexpensive price. The SP1 is just about the best deal you'll ever find for a mic like this and is subject to many mods to raise the quality. The 2001 is basically the same mic but with more QC and tighter tolerances.

Oktava MK012

A small-diaphragm condenser with interchangeable capsules for different patterns, the MK012 has become a favorite for cymbals, acoustic guitars, and choirs.

Rode NT1-A

Rode actually started as a Swedish company before finally settling in Australia, and it really doesn't fit into this category since all the parts except the capsules are manufactured there. That being said, they produce quality microphones for people on a budget. The NT1-A is the much improved, super-quiet successor to the original NT1.

sE Electronics sE2200A

Built by hand in their own factory in Shangai, sE Electronics mics are one of the few from this class that are finding use by everyday pros and big-name recording artists.

Studio Projects C1

The Studio Projects C series of large- and small-diaphragm condenser mics has become one that has a very high user-satisfaction rating, with the C1 being the first introduced.

Meet Microphone Designer David Bock

After stints repairing microphones (among other things) at such prestigious facilities as the Hit Factory and Ocean Way, Bock Audio Designs (formerly Soundelux) founder and managing director David Bock went from repairing vintage microphones to manufacturing them. David now utilizes his expertise to produce updated versions of the studio classic 251, although he made versions of the U 47, FET 47, M 49, and U 67 in the previous Soundelux incarnation of the company. David was kind enough to share some of his insights as to the inner workings and differences between classic microphones and their modern counterparts.

How did you get this interest in microphones?

From the very first time I put on a set of headphones and listened to that pair of Neumann M 269s that I used in college, the sound was very seductive. I was always searching to do a great record as an engineer and therefore had a fascination with microphones. Later, I was fortunate enough to have someone show me a little bit about how to open one up and not destroy it, which is kind of the first step. My interest evolved from there as I became a technician, and it became more and more obvious that there was a really small number of people that knew what made microphones tick, so it became a definite worthwhile specialization to me. Plus, there was a lot of other gear that was coming onto the market that was just no fun to work on, so that helped push me into the microphone direction anyway.

How did you get involved in designing your first mic?

I had been modifying some Chinese microphones that someone had brought into the country about 15 years ago, and some people got excited about the results. I had specialized in repairing microphones up until that point, so modifying them was the next step. Then saying, "Why are we always using the same single triode design for microphones? Let's do something different," was the final step.

Last we talked, you mentioned how people keep using the same old designs without knowing why they were used in the first place.

Well, at this point it's really out of control in terms of the copying. If you really want to see it on a larger scale, just look at guitar amplifier circuits. Every guitar amp circuit is a copy of every other guitar amp circuit, and the copy has passed through generations now to where you really have people that don't know why they're doing something. That's seriously true in the microphone world as well.

Isn't it true that people are copying the original "mistakes" that were made because of the limitations of the technology at the time?

That's a very logical conclusion and there's some truth to that, but there's also another element involved, which is that companies make decisions based on what they have to do to stay in business. They may have parameters handed to them by a broadcast network who is their primary customer. They might also base some of their design decisions on the "bean counters," where they ask if there is a cheaper way to produce the product. Suddenly, you might get a so-called "classic" design just because it's so easy to implement that everyone copies it. That's actually a bigger factor.

What actually makes a vintage microphone so special?

There are a couple of things that go into that. The bottom line is that the '50s were really the golden age of audio design. Those guys really did know what they were doing when they designed a lot of the key gear that people are still using. They used a lot of the correct techniques, and they had the luxury of decent materials and the time to research things properly.

There is a tone to these things that is harder and harder to duplicate. Not impossible, just harder and harder. They had tubes back then that are harder to get now. The available selection of materials was a lot greater back then. Then there's the element of chance. Why would someone pay $20,000 for a 251? Well, maybe that particular 251 really does sound unique because AKG's production was so sloppy and the capsules were so poorly machined that you're bound to get one that excels beyond everything else, and the rest are just kind of average. Now we have CNC machines that can make these tiny little holes on the capsule backplate all the same, which AKG really couldn't do.

When you set out to build a mic, how did you determine what you were going to copy?

If I was to have a studio, I know what I'd need to have in terms of vintage microphones, but the vintage market is such a disaster in that you pay too much for something that needs significant repairs and constant attention. So my goal was to build the products that I know I would need if I were to have that studio. If I were to make a record, I would need real microphones, but I couldn't afford $90,000 in vintage microphones.

When I started building microphones, there was no copying intended; it was merely to forge new ground. Everything was defined by economic and production parameters as well as a little ignorance, since I hadn't been in the manufacturing game that long. That's what I was able to do initially, but that wasn't my goal. So the first few microphones (the U 95 and U 99) established the company enough so I could get to that goal. Once I was able to get there, it was time to emulate a few of the classics that everyone used on great records. I had a client who was a 251 freak that kept bugging me to build one, and it became a several-year obsession for both of us. That's what led to that first copy, but it was not a short process.

In the case of the 47, which came after the 251, it was even a longer process. There were a lot of things that had to come together since it's such a complicated construction with a lot of parts. In some ways it was a little easier, though, since I had repaired so many of them, and as a result I had a better sense for what sounded good or bad.

What's the most common repair that you saw in vintage mics?

The range of problems goes from common to obscure, but the most common thing is a dirty capsule—but that can be true of even a new microphone. If you wanted to build a dust collector, you would build it similar to a condenser microphone, unfortunately.

As you were trying to build an updated version of a vintage microphone, were you trying to copy everything, including the circuitry, and trying to get it as close to the original as possible, or were you trying to just make it sound like the original?

The sound comes first, but that's not the whole story. The first thing I had to do was try to find what makes the microphone sound the way it does. There were at least 15 points that you have to look at, it turns out, if you're going to emulate the sound of a microphone. The first large problem is, "I want to copy the sound of a 251." Well, which 251? I rented about ten 251s here in town [Hollywood], and you know what? There's no such thing as a common 251. They're all totally different. I could hear it and I could measure it.

Among some of them there is a common thread, though. Frequency response is the primary guidepost because all microphones have their own signature. But frequency response curves don't always tell you everything. You have to take frequency response measurements not only far-field but also proximity [near-field], which strangely are not published and are completely critical to what we believe a microphone sounds like in the directional world. That's key, and it's somewhat of a disservice that most of the larger condenser-microphone manufacturers have not been publishing those graphs for many years. That's why most engineers will say, "Those graphs don't really mean anything." That's because you're always looking at a 1-meter graph, but you're not always putting your microphone 1 meter away from the sound source. So of course they don't mean anything, because they're not telling you what you're hearing. If you saw a proximity graph and a 1-meter graph, you'd have a much better idea of what the microphone sounds like.

So the dissection process continued through a lot of substitutions. You might take a power supply and substitute a different circuit topology and see what it changes, for instance. There are also a lot of measurements that you have to do. Our ability to test things today is definitely better than back when the classics were built, but it's not completely conclusive and opens up a can of worms that says, "If I can't measure it, then I can't hear it," which I completely disagree with. If you worked only toward measurements, you end up with something that actually doesn't sound particularly good compared to things that were designed with listening in mind.

Finally, there are listening tests. My primary listening test is to make a recording of a drum set in a large room. I've got a couple of key locations where I place the microphone to give me an idea about the close and distant pickup characteristics. That's where you start hearing the differences. Microphone capsules are related to drums. If you took 10 DW kits and you tuned them all the same, they'd still sound all different. There's a parallel you could draw toward microphones. You could tune all the snare drums and toms the same and even use measurement devices to be sure that they're the same, and yet the trained ear of an engineer can pick out the differences between them. We can lock onto things that are different about each one.

What was the hardest thing to get right?

Always the capsule, because it's so small, and if you make a tiny change, it makes a huge result. But that's not to say that the capsule is 99 percent of the sound. An 87 and a 67 don't sound that similar, yet they use the same capsule.

How do you deal with parts that are no longer made?

In some cases you can replicate them. In some cases you can improve them. In some cases you have to bite the bullet and say, "I just can't get that part, so I'll have to come up with the closest thing I can." For instance, something like transformer laminations. We don't have the exact laminations that they used in the original 47 transformer, but we came up with something that's a lot closer than an off-the-shelf Jensen [transformer].

But then again, you're not going so much for the part but for the effect of the part.

That's right. But in some cases we've found through the substitution method that some things just have to be duplicated. Like if you mounted the tube to a printed circuit board, it would have a different resonance than if you mounted it with two rubber mounts.

But in other cases, a substitution can be as good or even better. For example, in our 251 we use a large core output transformer with the same turns ratio as the small transformer used in the original. That gives us a little less distortion and a lot more headroom in the low end. At the risk of not being historically accurate but being a lot more useful for today's recordings, I made a decision saying, "I'd rather have the headroom," because it didn't affect anything else.

The original 251s were made out of plastic that could disintegrate in your hands. That's not acceptable, so ours are metal framed. And the way we power the heater on the tube is different than the way they did it in 1960, but we get 6 to 10 dB less noise overall because of it, so that's a useful improvement. So we try to maintain faithfulness to the vintage sound, and wherever that's not compromised we'll make an improvement where we can.

What's the biggest difference in the way microphones are made today from the way the classics were made?

Mass production and availability of quality materials. Also, the need for profitability on a corporate level seems to affect how things are made a lot. I've seen the way Neumann microphones are built, and they're very different from the way they used to be. The way they built their microphones in the '50s and early '60s, I'll be able to keep those microphones running for a long time. Not so with the newer microphones. They still make a great capsule, but they don't make the microphone the same in terms of construction. They're built for ease of production and lowest cost. It's true almost across the board.

So if we were to make a broad statement, microphones are not made as well today as they were 50 years ago.

No, they're not. If you had a "cost is no object" attitude, you still don't even have the same metals available. The quality of brass is different now from what they used in the '50s and '60s, for instance, and an equivalent can't be found.

What is the most critical part of a microphone?

The capsule is the most critical, but electronics play a big part. You can have a great capsule but crummy electronics, and the microphone will sound mediocre. If you have really great electronics but a crummy capsule, then you still won't have a good-sounding microphone. If you have a great capsule and great electronics, then you'll have a really good microphone at that point.

If you were to look in the future of microphone development, where would you like to see it go?

Unless someone comes up with a true digital transducer that's usable, I don't know how much more it can get refined.

What seems like an improvement sometimes doesn't work at all. There have been "improvements" along the way that were commercial flops. I'll give you a quick example. There was a microphone that AKG made, the lowly 414, which has descended into the depths of hell at this point. In their 14 revisions of this microphone, they made one called the P48 EB that used a transistorized cascode circuit. It is the most correct and stable circuit that you can use from a textbook standpoint. It is the only time that I've ever seen it used outside of a secret internal Neumann document from the early '60s, yet it's their most hated microphone of all the 414 versions. So in terms of serious evolution, I'd like to see some, but I'm a little worried the marketplace can't handle real useful advances.

Could it be that the amplifier circuit was exposing the faults of the capsule?

Possibly, since by that time they had migrated to the molded capsule that is generally accepted to be a disaster.

Tell me about developing a version of the 67?

The 67 was actually a fascinating research project because of the patent involved, which tells you exactly how to do it. There are two problems, though, and the capsule is the least of them. You could almost use any capsule because the circuitry is so complex that it will overwhelm whatever capsule you have in there. The circuitry was ingenious. They had simultaneously bass boost and cut in order to get a rumble filter. The big problem is the transformer, which is tricky because it has feedback windings, and the whole circuit is dependent upon the gain of the tube, so the individual tube completely matters in the sound of the microphone. If you have a tube that's getting old and is losing a little of its gain, then the circuit doesn't work as planned and the microphone doesn't sound right.

With the way the business seems to be going, with less and less emphasis on sonic quality, will there be enough people left to appreciate what you're doing?

Anybody who is serious about the profession either evolves to a point where they say, "I can use an SM57 for every track to make a record," or "I'd rather use a high-quality microphone to make a record." You're going to go one way or the other, and most people, if they stay in the business long enough, will usually gravitate to the more exclusive side.

CHAPTER 3

Basic Recording Equipment

Almost as important as the microphone is the microphone preamplifier, or *mic pre*, *mic amp*, or just *preamp*. This circuit boosts the extremely tiny output voltage from the microphone up to a level (called *line level*) that can be easily sent around the studio to consoles, DAWs, and tape machines (if you still use one).

The Microphone Preamplifier

Nearly every console and most DAW interfaces have mic preamps built into them, but in most cases the quality of this circuit isn't nearly as high (or as costly) as what's available as an outboard piece. Also, each mic pre has its own sound, and most engineers will select the mic pre and mic combination as a different audio color to fit the instrument and music.

WHY A SEPARATE MIC AMP?

So if every DAW interface and console has its own mic amp, why use an outboard one, you might ask? Because for the most part, a dedicated unit sounds a lot better. An outboard pre generally has higher highs and lower lows (meaning it has better frequency response), and is clearer and cleaner. But this comes at a price. While the parts of a typical mic amp in a console hover somewhere around $20 a channel, an outboard mic pre can cost anywhere from a hundred to several thousand dollars per channel. With the increased cost usually comes a superior design with better quality components, as well as a larger box to put them in (usually at least 1U high, or a single rack space, with a standard 19-inch rack mount).

MACK: *The actual sound of something is mostly determined by the initial instant of the sound. If you cut that off, then it could be any instrument. Just try cutting the attacks off most any instrument. You can't tell what it is any more. So that made a lot of sense to me, and I got really hooked on preserving the transients after that.*

As with microphones, some mic pres are solid state, while some use a tube for their amplification. Both methods are capable of doing the job well, but ultimately they sound different.

VINTAGE MIC PRES

They just don't make them like they used to. At least that's what a lot of engineers think when selecting a mic pre. There's a sound to these units that hasn't been duplicated in modern gear, except in rare exceptions. Because of this philosophy, the most desirable mic amps were all made in the '60s and are actually cannibalized sections of recording consoles from that era.

So why does the old stuff sound different ("better" is such a relative term) than the new? Very broadly speaking, it's the iron inside—iron meaning the transformers and inductors used routinely on older gear that is passed over for modern electronic equivalents because of size, weight, and cost. So why not make them like before? Although some companies try, the fact of the matter is that many of these transformers were custom-made for the particular unit and just aren't available any more. Another factor in the difference of sound can be attributed to the fact that the older units used discrete (individual) electronic components that could be properly matched to the circuit, while modern units utilize mostly cookie cutter–type integrated circuits (a complete circuit on a chip) to attempt to achieve the same end.

Following are some examples of outboard vintage mic preamps that are generally held in high esteem for their sonic qualities.

Neve 1071/1083

Of all the Neve modules (and there are many), the Neve 1071 is probably the most famous. This unit is far more than just a mic preamp; it is actually a channel strip pulled from a console and reconfigured for outboard use, and it features both a line input and an equalizer as well. The 1071 has a 3-band equalizer with fixed EQ points and a hi-pass filter. Another Neve module used often is the 1083, which differs from the 1071 in that it has a 4-band equalizer with two midrange bands and more frequency choices. Through the years, Neve made a lot of variations on this theme as most of their consoles required a custom design, but they all had the distinctive Neve sound. (See Figure 3.1.)

Figure 3.1
Neve 33115 module (like a 1071).

API 312/512

API preamps (circa 1970) are classics, and everyone uses them if they are available (especially on drums). They have tone that simply cannot be duplicated by anything else, vintage or modern, with a fat low end (due to the distortion in the old transformers) and a clear, slightly hyped high end. Although the more modern 512 sounds very similar, the older 312s are slightly fatter and smoother sounding. (See Figure 3.2.)

Figure 3.2
API 7600 channel strip. Courtesy of API.

Telefunken V72/V76

Consoles of the early '60s were vacuum tube–based, and German Broadcast set a standard for preamp modules used in their consoles that was copied and used all over Europe, most notably by EMI Records in England. The Telefunken V72, V72A, V76, and V78 are the most widely used and loved mic amplifiers from that period. The differences between the models are the numbers and types of tubes they employ. The V72 is a two-tube unit that uses two Telefunken EF804S tubes, while the V72A uses one E180F and one 5654 tube that provides a bit more gain and output as a result. The impossible-to-find V72S amplifiers were found in the famous EMI REDD 37 Abbey Road consoles that were used on the early Beatles recordings. The V76/78 uses four of the EF804S tubes and has the most gain of all the models as a result. (See Figure 3.3.)

Figure 3.3
Telefunken V72.

MODERN MIC PRES

There are many fine modern equivalents to these vintage mic amps, but again, each has its own special flavor that must be chosen to suit the microphone, instrument, and music. There are basically two categories of modern mic preamp—one that tries to emulate the unique sonic character of vintage, and one that tries to provide the cleanest amplification without adding any character (meaning distortion) at all. Some highly thought of modern brands are discussed in the following subsections.

Great River

Although Great River makes mic preamps in the "clean modern" category as well, they also make the MP-2NV, which emulates the classic circuitry and vintage sound of the Neve 1073 module. The circuitry allows for both transformer saturation and the soft distortions resulting from pushing the input level of the unit, just like the real thing. (See Figure 3.4.)

Figure 3.4
Great River MP-2NV.

Manley Labs

Manley produces an updated version of the historic Langevin AM-4 console channel. While not a completely faithful reproduction of the original unit, Manley's own discrete gain stage provides balanced outputs yet still retains that desirable tone that discrete circuitry delivers. (See Figure 3.5.)

Figure 3.5
Langevin dual mic amp. Courtesy
of Manley Labs.

Vintech

Vintech produces two models based on Neve classic designs: the X73 based on the Neve 1073 module and the X81, which is based on the 1081. (See Figure 3.6.)

Figure 3.6
Vintech X73. Courtesy of Vintech.

Daking

Daking manufactures the 52270B mic-pre/4-band equalizer, which differs from the others units mentioned in that it emulates the mic amp and equalizer of the famous and extremely rare Trident A Range console. (See Figure 3.7.)

Figure 3.7
Daking 52270B.

Universal Audio

The Universal Audio 2-610 is a new version of a channel from the legendary Universal Audio 610 modular console. The original model 610 was used on a host of '50s and '60s chart busters, including hits by the Beach Boys and Frank Sinatra. (See Figure 3.8.)

Figure 3.8
UA 2-610. Courtesy of Universal Audio.

Hardy

The Hardy M-1 is great example of simple and elegant design that results in sonic accuracy and transparency, yet is still capable of providing the "aggressive" sound so desirable in certain types of music. Introduced in 1987, the M-1 was one of the first dedicated outboard microphone pre-amps. Go to johnhardyco.com for more information. (See Figure 3.9.)

Figure 3.9
Hardy M-1. Courtesy of the John Hardy Company.

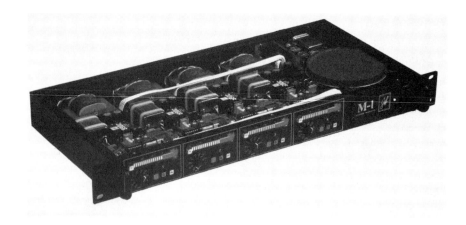

Millennia Media HV-3B

The HV-3B is an extremely wide bandwidth (up to 300 kHz) stereo microphone preamplifier that's become somewhat of a standard for classical and critical acoustic music recording. Go to www.mil-media.com for more information. (See Figure 3.10.)

Figure 3.10
Millennia Media HV-3B. Courtesy of Millennia Media.

GML

Designed by George Massenburg, who is not only one of the best audio designers in the world, but one of the best recording engineers as well, GML gear is renowned for its lifelike realism and reference-standard transparency. Go to www.massenburg.com for more information. (See Figure 3.11.)

Figure 3.11
GML 8304. Courtesy of George Massenburg Labs.

Grace

This boutique audio company has built a reputation for building ultra-reliable products that are extremely transparent. Now with a full product line that has grown out of their mic preamp models, anything from Grace can truly be considered "high fidelity." Go to www.gracedesign.com for more information. (See Figure 3.12.)

Figure 3.12
*Grace m201. Courtesy of Grace
Design.*

Mic Amp Setup

Mic preamps do only one job—amplify. Therefore, they usually have few controls, although the more expensive, exotic models might have extra features. The two items that every pre have in common are a gain control (sometimes called *trim*) and some type of overload indicator. Other controls you might see are output gain, impedance, input pad, phase, hi-pass filter, and more extensive metering.

PRIMARY CONTROLS

The primary controls on a preamp include the following:

▶ **Gain** (may be called *level* or *trim*) controls how much the microphone signal is amplified. Most mic preamps have about 60 dB of gain (which amplifies the mic signal a million times), but some have as much as 80 dB to accommodate low-output ribbon microphones or field audio recording where the signals captured by the mic are very quiet.

▶ **Metering** on a mic preamp can be something as simple as a single indicator that signals an overload to a full-on ladder-style LED peak meter, as found on consoles or DAWs. Many times there is a combination, with the overload indicator at the top of the full meter.

▶ An **input pad** (or *attenuator*) is usually a switch that attenuates the signal from the microphone from 10 to 20 dB (it's different for every mic pre) to keep the circuitry from overloading.

▶ A **phase switch** changes the polarity of the microphone signal due to either a misplaced or a miswired microphone. Set the switch to the position that has the most low end. (For more on phase, see Chapter 5, "Basic Stereo Techniques.")

▶ A **hi-pass filter** attenuates the low frequencies at anywhere from 40 Hz to 160 Hz to eliminate unwanted low-frequency noise (such as truck rumble). On most preamps the frequency is fixed, but many have a variable frequency.

▶ A few mic preamps feature an **impedance control**, which is used to properly match the impedance of a microphone. This is less important today than back in the days when audio equipment required a precise 600-ohm load in order to operate within specifications (in the '40s through the '70s). Experiment with the various settings and select the one that sounds the best (the fullest sound with the most low end).

The best way to set up the unit is to adjust the gain until the clip light flashes only on the loudest sections of the recording. In most cases, the overload indicator doesn't actually light at the onset of clipping, but just before, so it's okay if it flashes occasionally (but check the manual first to make sure that's what really happens). This gives you the best combination of low noise with the least distortion (unless, of course, you like distortion, in which case you want the clip indicator to remain on most of the time). If you set the gain of the mic amp too low, you might have to raise the gain at another place in the signal chain, which can raise the noise to unacceptable limits.

DIRECT INJECTION

Direct injection (*DI* or "going direct") of a signal means that a microphone is bypassed, and the instrument (always electric or electrified) is plugged directly into the console or recording device. This was originally done to cut down on the number of mics (and therefore the leakage) used in a tracking session with a lot of instruments playing simultaneously. However, a DI is now used because it either makes the instrument sound better (like in the case of electric keyboards) or is just easier and faster.

Why can't you just plug your guitar or keyboard directly into the mic preamp without the direct box? Because this might cause an impedance mismatch that will change the frequency response of the instrument (although it won't hurt anything), usually causing the high frequencies to drop off and therefore make the instrument sound dull.

The advantages of direct injection are:

▶ Direct box transformers provide ground isolation and allow long cable runs from high impedance sources, such as guitars and keyboards, without excessive bandwidth loss.

▶ The extremely high impedance of the DI ensures a perfect match with every pickup to provide a warmer, more natural sound.

▶ The length of cable can be extended to up to 50 feet without signal degradation.

Types

There are two basic types of direct boxes: *active* (which provides gain and therefore needs electronics, requiring either battery or AC power) and *passive* (which has no gain and doesn't require power). Which is better? Once again, there are good and poor examples of each. Generally speaking, the more you pay, the higher quality they are. (See Figure 3.13.)

Figure 3.13
Demeter VTDB-2 direct box.
Courtesy of Demeter
Amplification.

An active DI sometimes has enough gain to be able to actually replace the mic amp and connect directly to a storage device, such as a tape machine or DAW.

An excellent passive DI can be built around the fine Jensen transformer (www.jensen-transformers.com for do-it-yourself instructions), but you can buy basically the same thing from Radial Engineering in their JDI direct box (see Figure 3.14). Also, most modern mic pres now come with a separate DI input on a 1/4-inch guitar jack.

Figure 3.14
Radial JDI direct box. Courtesy of
Radial Engineering.

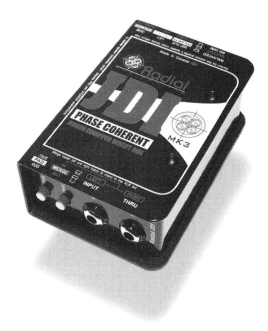

Setup

Not much setup is required to use a direct box. For the most part, you just plug the instrument in and play. About the only thing that you might have to set is the *gain* (which is usually only a switch that provides a 10-dB boost or so) on an active box or the *ground switch*. Most DIs have a ground switch to reduce hum in the event of a ground loop between the instrument and the DI. Set it for the quietest level.

Amplifier Emulators

The amplifier emulator, which is basically a glorified active direct box, has now been around for some time and has become a staple of almost any studio (see Figure 3.15). An emulator attempts to electronically duplicate the sound of different guitar and bass amplifiers, speaker cabinets, and even miking schemes. The advantages of the boxes are that they're quick and easy, give a very wide tonal variation, and provide the proper interface to just about any analog or (in some cases) digital recording device. Although they might not sound as realistic as a properly miked amplifier in a great studio with a terrific signal chain, they can provide a more than adequate substitute if you don't have any of those pieces available.

Figure 3.15
An amplifier emulator: Line 6
Guitar POD Pro. Courtesy of Line 6.

Compressor/Limiters

A compressor/limiter is frequently inserted into the microphone signal chain for two reasons: for dynamics control to prevent a signal overload or to change the tonal characteristics of the sound.

PRIMARY CONTROLS

The primary controls on a compressor are the following:

▶ **Threshold** sets the point at which the automatic gain reduction begins. Below that level, the compressor is essentially out of the circuit and does nothing. When the input gets above the threshold point, the compressor reduces the volume automatically and keeps the signal from getting louder.

▶ **Attack time** determines how quickly the volume is reduced when the input exceeds the threshold. If set too slow, then signal peaks can get through and possibly cause distortion. To prevent overload, a very fast attack time is selected. Sometimes a fast attack time is desirable, depending upon the instrument (such as drums, for instance).

▶ **Release time** determines how quickly the volume returns to normal after being reduced. If set too fast, this change becomes audible as the volume quickly swings up and down (called *pumping* or *breathing*). Setting the release time to fairly long (one second or more) eliminates this.

▶ **Compression ratio** determines the amount of compression that will occur. A setting of 1:1 does nothing (except maybe color the sound a bit due to the electronics of the compressor). A setting of 2:1 means that if the input rises 2 dB above threshold, the output level will increase by only 1 dB. A setting of 10:1 means that the input must climb 10 dB above the threshold before the output increases 1 dB.

A ratio of 10:1 or higher is usually considered to be limiting, with anything less considered compression. Generally speaking, compression is used to keep the level even, while limiting is used to prevent overload.

COMPRESSOR/LIMITER SETUP

For dynamics control, the compressor is usually set to limiting (a 10:1 or larger gain ratio) and set so that the signal doesn't exceed a certain level (usually just before clipping or distortion). In other cases, the unit is used mostly as a tone control and is set to compression (2:1 or higher but less than 10:1), with only a few dB of compression added.

As with microphones and preamps, the vintage units of the past are still the most desirable. Here are a few famous units that are frequently used during tracking.

Teletronix LA-2A

The Teletronix LA-2A may be the most popular of all tube limiters. Early LA-2s can be identified by their gray faceplate, while later models feature a brushed aluminum face with a switch on the back to swap between limiting and compression functions. (In the earlier models, this was accomplished through internal jumpers.) While not at all transparent, the LA-2A provides an airy sound (especially on vocals) heard on literally thousands of hits. There are only two controls—an input threshold control and a makeup gain control—but they're quite enough to do the job very well. (See Figure 3.16.)

Figure 3.16
LA-2A. Courtesy of Universal Audio.

There are numerous "clones" of the LA-2A available on the market, as well as a reissue of the unit by the descendant of the original manufacturer, Universal Audio.

Universal Audio LA-3A

A favorite in the vocal chain, the LA-3A was basically a solid-state LA-2A, although it has a bit more of a midrange sound. (See Figure 3.17.)

Figure 3.17
Universal Audio LA-3A.

UREI LA-4

The LA-4 was an improved LA-3A, with cleaner audio, variable ratio control, and separate input and output controls. Despite its cleaner audio (or maybe because of it), the LA-4 was never as desirable as its predecessors. (See Figure 3.18.)

Figure 3.18
UREI LA-4.

UREI 1176

From its introduction in 1967, the 1176 became one of the most storied pieces in audio history, being a staple in every rack in every studio since. Released in eight versions (from A to H), the earliest 1176A and B models were silver-faced with a blue stripe around the meter and featured push-button ratio selection of 4:1, 8:1, 10:1, and 20:1, as well as attack and release controls. These attack and release controls actually work backward, with the higher numbers (7 is highest clockwise) being faster than the lower numbers. One of the neat tricks with any version of 1176 is pushing in all four buttons simultaneously, which makes the meter go crazy but sure sounds cool. (See Figure 3.19.)

Figure 3.19
UREI 1176. Courtesy of Universal Audio.

The original blue-stripe models were replaced by the black-face C model and the 1176LN (the LN stands for *low noise*), which employed low-noise circuitry encased within an epoxy module. The next model, D, integrated these improvements into the main circuit board. The model E, introduced in the early 1970s, was the first to accommodate European 220V mains power with a voltage selector on the rear panel.

The classic transformer front end of the 1176 was discarded with the model G, and the unit never had its same rich tone again as a result. The final update, the model H, simply marked a return to a silver faceplate.

Of all the versions, model D or E variants are the most desirable. The 1178 is a stereo/dual-mono version of the 1176 with single controls.

New versions of the 1176 can now be purchased once again, since Universal Audio has reissued the black-face model E version of the unit, and Purple Audio has introduced a version based on that model as well.

CHAPTER 4

DAW Recording

It's difficult to find a musician who doesn't have some type of recording capability at home these days. It's so easy to put together the kind of studio that only a few years ago you could only dream about that just about everyone can now get into the recording game at very little cost. But there are a few concerns beyond microphone choice and placement that you need to address before you hit the Record button.

Getting Sound into the Computer

In the days of recording consoles and tape machines (and in those studios that still have those units today), recording was actually a little easier than what you find in a typical DAW these days. What you heard in the headphones or on the speakers was always in sync, thanks to the miracle of analog. (I say that in jest, of course.) You still had to deal with getting a signal to the phones and setting up a phone mix, but you have those kinds of issues in the digital domain as well.

ADCS AND DACS

Besides the mic and microphone preamp, the next most important devices that have an impact on the sound quality are the analog-to-digital convertor (shortened to ADC, which is a unit that converts the analog signals into the digital language of the DAW) and the digital-to-analog convertor (shortened to DAC, which is a unit that converts the digital signal back to analog for playback). In most lower-end DAW interfaces by manufacturers such as Digidesign, M-Audio, and MOTU, the ADCs and the DACs are built into the same box along with the mic preamps (see Figure 4.1). As you get into higher-end systems, such as Pro Tools|HD, the ADCs and DACs are separate higher quality units capable of greater fidelity, and specialized outboard units capable of even higher fidelity are available from a number of manufacturers, such as Apogee or Lavry.

Figure 4.1
Digidesign Mbox. Courtesy of
Digidesign.

The fact of the matter is that most convertors sold today, even at a budget, all-in-the-same-box price, sound pretty good compared to what was available in the early '90s, when digital recording was in its infancy. That being said, most DAW software (like Nuendo, Cubase, Logic, Cakewalk, or Sound Forge, for instance) allows you to mix and match the hardware to the level of quality that you need and can afford.

As with most everything else in the audio world, price usually does buy you increased quality, but it still depends upon the weakest link in your signal path just how much of that quality you'll actually hear.

LATENCY

One of the biggest problems in the digital world is latency. *Latency* is a measure of the time it takes (in milliseconds) for your audio signal to pass through your system during the recording process. This delay is caused by the time it takes for your computer to receive, understand, process, and send the signal back to your outputs.

High latency (which means you hear a note long after you play or sing it) is what you want to avoid, especially if you're doing overdubs. High latency means it's taking too long for the audio input to become audio output, giving a lag time between the time you play a note and when you hear it. A very small lag time (3 to 6 milliseconds) is tolerable, but anything beyond that creates everything from a phasing sound to a full echo, which makes it anywhere from distracting to impossible to sing or play with.

The lower your latency, the better the music you're recording will stay in sync with the music you're playing back, up to a point. If you try to set the latency parameter too low, the audio stream can break up into random static because the computer doesn't have the time to process it.

The key is to adjust your latency (through either your soundcard or your interface settings, or through third-party audio drivers) as low as it can go without causing the computer to stutter. How low your latency can be set is dependent upon such factors as computer speed, system bus speed, soundcard performance, and system memory. Most computers purchased today are powerful enough that you can get the latency pretty low, but you still have to experiment to find the settings that provide the best performance.

The parameter that most computer audio interfaces use to set the latency is called the *input buffer*. The smaller the buffer, the lower the latency, but the harder the CPU has to work. If you lower the buffer size too much, the setting can produce crackling noises, although this is a function of the horsepower of the computer. These noises crop up when the CPU literally has to drop audio bytes because it can't keep up with the audio stream.

Today's fast computers can get the I/O buffer size down to 64 samples (1.3 ms at a 48k sampling rate) without too much trouble, but the more tracks and processing you add (especially when running at sampling rates higher than 48 kHz), the harder the computer's CPU will have to work, which means you may need to increase the buffer size to prevent dropouts.

It should be noted that it's best *not* to use any software processing, such as compressors or EQ, when recording because each plug-in adds any-where from a little to a lot of latency. Keep the signal path as efficient as possible with as few things between the mic and the recorder as you can, and your signal will not only sound better, but it will stay in sync as well.

Many audio interfaces are equipped with zero-latency monitoring, which is an analog bus that loops directly from the interface's input to its output without passing through the computer. Once you've set up this routing in your interface's control panel applet (it comes with the inter-face), the player or singer will be able to monitor the backing tracks and get his or her performance in sync without any time delay whatsoever.

If your interface doesn't have zero-latency monitoring, you can accom-plish the same thing if you have an analog or digital hardware console. Just connect the interface input to an aux, bus, or direct output on the mixer to avoid recording the entire temp mix into the new track. Although there is some latency in digital mixers, it's kept very low (to 2 ms or less) thanks to an operating system that's specifically optimized for the task.

To lower latency:

▶ Lower the input buffer size.

▶ Use zero-latency monitoring.

▶ Use an outboard console.

▶ Avoid the use of plug-ins.

FIREWIRE VERSUS USB

Most audio interfaces have either a FireWire or a USB connection to your computer, and many users aren't sure what's right for them, given the wide range of products available. On the surface it seems that USB 2.0 is the faster interface, with a speed of 480 kbs compared to FireWire's 400 kbs, but more than just that one parameter determines which is best for your application.

The circuit architecture between FireWire and USB 2.0 is different. FireWire uses what's known as a *peer-to-peer* configuration, where each device has some built-in intelligence that can determine the best way for data to transfer. High-speed USB 2.0 (as compared to low-speed USB 1.0) uses a *master-slave* configuration that adds system overhead that results in slower data flow. What this really means is that if you really want to record more than a few tracks at a time, then FireWire is the way to go. USB is too unreliable in that you might have dropouts and ruin that perfect take.

For very high track counts (greater than eight), an interface card that plugs directly into your computer's PCI bus is required, which is what the large Digidesign Pro Tools|HD and the older TDM packages do.

Headroom and Gain Staging

Gain staging is the proper level setting of each section of the signal path so that no one section overloads. On an analog console, you would make sure that the input gain wouldn't overload the equalizer section, which wouldn't overload the panning amplifier, which wouldn't overload the fader buffer, which wouldn't overload the bus, which wouldn't overload the master bus. This is the reason why a pre-fader and after-fader listen (PFL and AFL) exist: to monitor each gain stage to make sure there's no distortion.

While all of these stages are slightly tweakable, one rule exists in the analog world that aptly applies in the digital world as well.

The level of the channel faders should always stay below the subgroup or master fader.

This means that the level of the master fader should always be placed higher than each of the channel faders (see Figures 4.2, 4.3, and 4.4). Although it might be okay if one or two channels are slightly above (it's almost inevitable in every mix), just a single channel with big chunks of EQ (like +10 of a frequency band) or an insert with an effects plug-in that's maxed can destroy any semblance of a good-sounding mix.

Figure 4.2
Channel faders too high, subgroup fader too low.

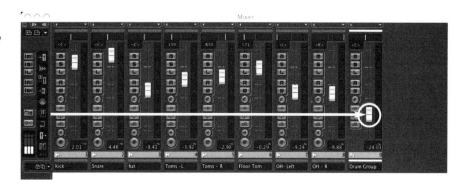

Figure 4.3
Subgroup too high, master fader too low.

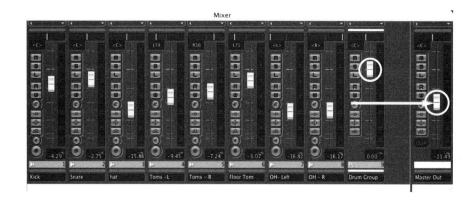

Figure 4.4
Channel and subgroup faders at correct levels.

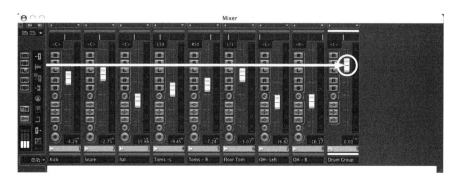

Because many analog consoles have sufficient headroom these days, the rule hasn't been religiously followed, but it has been a golden rule since day one of modern consoles. Not following this rule is the main reason for lack of fidelity in the DAW, however. The master bus is overloaded!

Speaking of headroom, that brings us to the second rule:

Leave lots of headroom!

HEADROOM

Recording engineers in the digital world have been taught to increase the level of anything recorded or mixed to as close to 0 dB full scale as possible in an effort to "use all the bits," which means that, in theory, full 24-bit resolution is achieved only at 0 dB full scale. Although this might have been useful back in the days of 16-bit recording, when you needed all 16 to get the best sound quality, it doesn't apply as much today in the 24-bit and beyond world. The short reason for this is that if we didn't record hot enough in the 16-bit days, we'd get more noise. That's not so much true in our 24-bit world. Today we can record at a level a lot less than 0 dB FS and not have to worry about noise, and there's a great advantage in doing so—lots of headroom and therefore less distortion.

Headroom is our friend. We need it to preserve the super-fast transients that make up the first part of almost any instrument (but especially instruments such as tambourines, drums, and percussion). These transients can typically range as high as 20 dB above what a VU meter might be telling you (peak meters are much closer to the actual true recording level), and recording too hot means cutting those transients off the signal by going into overload, if only for a millisecond or two. This results in not only a slightly dull recording, but one that sounds less realistic as well. The solution: *more headroom.*

Headroom means that our average level might be –10 dB or less on the meter, leaving plenty of room for transients above that. This concept is actually a holdover once again from the analog days, where a really good console might have a clipping point of +28 dB. Since 0 dB VU = +4 dB (trust me, it does), that means that you had a full 24 dB of headroom before you ran into distortion as long as you kept your mix hovering around 0 VU.

While leaving 24 dB for headroom might be excessive in the digital world, leaving 10 or 15 dB may not be. Since it's easy enough to make up the gain later, you won't increase the noise, and your mix will be cleaner, why not try it?

Rules for Gain Staging

1. Keep all channel faders below the subgroup or master fader.

2. When using large amounts of EQ or a plug-in with gain, lower the channel fader rather than bringing up the others around it.

3. Leave lots of headroom; you can raise the level later.

Interview with Gannon Kashiwa:
Digidesign's Professional Products Market Manager

DAW fidelity is so important that it's a really good idea to get some insight directly from the source, so here's a brief interview with Gannon Kashawi of Digidesign that will provide a manufacturer's perspective on the subject.

What are the common things that you see that cause a decrease in fidelity?

There's a bunch of things that people do to degrade their sound. One of the things is overcompressing and using way too much processing in order to get that CD sound too early in the process. I see mixes that are totally squashed and maximized up to the top of the digital word leaving the studio heading to mastering. There's nothing wrong with putting a mastering chain on your master fader so you can check it out, but if you leave it on, you're not giving the mastering engineer any choices to work with dynamically and sonically. If you pack the word up into the final 2 bits of a 24-bit word [that's anything hotter than −12dB FS], there really isn't much left for those guys to do. You can't uncompress something once it's already maximized.

It seems to me that's a holdover from the days of 16 bit, where you needed to get as close to 0 dB FS to keep the signal from getting noisy. That doesn't seem needed today.

Exactly. You've got 24 bits of audio dynamic range to use. That's 144 dB of dynamic range that is available to you. There's no reason to record up in that top 2 bits (12 dB) and keep the mix there the whole time.

As a matter of fact, if you record everything really hot, then you're going to have to start pulling the channel faders down and the master fader down in order to avoid clipping. I always recommend for people to leave 3 to 6 dB of headroom, or even more depending upon the kind of music, in their recorded files in their mix. Again, if you maximize it out, you don't have the dynamic range later in the game.

Also, if you're always working towards 0 dB FS, with highly dynamic material with a lot of fast transients there's a chance that you're going to have inter-sample clipping that you wouldn't ordinarily see when the waveform gets reconstructed. If you have a couple of samples that are right at 0 dB FS, in between those samples you might have something that's an overage.

I hadn't heard of that. It's really in between the samples?

It's what happens with the reconstruction filter. It's only getting its information at the sample points, but it's possible to clip the reconstructed waveform in between those samples.

Coming back to overprocessing, do you have a recommended method for keeping everything as clean as possible?

As I said, part of the sound today is to make things compressed and loud, but I think what people do is overcompress. They're listening to a mastered final mix of a CD, which is already mastered, and comparing what they're doing as they go along in the recording process. People try to get to the finished sound too quickly.

What I recommend is to mix in groups (drums in one group, vocals in another, and so on) and try to distribute any EQ and compression across a number of stages so you're not trying to get any one equalizer or any one compressor to do a huge amount of work. If you distribute it across a couple of different compressors or EQs where nothing is used to its extreme, you'll get a much cleaner result.

So use bus compression and compression on the instruments, but don't work any one of them too hard unless you want that real "effect" kind of sound, because the non-linearities of a compressor are going to become more extreme and more audible as you push it harder. A little bit at a time is the key. Don't work any of the processors or EQs too hard.

One other thing about making a cleaner mix: Filtering makes a difference. Being bright is sometimes not your friend because you have all this stuff that's competing for the air in your mix, so using the low-pass filters and removing some of the high-frequency content sometimes cleans things up considerably. Sometimes you have all this high-frequency garbage that you don't need, and you have to make space for the stuff that really belongs up there.

How about the theory that you degrade the sound if you move the faders off of unity gain?

Ah, total BS. Pro Tools calculates all volume and pan coefficients as 24-bit coefficients. It doesn't matter where your fader is. Whether your fader is down 5 dB or up 5 dB, there's no mathematical or sonic consequence.

Does gain staging make a difference? Is it like analog, where you can't have the channel or group faders way above the master?

Sure. Extremes in any of those cases will affect the output. You still have to observe good gain structure throughout the system, especially when you're doing heavy processing. Good analog engineering practices are still good digital engineering practices.

CHAPTER 5

Basic Stereo Techniques

Even if you never intend to record an ensemble larger than a standard rock-and-roll rhythm section, a good grasp of the many techniques for stereo recording is essential and will come in handy sooner or later. Stereo miking is commonly used when recording drum kits, pianos, string sections, Leslies, and the like, and can certainly be applied to just about any recording situation.

So although we won't discuss these techniques in an orchestral music sense (where a lot of knowledge beyond the scope of this book is a necessity), this chapter will provide a basic overview of the many methods of stereo miking.

First of all, stereo miking is an improvement over mono miking because it provides:

▶ A sense of the soundfield from left to right

▶ A sense of depth or distance between each instrument

▶ A sense of distance of the ensemble from the listener

▶ A spatial sense of the acoustic environment—the ambience or hall reverberation

Types of Stereo Miking

There are four general mic techniques used for stereo recording, each with a different sound and different sets of benefits and disadvantages:

▶ Coincident pair (including X/Y, M-S, and Blumlein)

▶ Spaced pair

▶ Near-coincident pair (the famous ORTF method)

▶ Baffled-omni pair or artificial head

COINCIDENT PAIR

A coincident pair consists of two directional mics mounted so that their grilles are nearly touching, but with their diaphragms angled apart in such a way that they aim approximately toward the left and right sides of the ensemble. For example, two cardioid microphones can be mounted angled apart, their grilles one above the other. The greater the angle between microphones and the narrower the polar pattern, the wider the stereo spread.

X/Y

While there are several variations of the coincident pair, the X/Y configuration is the easiest and mostly widely used. X/Y requires two identical directional microphones.

Unlike what you may think, the mics are not crossed in an X pattern in this configuration. In fact, the mic capsules are placed as close as possible to one another in a 90-degree angle. (See Figure 5.1.)

Figure 5.1
Two AKG 451s in an X/Y configuration.

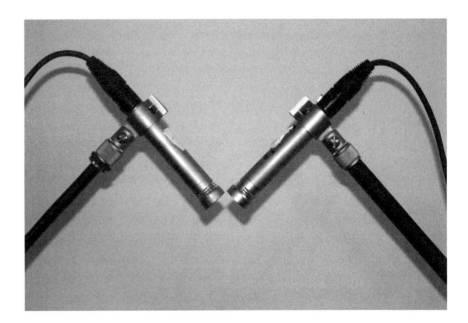

M-S

M-S stands for mid-side and consists again of two microphones—a directional mic (an omni can be substituted as well) pointed toward the sound source and a figure-8 mic pointed toward the sides. Once again, the mics are positioned so their capsules are as close to touching as possible. (See Figure 5.2.)

Figure 5.2
M-S miking.

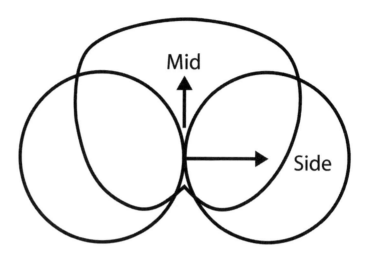

M-S is great for stereo imaging, especially when most of the sound is coming from the center of the ensemble. Because of this, it's less effective on large groups, favoring the middle voices to which the mics are closer.

M-S has no phase problems in stereo, with excellent mono compatibility, which can make it the best way to do room and ambience miking under the right circumstances. In many cases it can sound more natural than a spaced pair. If the source is extra large, sometimes using M-S alone will require too much distance to get the whole section or choir into perspective, so multiple mic locations must be used. If a narrower pickup pattern is required to attenuate hall sound, then a directional mic, such as a cardioid or even a hypercardioid, will work for the M mic. Just be aware that you may be sacrificing the bottom octaves as a result.

For best placement, walk around the room and listen to where the instrument or sound source sounds best. Note the balance of instrument to room, and the stereo image of the room as well. Once you have found a location, set up the directional mic where the middle of your head was.

Listening to either of these mics alone may sound okay, or they may even sound horribly bad. In order to make this system work, the mic's output signals need an additional "decoding" step to reproduce a faithful stereo image. The directional creates a *positive* voltage all the way around, and the bidirectional mic is nulled to the front (of the source, the side of the mic) and creates a positive voltage from anything coming from the left and a *negative* voltage from anything coming from the right.

While you can buy an M-S decoder, you can easily emulate one with three channels on your console or DAW. On one channel, bring up the cardioid (M) forward-facing mic. Bring up the figure-8 mic (S) on two additional channels, either by multing the outputs or by patching from the "insert out" of the S channel to the "insert in" of an adjacent channel. Pan both channels to one side (like hard left), then run a tone down the first S channel, flip the phase of the second S channel, and bring up the level until the two channels cancel 100 percent.

Now pan the first S channel hard left and the second S channel hard right, balance the cardioid (M) channel with your pair of S channels, and you have your matrix.

A nice additional feature of this method is that you are able to vary the amount of room sound (or change the focus) by varying the level of the bidirectional S mic.

Blumlein Array

Developed for EMI Records in 1935 by audio pioneer Alan Blumlein, the Blumlein stereo setup is a coincident stereo technique that uses two bidirectional microphones angled at 90 degrees to each other. This technique provides the best results when placed close to the sound source, since the low frequency response will decrease as the distance is increased. Blumlein stereo has a higher degree of separation between the channels than X/Y stereo, but must be used with care since it also picks up sound sources located behind the stereo pair.. (See Figures 5.3 and 5.4.)

Figure 5.3
A Blumlein array.

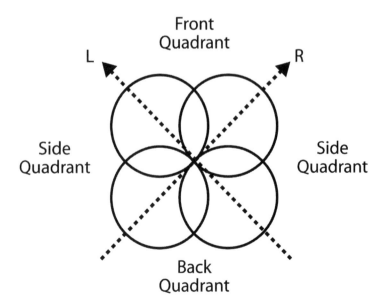

Figure 5.4
Bruce Swedien with a Royer
R-121 Blumlein array. Courtesy of
Royer Labs.

Stereo Mic

Although not normally thought of as a coincident mic pair, a stereo mic uses two coincident mic capsules mounted in a single housing for convenience. Because of their close proximity to one another, this method may provide the easiest coincident mic setup. (See Figure 5.5.)

Figure 5.5
Royer SF-12 stereo microphone.
Courtesy of Royer Labs.

Coincident-Pair Technique

The coincident-pair technique has the following features:

- Imaging is very good.

- Stereo spread ranges from narrow to accurate.

- Signals are mono-compatible.

- Stereo is not as wide as other methods.

SPACED PAIR

With the spaced-pair technique, two identical mics are placed several feet apart, aiming straight ahead toward the musical ensemble. The mics can have any polar pattern, but the omnidirectional pattern is the most popular for this method. The greater the spacing between mics, the greater the stereo spread. (See Figure 5.6.)

Figure 5.6
Spaced-pair diagram.

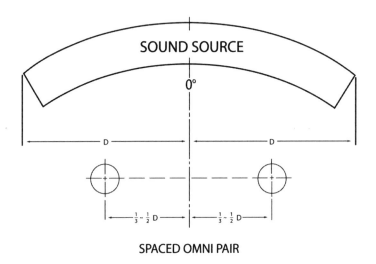

SPACED OMNI PAIR

If the spacing between mics is too far apart, the stereo separation seems exaggerated. On the other hand, if the mics are too close together, there will be an inadequate stereo spread. In addition, the mics will tend to favor the center of the ensemble because the mics are closest to the center instruments.

In an attempt to obtain a good musical balance, the mics are usually placed about 10 or 12 feet apart, but such spacing results in exaggerated separation. One solution is to place a third microphone midway between the original pair and mix its output to both channels. That way, the ensemble is recorded with a good balance, and the stereo spread is not as exaggerated.

The spaced-pair method tends to make off-center images relatively unfocused or hard to localize. In addition, combining both mics to mono sometimes causes phase cancellations of various frequencies, which may or may not be audible.

The advantage with spaced miking is a warm sense of ambience in which concert hall reverberation seems to surround the instruments and sometimes the listener. Another advantage of the spaced-mic technique is the ability to use omnidirectional microphones. An omni condenser mic has more extended low-frequency response than a unidirectional condenser mic and tends to have a smoother response and less off-axis coloration.

Spaced-Pair Technique

The spaced-pair technique has the following features:

- Off-center images are diffuse.

- Stereo spread tends to be exaggerated unless a third center mic is used.

- Provides a warm sense of ambience.

- Phasing problems are possible.

THE DECCA TREE

A variation of the spaced pair is the Decca Tree, which is essentially a spaced pair with a center mic connected to a custom stand and suspended over the conductor (see Figure 5.7). Decca Records, who had a long tradition of developing experimental recording techniques, including surround sound and proprietary recording equipment, developed the Decca Tree as a compromise between the purist stereo pair and multi-mic arrays for orchestral recording by Decca engineers in 1950s. Apart from individual engineer's choice of mic, it remains unchanged to this day. It is still in use in film scoring/classical orchestral and opera recording because it produces a very spacious stereo image with good localization.

Figure 5.7
The Decca Tree.

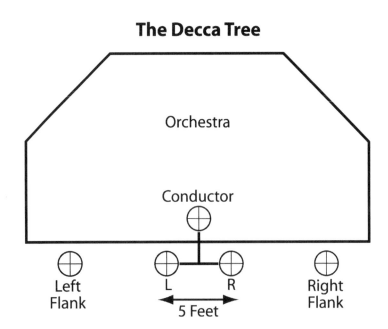

The classic Decca Tree setup uses three Neumann M 50s arranged in a triangle 10 to 12 feet above the conductor's position, although the spacing varies with venue and size of ensemble. The left mic is panned left, the right mic panned right, and the center mic panned to the center, with additional mics ("spot" mics or "sweeteners") used over violins (usually panned to the left), cellos (usually panned to the right), and harp/timps and soloist.

The distance between mics depends on the size of the ensemble. For orchestra, the left and right mics are 8 to 10 feet apart, with the center about 6 to 7 feet in front of the left-right axis.

It is a little-known fact that Decca has used (and maybe still uses) mics other than the M 50 on the tree. In particular, Decca has used M 49s and KM 56s on the tree, but modern substitutions include the TLM 50 or M 150, the Brauner VM1, or the DPA 4003 with APE spheres.

NEAR-COINCIDENT PAIR

The most common example of the near-coincident method is the ORTF system, which uses two cardioids angled 110 degrees apart and spaced 7 inches (17 cm) apart horizontally. (ORTF stands for *Office de Radiodifusión Television Française* or the *Office of French Radio and Television Broadcasting*.) This method tends to provide accurate localization; that is, instruments at the sides of the orchestra are reproduced at or very near the speakers, and instruments halfway to one side tend to be reproduced halfway to one side. ORTF provides a much greater sense of space due to time/phase differences since the capsules are as far apart as your ears. (See Figure 5.8.)

Figure 5.8
An ORTF setup using AKG 451s.

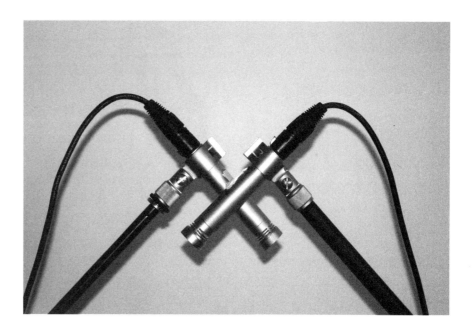

Near-Coincident Pair Technique

Near-coincident pair features include the following:

- Sharp imaging.

- Accurate stereo spread.

- A greater sense of air and depth than coincident methods.

- Wide image and depth of Blumlein without as much of the reverberant field.

BAFFLED-OMNI PAIR

A baffled-omni pair, whether using two mics or a dummy head, is simply trying to emulate the way our ears are placed on our heads, and therefore the way we hear.

In this method, two omnidirectional mics are separated a few inches by a baffle between them. The baffle is a hard disk covered with absorbent foam (as in the Jecklin Disk; see Figure 5.9). Or, the baffle is a hard sphere with the mics flush-mounted on opposite sides (as in the Schoeps spherical mic; see Figure 5.10).

Figure 5.9
Jecklin Disk. Courtesy of Josephson
Engineering.

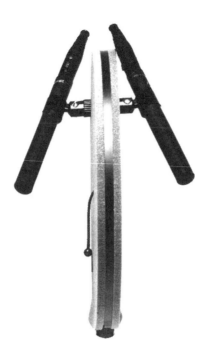

Figure 5.10
Schoeps KFM 360 spherical mic.
Courtesy of Schoeps GmbH.

With the baffled-omni pair, the level, time, and spectral differences between channels create the stereo images. The omni condenser mics used in this method have excellent low-frequency response.

Also falling into this category are dummy heads, such as the Neumann KU 100. (See Figure 5.11.)

Figure 5.11
Neumann KU 100 dummy head.
Courtesy of Neumann USA.

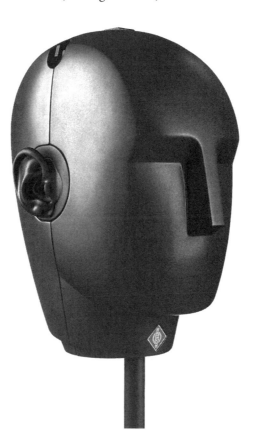

Baffled-Omni Pair Technique

The baffled-omni pair technique has the following features:

- Images are sharp.

- Stereo spread tends to be accurate.

- Low-frequency response is excellent.

For more information on stereo recording:

▶ www.kellyindustries.com/microphones/stereo_miking_techniques.html

▶ www.tape.com/Bartlett_Articles/stereo_microphone_techniques.html

▶ www.josephson.com (click on Tech Notes and then Jecklin Disk)

▶ www.csun.edu/~record/stereo

▶ www.prosoundweb.com/studyhall/shure/mics/stereo/techniques.php

▶ homerecording.about.com/od/microphones101/ss/stereo_mics.htm

▶ www.shurenotes.com/issue25/article.asp?flash=true

CHAPTER 6

Basic Multichannel Tracking

Although it's possible to get a good sound by just randomly placing a mic in front of an instrument or vocal, it can sound so much better with a little forethought regarding the many concerns involved. And, the more mics you record with, the more complex these concerns become. This chapter will give you some insights on how to get good sounds quickly.

Choosing the Right Mic

While it's safe to say that most engineers rely on experience when choosing microphones, there are some things to think about when selecting a microphone.

MICHAEL BEINHORN: *There's no one microphone that does every single thing.*

▶ **Select a microphone that complements the instrument you'll be recording.** For instance, if you have an instrument that has a very edgy top end, you wouldn't want to choose a mic that also has that quality, since those frequencies will be emphasized. Instead, choose a mic that's a bit mellower, such as a ribbon. This is one of the reasons why a ribbon mic works so well on brass, for instance.

▶ **Is the mic designed to be used in the free field or in the diffuse field?** *Free field* means that the sound source dominates what the mic hears. *Diffuse field* means that the reflections play a large role in what the mic hears. Mics designed for free-field use have a very flat frequency response in the high frequencies and, as a result, can sound dull when placed farther away. Diffuse-field mics have a boost in the upper frequencies that makes them sound flat when placed farther away.

▶ **Select a mic that won't be overloaded by the source.** You wouldn't want to put a ribbon mic or many condensers on a snare drum with a heavy-hitting drummer, for instance.

▶ **Choose the right polar pattern for the job.** If leakage is a consideration, then choose a mic with the proper directional capabilities for the job. If a mic is flat on-axis, it will roll off the highs when it's 90 degrees off-axis. If it's flat 90 degrees off-axis, it will have a rising high end when it's on-axis.

▶ **Is proximity effect an issue?** If you're close-miking, will the bass buildup from proximity be too much? If so, consider an omni.

Microphone Considerations

1. Condensers of a given polar pattern will tend to give you more room sound than dynamics of the same polar pattern.

2. Omnis will give you lower bass extension than cardioids.

3. Large-diaphragm condensers have lower self-noise than small-diaphragm condensers.

4. Small-diaphragm condensers are generally less colored off-axis than large-diaphragm condensers.

The Secret to Getting Good Sounds

Contrary to what many who are starting out in recording might think, just having great equipment doesn't guarantee a great sound. While you can't really quantify how much each variable contributes to how something ultimately sounds (because each situation, even within the same project, is unique), you can generally break it down to something like this:

▶ The player and the instrument contribute about 50 percent to the overall sound (sometimes a little more, sometimes a little less—but always the greatest portion).

▶ The room contributes about 20 percent to the overall sound. (Even on close-miked instruments, the room is far more responsible for the ultimate sound than many engineers realize.)

▶ The mic position contributes about 20 percent to the overall sound. (Placement is really your acoustic EQ and is responsible for the instrument's blend in the track.)

▶ The mic choice contributes about 10 percent to the overall sound. (This is the last little bit that takes a good sound and makes it great.)

If something doesn't sound right, there are many things to change before you reach for the EQ. Try the following in this order:

1. Change the source (the instrument you are miking), if possible.

2. Change the mic placement.

3. Change the placement of the instrument in the room.

4. Change the mic.

5. Change the mic preamplifier.

6. Change the amount of compression and/or limiting (from none to a lot).

7. Change the room (the actual room you are recording in).

8. Change the player.

9. Come back and try it another day.

AL SCHMITT: *I don't use any EQ when I record. I use the mics for EQ. I don't even use any compression. The only time I might use a little bit of compression is maybe on the kick, but for most jazz dates I don't.*

MACK: *One of my big things is not to use EQ, or as little as possible, and not to add any, but find what's offensive and get rid of that as opposed to cranking other stuff to compensate.*

SECRETS OF MIC PLACEMENT

Quickly finding a mic's optimum position is perhaps the single most useful talent an engineer can have. Bruce Sweiden says mics are the voodoo magic of recording. Steve Albini says every mic has someplace where it will sound best. Sometimes the search resembles questing for the Holy Grail. You should always trust your ears and begin by listening to the musician in your studio, find a sweet spot, and then begin your microphone placement there. If you don't like the resultant sound, then move the mic or swap it with another. EQ is the last thing you should touch.

FRANK FILIPETTI: *I've been doing this long enough to know that a change in microphones or position is worth a lot more than tweaking EQs. I have a tendency to think that if you start tweaking EQs too soon, you're going to miss some obvious things, so the first thing I do is get the session sounding great flat.*

Remember: Mics cannot effectively be placed by sight, which is a mistake that is all too easy to make (especially after reading a book like this). The best mic position cannot be predicted, it must be found.

To Find the Sweet Spot

- To correctly place an omni microphone, cover one ear and listen with the other. Move around the player or sound source until you find a spot that sounds best.

- To place a cardioid microphone, cup your hand behind your ear and listen. Move around the player or sound source until you find a spot that sounds best.

- For a stereo pair, cup your hands behind both ears. Move around the player or sound source until you find a spot that sounds best.

Before you start swapping gear, know that the three most important factors in getting the sound you want are *mic position*, *mic position*, and *mic position*.

1. Get the instrument to make the sound you want to record first. If you can't hear it, you can't record it.

AL SCHMITT: *The major trick in all of this...is that you go out in the studio, stand next to the conductor, and listen to what's going on. Your job is to go in and capture exactly what he wants to hear out there. So my microphone techniques are still the same as they were 30 years ago.*

2. Use the cover-one-ear-and-listen technique described a moment ago to find the best place to start experimenting with mic position.

3. Position the mic and listen. Repeat as much as necessary.

Placement Considerations
The following are some issues to consider before mic placement:

▶ The only reasons for close-miking are to avoid leakage to other mics so that the engineer can have more flexibility in balancing the ensemble in the mix. If at all possible, give the mic some distance from the source in order to let the sound develop and be captured naturally.

EDDIE KRAMER: *In regard to mic techniques, what I adapted was this classical idea of recording—i.e., the distance of the microphones to the instruments should not be too close if you wanted to get anything with tremendous depth. Obviously, I used close-miking techniques as well, but it started with the concept that "distance makes depth" that Bob Auger taught me. Generally, the basic philosophy of getting the mics up in the air and getting some room sound and some air around the instrument was what we used. Then you'd fill in with the close mics.*

▶ Mics cannot effectively be placed by sight. The best mic position cannot be predicted, it must be found. It's okay to start from a place that you know has worked in the past, but be prepared to experiment with the placement a bit because each instrument and situation is different.

▶ If the room ambience will be the majority of the sound you want to record, start with those mics that pick up the room and then add mics that act as support to the room mics.

▶ To overcome phase problems, consider inserting an X/Y phase scope on your stereo bus. Leave it running all the time so your eyes and ears get in sync with what is in phase and what is not. Monitoring phase this way does not guarantee good mic placement, but it does allow bad placement to be spotted more easily.

▶ Around 300 Hz is where the proximity effect often shows up and is why many engineers continually cut in this range. If many directional microphones are being used, they will be subject to proximity effect, and you should expect a buildup of this frequency range in the mix.

ED CHERNEY: *"If something is a little dark, then it might be because 2 or 300 is building up, so you dip a little of that out....*

▶ A huge sound is a larger-than-life sound. One way to accomplish a larger-than-life sound is by recording a sound that is softer than the recording will most likely be played back. Ever listen to the guitar sounds on Eric Clapton's seminal recording of "Layla?" Both he and Duane Allman used little Fender Champ and Princeton Reverb amplifiers (the Champ is 6 watts into an 8-inch speaker, and the Princeton is 12 watts into a 10-inch), but the guitar sounds are huge.

The 3-to-1 Principle

The 3-to-1 principle is pretty important when considering any multi-mic setups because, if you observe the rule, you can stop any phase problems before they start. Simply put, the 3-to-1 principle states that in order to maintain phase integrity between microphones, for every unit of distance between the mic and its source, the distance between any other mics should be at least three times that distance. For instance, if a pair of microphones were placed over the sound board of a piano at a distance of 1 foot, the separation between the two mics should be at least 3 feet. If the distance from the source were 2 feet, the distance between mics should be at least 6 feet. (See Figure 6.1.)

Figure 6.1
The 3-to-1 principle.

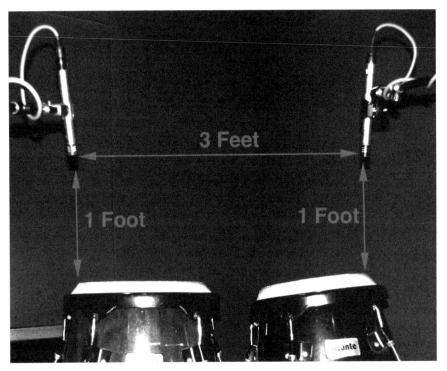

This principle is not a hard-and-fast rule, but it certainly is a good guideline for eliminating phase problems. Remember, if you record something with a phase problem, no amount of EQ or processing afterward can ever make it right.

CHECKING PHASE

Checking microphone phase should be one of the first things that an engineer does after the mics are wired up and tested. This is especially the case in a tracking session where a lot of mics will be used, since having just one mic out of phase can cause uncorrectable sonic problems that will haunt the recording forever. A session that is in phase will sound bigger and punchier, while just a single out-of-phase mic will make the entire mix sound tiny and weak.

If you're going to be absolutely thorough, there are actually two tests—one for polarity and one for phase. The polarity check is used mainly to be sure that all mics are pushing and pulling the same way and to check for miswired cables. (Yes, they're out there, especially if you build your own.) The phase check will make sure that you minimize the interference between the mics when they're placed.

Remember that the phase switch on the mic preamp, DAW interface, or console is really a polarity switch that changes the phase by 180 degrees at all frequencies by swapping Pins 2 and 3 of a balanced microphone line. It may get the problem frequencies closer to being in phase, or it may get them further away. It depends on what the problems are and what the placement of the mics is.

HOW TO CHECK POLARITY

1. After the mics are set up, wired, and checked, but not necessarily placed, pick one mic that can be easily moved. This can be a scratch vocal mic, a hat mic, a guitar mic—it doesn't matter as long as it works, sounds good to begin with (it's not defective), and can move next to the farthest mic used in the session. This mic will become your "gold standard."

2. With the gold-standard mic in hand, move it next to the kick drum mic (or any other mic that you wish to test, for that matter). Put both mics together so the capsules touch and speak into them from about a foot away (the distance isn't critical). See Figure 6.2.

Figure 6.2
Checking polarity.

3. Bring up the faders on both mics so the audio level (not the fader position) is equal on both.

4. Flip the phase of the mic under test (in this case, the kick mic) and choose the position that gives you the most low end.

5. Repeat for all the other mics.

Remember, you're not flipping the phase of the gold-standard mic, only the one that you're testing.

CHECKING PHASE BY LISTENING

This is essential not only on the drums, but on any instrument being miked with more than a single microphone. However, the chances for a phase problem are far greater on the drum kit because it usually has more mics on it than any other instrument. Understand that you will never have all microphones completely in phase, but some problems will be diminished by reversing polarity on some of the channels. The only way to determine this is through experimentation and listening.

1. Listen to the overheads in stereo and then listen to them in mono. If they still sound okay, go on to the next step. If the overheads sound thin or swishy and you know their polarity is correct (they're pushing and pulling at the same time), then place them in a different position, perhaps using them as a coincident pair or placed farther apart.

2. Once you are pleased with the overheads, add the kick. Switch the polarity on the kick and stay with the position that has the fullest sound.

3. Bring up the snare mic. Press the phase button on the console. Does it sound better inverted or not? Now, listen in mono and see whether it still sounds better.

4. Keep doing this for each microphone. On each one, listen to how the mic sits in the mix, then listen to it with the phase inverted, and then do the same thing in mono. In each case, use the phase switch position that gives you the fullest sound with the most low end.

5. If you have two kick mics, check the phase of the inside kick mic against the overheads and then the outside kick against the inside. Sometimes you might need to move the outside mic because neither position is good.

Ultimately, you cannot avoid phase cancellation; you can only make sure it has as little effect on the overall sound as possible.

Remember: One position of the phase switch will always sound fuller than the other.

> ## Mic Placement Most Likely to Cause Problems
>
> - Mics that are facing each other (like on the opposite sides of a drum).
>
> - Mics that are facing the floor. (Just angle them a bit.)
>
> - Mics that are pointing at one source where there is another much louder source nearby with its own mic.

CHECKING PHASE WITH AN OSCILLOSCOPE PLUG-IN

One way to be absolutely certain about phase is to look at either a phase meter or an oscilloscope. Remember that the nature of music is that there will always be some phase difference between any two mics picking up the same sound from different positions, so you will never see perfect phase alignment.

1. You need an oscilloscope plug-in that has an external norizontal input with sufficient sensitivity so that you can get full-scale deflection from the nominal operating voltage of your system. Route the main left output channel of your console or DAW to the vertical input and the right channel to the horizontal output and adjust the scope's gain so that a mono signal (same program on both channels) shows a straight, diagonal line slanting to the right. (See Figure 6.3.)

Figure 6.3
An in-phase scope signal.

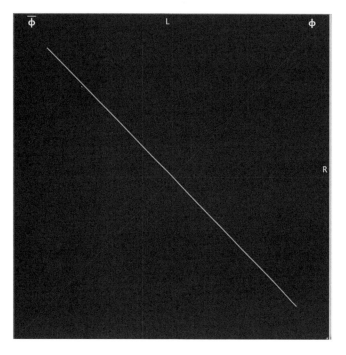

2. Now play your stereo mix, and you'll see "scrambled eggs" as the line opens up into an irregular and constantly changing circle. The more "open" the circle, the greater the phase difference between the mics. You want to avoid the condition where the circle starts slanting to the left. (See Figure 6.4.)

Figure 6.4
An out-of-phase scope signal.

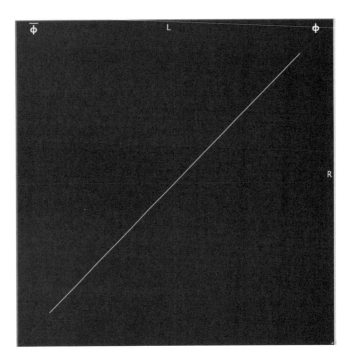

CHECKING PHASE WITH A PHASE METER

Many traditional hardware consoles have a built-in phase meter (and many DAWs have a phase meter plug-in). Being able to properly read it can go a long way in determining whether you have any phase problems.

If the left and right channels are identical and in phase, the needle should read all the way to the right, or +. (See Figure 6.5.) If the level of both channels is identical and out of phase, the needle will read all the way to the left, or –. This is the condition that you're trying to avoid, because if you sum the two channels together, they will cancel out in mono. If there's no relationship between the two channels, the needle will sit in the middle. For most stereo program material that has a lot of identical content on both channels, it will wander around in the + side of the scale (which is okay).

Figure 6.5
A phase meter with an in-phase signal.

The degree to which the needle stays to the right is the degree to which the parts of the mix that are in both channels will sum to mono. For instance, suppose you have a singer panned to the center. The meter should poke to the right on peaks, indicating that this common content is in phase. If the meter nudges to the left on voice peaks, something is inverting phase in one channel or the other, which will make that vocal content softer when summed to mono.

CHAPTER 7

Preparing the Drum Kit for Recording

If there's one instrument that engineers seem to obsess over, it's the drum kit, and well they should. Drums are the heartbeat of virtually all modern music. Wimpy-sounding drums can make for a wimpy recording regardless of how well everything else is recorded.

The problem is that most drummers' kits simply don't record well for any number of reasons. Whether it's because of old beat-up heads (the worst offender), bad tuning, uneven bearing edges of the shells, or defective hardware, drums that might be adequate or even great-sounding in a live situation don't always make the cut when put under the scrutiny of the recording studio.

While many engineers are willing to spend whatever time it takes to make the drums sound great, most just don't have the know-how or the time to improve the sound of the set before it gets under the mics. As a result, virtually all big-budget projects either rent a kit specifically for recording or hire a drum tuner, because no matter how great your signal chain is, if the drum sound in the room doesn't cut it, there's not much the engineer can do to help.

Since this book is about getting great sounds, it's important to make the drums sound their best before you even turn on a mic. But before we go there, just what constitutes a great-sounding drum kit?

The Recording Engineer's Handbook, Second Edition

The Keys to a Great-Sounding Drum Kit

While the definition of *great* is different to each person on a general level, in the studio it usually means a kit that is well tuned and free of buzzes and sympathetic vibrations. This means that when you hit the rack tom, for instance, the snare doesn't buzz, and the other toms don't ring along with it. Or if you hit the snare, the toms don't ring along. So how do you achieve this drum nirvana? It's all in the tuning and the kit maintenance, which we'll check out in depth later in the chapter. But first, let's learn a little bit about drums themselves, since it helps to have a basic idea of why they sound the way they do.

Here are the things that affect the sound of a drum:

► **Shell size** has the most impact on the natural pitch of a drum. The larger the diameter, the lower the natural pitch, although you can obviously change this a bit by tuning the heads.

► **Shell depth** is mostly responsible for how loud the drum will be and, to some degree, the articulation of the sound. This means that a shallow shell (say a 9-inch tom) doesn't have as much surface area as a larger one, so the sound is a bit shorter with a sharper attack.

► **Shell thickness** is usually overlooked as a contributing factor to the sound of a drum. Thinner shells actually are more resonant since they're easier to excite because they have a lower mass than a heavier, thicker shell.

► **Shell material** used to make the drum shell is the most responsible for the tone of the drums. Here are the most commonly used drum shell materials:

  ► **Maple** is the most prized construction material by drummers, primarily because the sound is so even across the drum frequency spectrum.

  ► **Mahogany** sounds warmer than maple because the low end is increased.

  ► **Birch** is very hard and dense, which results in a brighter drum with a lot less low end than maple.

  ► **Poplar** has a sound very similar to birch, with a bright top end with less bottom.

- ► **Basswood** exhibits an increased low end that's similar to mahogany.

- ► **Luaan** has a warmer sound with less top end, similar to mahogany.

► **Shell interior** has a lot to do with the pitch of the drum. A rough interior produces a less resonant drum, since the roughness breaks up the interior reflections. A smooth interior results in a more resonant drum, which means it's easier to tune and control.

► **Bearing edges** refers to the cut at the edge of a drum shell where the hoops are attached. The way the bearing edge is cut can not only affect the pitch of the drum, but the tuning as well. The sharper the cut, the brighter the drum.

► The type of **hoop** and the number of lugs used to seat the drum heads determine how the drum will sound. In general, the thicker the hoop, the easier the drum will be to tune. Fewer lugs provide more complex overtones. Stamped hoops get a warmer tone than die-cast hoops. Aluminum gives a high pitch, while brass provides more overtones. Die-cast hoops are generally both thicker and stronger than stamped hoops, so the drum becomes easier to tune. There are fewer overtones as a byproduct. Wood hoops come in different thicknesses, so they can be made to sound like either a stamped or a cast hoop, only brighter.

The Snare

Since the snare is the most important drum in the kit, it's best we take a look at it on its own, because there are so many other factors that influence the tone besides what we just discussed.

SNARE CONSTRUCTION

There are a lot of other materials used for snare drums, but first, here are a couple of things to consider. Metal snare drums are generally very loud, resonant, and bright. The thickness really makes a difference, with 3mm and thicker having more low end and midrange.

THE SNARE UNIT

Another important aspect is the snare unit itself. The snare count, type of material, curl, and diameter all determine the volume of the snare, as well as any sympathetic vibrations that may occur. Make sure that the snare unit is flat against the head and has no sharp or uneven protrusions. Less curl will mean less volume, while a wider snare unit will have more volume. Too much snare volume will mean that the snare is hard to control when other drums are hit, though.

You might also want to check out one of my other books, *The Drum Recording Handbook* (Hal Leonard, 2008), for more tips and tricks.

TUNING TIPS

If the snares buzz when the toms are hit:

1. Check that the snares are straight.

2. Check to see whether the snares are flat and centered on the drum.

3. Loosen the bottom head.

4. Retune the offending toms.

   If the kick drum isn't punchy and lacks power in the context of the music:

1. Try increasing and decreasing the amount of muffling in the drum, or try a different blanket or pillow.

2. Change to a heavier, uncoated head, such as a clear Emperor or Powerstroke 3.

3. Change to a thinner front head or one with a larger cutout.

4. Have the edges re-cut to create more attack.

   If one or more of the toms is difficult to tune or has an unwanted "growl":

1. Check the top heads for dents and replace as necessary.

2. Check the evenness of tension all around on the top and bottom heads.

3. Tighten the bottom head.

4. Have the bearing edges checked and re-cut as required.

Interview with the "Drum Doctor" Ross Garfield

Anyone recording in Los Angeles certainly knows about the Drum Doctors, *the* place in town to either rent a great-sounding kit or have your kit fine-tuned. Ross Garfield is the Drum Doctor, and his knowledge of what it takes to make drums sound great under the microphones may be unlike that of anyone else on the planet. Having made the drums sound great on platinum-selling recordings for the likes of Alanis Morissette, the Black Crowes, Bruce Springsteen, Rod Stewart, Metallica, Marilyn

Manson, Dwight Yoakam, Jane's Addiction, Red Hot Chili Peppers, Foo Fighters, Lenny Kravitz, Michael Jackson, Rage Against the Machine, Sheryl Crow, Nirvana, and many more names than can comfortably fit on this page, Ross agreed to share his insights on drum tuning. Here are some tips and tricks on making any drum kit come to life in the studio from an acknowledged master on the subject—Ross Garfield, the Drum Doctor.

How did you become the Drum Doctor?

I started out as a drummer, and I was always good at drum tuning. When I first moved to LA, I went into a drum shop and asked for a day job. The owner was sort of indifferent, so I walked around the shop and went from one drum set to the next and spent maybe half an hour tuning them up. After I was finished, I hit them a little bit, and the owner came over and said, "You can have a job because those drums have never sounded that good." I soon went from being just a worker to managing the shop and doing all the repairs.

One day somebody called for me, and one of my buddies on the guitar side of the shop answered the phone and called out to me, "Hey Drum Doctor, Line one!" and the name stuck. I took the name, eventually trademarked and copyrighted it, and ran with the idea. That was in 1981.

How did you get into doing your thing in the recording studios?

A friend of mine was a guitar tech in the studios. Everybody used to hire him because they liked the sounds that he helped them get. I was just playing in a band at the time, and one day he took me aside and said, "If you keep on trying to play drums in a band, one day you're going to be too old to do it. You can be doing this [drum tuning] until you're 60." Those words sunk in, so I sort of followed his lead. I started collecting drums and got to the point where I had about 10 sets and 20 snares, and I just went around and talked to people. I went to studio and live gigs until I found some people who were interested in what I did.

Before long I was introduced to [legendary session drummer] Jim Keltner. I was doing a session in one studio with Vinnie Colaiuta, and someone introduced me to him. He said, "If you can do that for Vinnie, then you must be good, so I'll give you shot." When Jim started using me, then Jeff Porcaro called me out of the blue and tried me. When I started to work with Jeff [in 1985 or so], he was hot. He was everyone's hero at the time.

I think I offer a certain edge to the client. All I do is tune, and all they do is practice and play drums. My thing is to make it the way they want it, whoever "they" are, because it may be the producer, drummer, engineer, or artist. Whoever it is that is giving me direction, my gig is to make them happy and make the drums sound the way they want. I really go at it with that approach most of the time. Actually, it's gotten to the point now where producers will ask me what I think it should be. I'll set up a tuning for a particular song and wait for them to ask me to take the snare up or down or try something different.

I'm really into changing stuff around from song to song, but I have some producers who don't want the sound to change so the record has continuity. I can understand that too, so I'll go that route if that's what they want.

Do you find that you're mostly tuning someone else's drums or you're renting them something of yours?

At this point it's mostly my gear. I've got over 160 sets of drums, and most of them are highly collectable. Most are not what you find off the shelf. The collection is sort of broken down by decades. I have 1920s and '30s sets, '40s and '50s sets, '60s sets, '70s and '80s sets, and a few modern-day drums. I have 17 DW sets and 6 Yamaha sets for current drums. But we put mostly old classic sets in the studios because most producers know that I can give them a really current sound from the set as well if that's what they want.

Each project is its own entity to me. It's not like I take what I just did on a Linkin Park session to an Offspring session. I try to do my homework by listening to the artists' previous releases prior to the session, just so I know what worked or didn't work on the last session. Like with Offspring—I've done four or five records with them, so I'll listen to the past records. Sometimes that helps and sometimes it doesn't, because the producer might have an idea of what he wants that might be different. It's really important to me that I'm able to give the producer what he's going for.

What's the one thing that you find wrong with most drum kits that you run into?

I think most guys don't know how to tune their drums, to be blunt. I can usually take even a cheap starter set and get it sounding good under the microphones if I have the time. It's really a matter of people getting in there and changing their heads a lot. Not for the fact of putting fresh heads on as much as the fact that they're taking their drums apart and putting them back together and tuning them each time. The repetition is a big part of it. Most people are afraid to take the heads off their drums.

When I get called into a session that can't afford to use my drums, and they just want me to tune theirs, the first thing I'll do is put a fresh set of heads on.

Top and bottom heads?

Yeah, usually top and bottom. Nine times out of ten, I'll put white Remo Ambassadors on the tops, clear Remo Ambassadors on the bottoms, and a Remo clear Powerstroke 3 on the kick drum. I'll use a white Ambassador or a coated black-dot Ambassador on the snare top and either a clear Diplomat or a coated Ambassador on the bottom. A lot of it has to do with how deep the drum is. If it's 5 inches or less, I'll usually go with an Ambassador, and if it's 6 1/2 or bigger, I'll usually go with a Diplomat. Just this little bit of information really makes a difference in how the kit sounds.

How did you come up with this combination?

I've experimented a lot and picked things up along the way. Having worked with people like Jeff Porcaro, Jim Keltner, Charlie Watts, Terry Bozzio, Jeff Hamilton, Steve Jordan, Charlie Drayton, and Peter Erskine, I really learned some stuff.

How long does it take you to tune a set that needs some help?

Usually well under an hour. If I have to change all the heads and tune them up, it'll take about an hour before we can start listening through the mics. I try to tune them to what I think they should be, then when we open up the mics and hear all the little things magnified, I'll modify it. Once the drummer starts playing, I like to go into the control room and listen to how they sound when he plays. Then once the band starts, I'll see how the drum sound fits with the other instruments.

What makes a drum kit sound great?

I always look for a richness in tone. Even when a snare drum is tuned high, I look for that richness. For example, on a snare drum I like the ring of the drum to last and decay with the snares. I don't like the ring to go past the snares. And I like the toms to have a nice, even decay. Usually I'll tune the drums so that the smallest drums have a shorter decay and the decay gets longer as the drums get bigger. I think that's pleasing.

What's the next step to making drums sound good after you change the heads?

I tune the drums on the high side for starters. For tuning, you've got to keep all of the tension rods even so they have the same tension at each lug. You hit the head an inch in front of the lug, and if you do it enough times you'll hear which ones are higher and which are lower. The pitch should be the same at each lug. Then when you hit it in the center, you should have a nice, even decay. I do that at the top and the bottom head.

Are they both tuned to the same pitch?

I start it that way, and then take the bottom head down a third to a fifth below the top head.

I've been in awe of the way you can get each drum to sound so separate without any sympathetic vibrations from the other drums. Even when the other drums do vibrate, it's still pleasing. How do you do that?

Part of that is having good drums, and that's the reason why I have so many—so I can cherry-pick the ones that sound really good together. The other thing is to have the edges of the shells cut properly. If you take the heads off, the edges should be flat. I used to check it with a piece of glass; now I check it with a piece of granite that I had cut. It's perfectly flat and about 2 inches thick. I'll put the shell on the granite and have a light over the top of the shell. Then I'll get down to where the edge of the drum hits the granite. If you see light at any point, then you have a low spot. So that's the first thing, to make sure that your drums are "true."

The edges should be looked at anyway because you don't want to have a flat drum with a square edge; you want it to have a bevel to it. If you have a problem with a drum, you should just send it in to the manufacturer. I don't recommend anyone trying to cut the edges of their drums themselves. It's like operating on one of your family members. It doesn't cost that much and it's something that should be looked at by someone who knows what to look for.

Once you get those factors in play, then tuning is a lot easier. I tend to tune each drum as far apart as the song will permit. It's easy to get the right spread between a 13- and a 16-inch tom, but it's more difficult to get it between a 12 and a 13. What I try to do is to take the 12 up to a higher register and the 13 down a little. The trick to all that is the snare drum, because the biggest problem that people have is when they hit the snare drum, there's a sympathetic vibration with the toms. The way I look at that is to get the snare drum where you want it first, because it's way more important than the way the toms are tuned. You hear that snare on at least every two and four. The kick and snare are the two most important drums, and I tune the toms around that and make sure that the rack toms aren't being set off by the snare. For me, the snare is probably the most important drum in the set because for me it's the voice of the song. I try to pick the right snare drum for the song because that's where you get the character.

Another thing that makes the drum sound special to me is if there's something quirky about it. I always loved Charlie Watts' snare sound because it always had that clang to it. It was so distinctive that you knew it was Charlie Watts right away. I always liked John Bonham because he had a very distinctive kick and snare sound as well. I always liked Def Leppard's and AC/DC's snare sound. Mitch Mitchell always had a distinctive snare sound. So getting the right snare sound for the song is a big part of what I do.

Do you tune to the key of a song?

Not intentionally. I have people who ask me to do that, and I will if that's what they want, but usually I just tune it so it sounds good with the key of the song. If there's a ring in the snare, I try to get it to ring in the key of the song. But sometimes I want the kit just to stand on its own because if it is tuned in the key of the song and one of the players hits the note that the snare or kick is tuned to, then the drum kind of gets covered up. So I tend to make it sound good with the song rather than in pitch with the song.

Would you tune things differently if you have a heavy hitter as opposed to someone with a light touch?

Yeah, a heavy hitter will get more low end out of a drum that's tuned higher just because of the way he hits, so I usually tune a drum a little tighter with a heavy hitter. I might move into different heads as well, like an Emperor or something thicker.

How about the kick drum? It's the drum that engineers spend the most time on.

It's weird for me because I always find them to be pretty easy because you muffle the kick drum on almost every session, and when you do, it makes tuning easier. On the other hand, a tom has as much life as possible with no muffling.

What I would recommend is to take a down pillow and set it up so that it's sitting inside the drum touching both heads. From there you can experiment, so if you want a deader, drier sound, then you push more pillow against the batter head, and if you want it livelier, then you push it against the front head. That's one way to go.

Another way to go is to take three or four bath towels and fold one of them so it's touching both heads. If that's not enough, then put another one in against both heads on top of the first one. If that's not enough, then put another one in. Just fold them neatly so that they're touching both heads. That's a good place to start, then experiment from there.

Do you prefer a hole in the front head?

It makes it easier. I do some things without holes in the front head, but having it really makes it easy to adjust anything on the inside. Ninety-nine out of a hundred have a hole. No front head is good, too. It's usually a drier sound, and you're usually just packing the towels against the batter head. You have much more access to the drum. Just put a sandbag in front to hold the towels against the head.

How about cymbals?

I like all kinds of cymbals and I've got all different makes. I've got some cymbals that are really cheap beginner's types that might make just the perfect pair of hip-hop hi-hats. I've got some old Zildjians from the '50s and '60s, but some of the new Zildjians sound really good. I've got a lot of Paiste; I really like the Signature series. I'm really open-minded and I like to experiment a lot.

One thing for recording is that you probably want a heavier ride, but you don't want that heavy of a cymbal for the Crashes. You also have to be careful when you mix weights. For example, if you're using Zildjian A Custom Crashes, you don't want to use a medium. You want to stay with the thins rather than try to mix in a Rock Crash with that, because the thicker cymbals are made for more of a live situation. They're made to be loud and made to cut, and sometimes they can sound a little gong-like to the mics. On the other side of the coin, if you play all Rock Crashes, and the engineer can deal with the level, that's not so bad either because the volume is even. But a thinner cymbal mixed in with those would probably disappear.

Any specific recommendations?

I think the Paiste Signature heavy hi-hats record really well. I like the dry heavy ride in a 20- or 21-inch. I like the Power Ride in a 22-inch size. I like the Full Crashes in basically every size. I really like the Zildjian A Custom line from top to bottom and the K Custom Hats in either 13-, 14-, or 15-inch. The 22-inch K Custom Ride in a heavy sounds good. If you want it to sound a little more retro, maybe you can find a pair of '60s Zildjian 14-inch New Beats or something like that.

Which records better, big drums or smaller ones?

It depends what you want your track to sound like. When I started my company, people would always say to me, "Why would someone want to rent your drums when they have their own set?" For one simple reason: Most drummers have a single set of drums. If they're going for a John Bonham drum sound, they're not going to get it with, say, a "Ringo" set. A lot of times when they go into the studio, the producer says, "You know, I really heard a 24-inch kick drum for this band. I hear that extra low end," but the drummer's playing a 22. So it's important to have the right size drums for the song. If you're going for that big double-headed Bonham sound, you really should have a 26. If you're going for a Jeff Porcaro punchy track like "Rosanna," then you should probably have a 22. That's my whole approach; you bring in the right instrument for the sound you're going for. You don't try to push a square peg into a round hole.

How much does the type of music determine your approach?

The drums that I bring for a hip-hop session are actually very close to what I bring for a jazz session. Usually, the hip-hop guys want a little bass drum, like an 18-inch, and that's what's common for a jazz session, to have an 18 or a 20. Then maybe a 12- or a 14-inch rack tom, which is also similar to the jazz setup. The big difference is in the snare and hi-hats and the tuning of the kick drum and the snare.

On a jazz session I would keep the kick drum tuned high and probably not muffled. On a hip-hop record I would tune the kick probably as low as it would go and definitely not have any muffling so it has that big "Boom" as much as possible. I would also have a selection of snares from like a 4×12-inch snare, 3×13, and maybe a 3×14. On a jazz record, I'd probably send them a 5×14 and a 6 1/2×14-inch. The hi-hats on a jazz record would almost definitely be 14s, where on a hip-hop record you'd want a pair of 10s or 12s, or maybe 13s.

Obviously, it's open to interpretation, because I'm sure a lot of hip-hop records have been made with bigger sets, but when I've delivered what I just said, it usually rocks their boat.

Why a smaller kick tuned down rather than just a bigger drum to begin with?

I think it all goes back to James Brown. I think he used a smaller kick tuned low, so we try to emulate that today. He brought that whole "funky drummer" thing around.

You've probably seen more miking setups than most engineers. What do you normally see?

They're all pretty close, believe it or not. There are the guys where budget is no problem, where they have U 87s on the kick with 67s for overheads and Telefunkens on the toms, but that's the exception. Normally what I see, and I see this on major sessions all the time, is Sennheiser 421s on the toms (sometimes on the top and bottom as well), an SM57 on the snare top, or once in a while a 451. On the kick I see a lot of 421s and AKG D 12s or 112s. Overheads vary a lot, but I see a lot of 451s and lately a lot of Royer ribbon mics. I really like the way they sound. I see 67s for overheads.

People experiment the most with overheads. Lately I've been seeing a lot of ATM25s on the toms. We used those for Linkin Park and Staind.

Which do you think sounds better: when you use the overheads as the primary sound of the kit or when they're just used as cymbal mics?

It depends on the situation, really. Sometimes you don't want the air and you want it to be a tight sound. That's an artistic call, and I don't want to limit someone by saying that it's got to be one way or another. It's just like when people ask me, "You've got all these drums, so what's your favorite?" I don't really have a favorite drum. I like them all, so it really depends on what the situation calls for.

For more on the Drum Doctors, go to www.drumdoctors.com.

CHAPTER 8

Miking Individual Instruments

This chapter contains a variety of miking approaches for individual instruments and ensembles that I've collected over some 25 years from other engineers, producers, mentors, manufacturer's reps, and musicians. (Unfortunately, in most cases I can't remember who showed me what and in some cases, I was sworn to secrecy never to tell.) They all work, at least to some degree. What will work for you depends upon the project, the song, the player, the room, and the signal chain. Since no two situations are the same, use these approaches as merely a starting point. Experiment, take what works, and leave the rest.

Since there are a lot of factors that go into getting something to record well, this section is treated somewhat differently than you might expect. First of all, unless there is a very specific need to use a particular microphone for an application, just the general type of mic (in other words, ribbon, dynamic, or condenser) will be suggested. One of the reasons for this is the fact that not everyone has such a wide variety of high-end microphones available to them that many of the applications might suggest. Second, the mic itself usually has less to do with the ultimate sound than the placement, the room, the player, and ultimately, the project itself. Even if all you have are inexpensive mics, the techniques will still work.

Accordion

Accordion is a central instrument in zydeco, Cajun, and polka music, although it's played in indigenous music throughout the world.

CONSIDERATIONS

► Like many instruments, an accordion radiates a different tone in every direction, and each accordion surface produces a distinct timbre. And as with most other instruments, the tonal balance can be dramatically altered depending upon where a mic is placed.

▶ Just to show that all roads sometimes lead to the same destination when it comes to the type of microphone used, it's interesting to look back at some of the mics used on the albums by accordionist extraordinaire Dick Contino back in the '50s and '60s. On an album engineered at Universal in Chicago by the legendary Bill Putnam, a U 47 was used. On an album tracked by Malcolm Chisholm at United Western in Hollywood, an RCA 77DX was used. On another Universal/Chicago date, engineer Bernie Clapper used a 251.

▶ When playing with a rhythm section, many accordionists play only with the right hand.

PLACEMENT

1. Place a mic about 2 or 3 feet away from the bellows of the accordion.

2. Use a stereo mic or a coincident pair rather than just one mic. The sound will no longer come from just one point in space, plus it will sound more natural. Experiment with a little more distance than the 3 feet mentioned a moment ago when using a stereo pair.

3. Place a large-diaphragm on the keyboard side about a foot or so back. Find out whether the accordionist will be playing treble only or bass and treble together, as that will dictate whether you have to be concerned with miking the bass end. First choice again would be a large-diaphragm condenser.

4. If button and air noise are concerns, try a single dynamic mic (like an SM57) because it won't pick up as much of the noise as a condenser mic. This is also a good choice for the button-type instruments used in Tejano and Norteno music.

5. Use a miniature lavaliere condenser mic clipped to the wrist strap of the accordion.

6. Standard pickup arrangement for a Cajun accordion is an SM57 capsule mounted on a bracket at the bottom of the accordion, facing upward. These are usually 4-reed accordions played with all the stops out so the sound is quite full.

7. For internal miking of the reeds, a favorite is a miniature lavaliere with three on the treble side, two on the bass for a full-sized piano accordion.

Audience or Crowd

Audience recording is both the key and the problem with live recording. It's sometimes difficult to record the audience in a way that captures its true sound. The transient peaks of the audience make it difficult not only to capture well, but also to keep out of the stage mics.

CONSIDERATIONS

It's very easy to have audience microphones overload either from the stage volume of the band or the peaks of the audience response. Therefore, it's a good idea to heavily compress or limit them to prevent overload.

MARK LINETT: *I compress the audience mics so when the band plays they don't overshoot, and when they stop playing the audience is good and loud.*

PLACEMENT

1. Set up two shotgun mics on either side of the stage, pointed out into the audience.

> **Variation:** Place the mics *behind* the band, pointing out toward the audience.

2. Set up a stereo pair over the audience and about halfway back from the stage, pointed at the stage. Be aware that you might need to advance the phase on this pair to match the stage mics.

3. Set up a pair of omnis near the rear of the hall and a second pair of omnis about a third of the way back from the stage.

Bagpipes

Bagpipes use enclosed reeds fed from a constant reservoir of air in the form of a bag. The chanter is the melody pipe played with either one or two hands. Most bagpipes also have at least one drone pipe, which has a single reed.

CONSIDERATIONS

▶ The ambience from the surrounding area is a bigger part of the sound than for most instruments.

▶ Bagpipes have no dynamic range but extremely high SPL. It's common to read levels as high as 108 dB SPL at the piper's head.

PLACEMENT

1. Place a small-diaphragm omni condenser at least 3 feet above the piper, pointing down.

2. For stereo, try a pair of baffled omnis (like a Jecklin Disc) or a set of cardioids in ORTF configuration. Place on a high stand or boom 2 to 3 feet above the piper, pointing down.

Banjo

Although the banjo is mostly identified as a country or bluegrass instrument, its origin is actually with African slaves brought to America. Banjos come in four-, five-, or six-string variations.

CONSIDERATIONS

▶ The banjo will tend to sound middy and harsh because, after all, it is a banjo, and they do sound middy and harsh by nature! Try a ribbon mic to mellow out the sound a bit.

▶ Since all the tone comes from the drum head resonator of the banjo, the techniques used to mic an acoustic guitar will not apply. Banjos don't resonate like guitars, so it's better to try to get a good attack sound from the picking. Usually close-miking is a good technique for this.

▶ Bluegrass banjos tend to be a good deal brighter than the old-time open-back banjos.

▶ Because bluegrass players usually use metal fingerpicks, there tends to be a good deal of pick noise. Try placing the microphone away from the player's hand, perhaps below the bridge, so that you're aiming at the skin of the hand, not the pick. Also try aiming directly below the hand at a distance of 8 to 10 inches.

▶ Most banjos do have some kind of adjustment on the tailpiece that changes the amount of downward pressure the bridge puts on the head. This will have some effect on the attack and tone of the instrument.

▶ Don't neglect your microphone preamp. A bluegrass banjo is about as good a torture test of a preamp as there is. The better your preamp, the less trouble you'll have getting the sound.

PLACEMENT

1. Place a large-diaphragm condenser 8 to 10 inches away, aimed right in front of the bridge, which captures the sound of the whole body.

2. Place a mic facing down about 2 1/2 feet above banjo and 1 foot in front of the player's head.

3. Place a mic 6 to 8 inches from the base of the picker's hand or just above, depending on the instrument and the picker.

4. Place two mics between 6 and 18 inches from the front of the banjo. Point one mic in the proximity of where the neck meets the body (or even a little higher up the neck) and then point the other mic in the proximity of the center of the resonator head (where the bridge and the player's picking hand are). Experiment with the mic pointed at the head, as different angles and slightly different positions can produce quite different sounds.

5. To reduce the noises that occur from the picking hand brushing against the head, clip an omni lavaliere mic to the strap down by the neck.

Acoustic String Bass (or Upright Bass)

Acoustic string bass is one of the hardest instruments to capture well, usually because it's being played in a live setting (such as a jazz trio) very close to other instruments. If you get it to sound good, you might have a lot of drums and piano bleeding onto the track, which then limits your control in mixing. It doesn't have to be this way, though, as there are a number of tried-and-true methods that work great and give you the isolation needed.

CONSIDERATIONS

► Position is everything when recording string bass. Close-miking the F-hole makes the sound muddy with no definition.

► Perhaps more than any other instrument, the upright bass needs space to really sound right. Tight-miking it can kill it if not done with care.

PLACEMENT

1. Place a ribbon mic about 18 to 24 inches away and aimed below the bridge. (See Figure 8.1.)

2. Place a large-diaphragm condenser in omni about 2 feet away pointed near where the neck meets the body.

Figure 8.1
Royer R-121 on upright bass.

3. Place a small-diaphragm condenser about halfway between the bridge and the end of the fingerboard, about 18 inches away.

4. Use a combination of a condenser mic placed as above and an SM57 wrapped in foam under the fingerboard overhang.

5. Place a large-diaphragm condenser aimed at the strings from about 8 to 12 inches above the strings but below the bridge. (See Figure 8.2.)

Figure 8.2
Soundelux U95 on upright bass.

6. Place a ribbon mic behind the bass at the bridge or soundpost height to capture the warmth of the wood.

7. Place a small-diaphragm condenser about even with the end of the fingerboard, pointed down, halfway between the fingerboard and the bridge, about 18 inches away.

8. Place a dynamic mic wrapped in a piece of foam and nestled in the tailpiece (pointing up at the bridge).

9. Here's a trick from Paul Langosch, bassist extraordinaire with Tony Bennett for many years. Wrap a small-diaphragm condenser in foam and wedge it between the A and D strings, aimed between the feet of the bridge. You may need the –10-dB pad if it's a loud bass.

10. You can see in pictures from Rudy Van Gelder (engineer for all the famous Blue Note recordings of the '50s and '60s) sessions that he was fond of using a 77DX placed near the floor, angled up toward the bridge at about a 45-degree angle. This can greatly reduce leakage from other instruments since the null of the mic is pointed outward.

11. Place a ribbon mic 4 inches above the right hand on an upright. Orient more toward the higher strings.

Electric Bass

Just like the acoustic bass (and almost all instruments), a great bass sound is dependent upon the bass, the player, the amp, and the room. The player has to be able to achieve the tone you're trying to record with his hands first and foremost.

CONSIDERATIONS

▶ Although just a DI can sound good for bass, using an amp (or both together) can really make it easier to dial in a great sound. However, many times the frequency band of the amp can step on the frequency bands of other instruments, such as guitars.

▶ Always check the phase relationship between the amp and the DI to make sure there's no cancellation of the low end. Flip the polarity switch to the position that has the most bottom.

▶ If recording into a DAW, align the bass amp track with the DI track so they are more in phase. (You really have to zoom in tight for this.)

PLACEMENT

1. The simplest and cleanest way to record an electric bass is with a direct box (or as it's sometimes called, a DI). Be careful which one you use because they're not all created equally, and some will not give you the low fundamental of bass that you want from recording this way. Active DIs do a better job of this than passive, although some passive boxes (like the ones made by Radial) do an excellent job because of the large Jensen transformer used in the circuit.

2. Place a large-diaphragm dynamic like D 112, RE20, or B52 a little off center and a couple of inches away from a cone of the bass cabinet. Depending on the sound that fits the track best, mix with a DI track. The sound will change substantially depending upon the balance of the DI and the miked amplifier.

3. Same as #2, but add an SM57 to the large-diaphragm mic for more bite. Mix the D 112 predominantly with just the slightest bit of 57. (See Figure 8.3.)

Figure 8.3
Shure Beta 52 and SM57 on bass cabinet.

4. For a metal bass sound, try this:

   ▶ Split the bass signal with a DI into the normal bass amp, and mic this with a large-diaphragm condenser. Make sure 100 Hz is not too loud. Bass players have a tendency to crank up lower frequencies on the amp in order to hear themselves or feel the bass.

> ▶ Send the other signal into a guitar amp and set it to distort. Make the sound a little dirtier than you actually like. It'll sit better in the mix.

> ▶ Adjust the EQ of the guitar amp to taste. The highs will give you that string-twang sound (Joey DeMaio of Manowar, Queensryche, and so on).

> ▶ Add the DI to taste.

5. Raise the cabinet about 3 feet off the floor. Mike with a ribbon mic or a large-diaphragm condenser from 3 to 6 inches away from the cone.

6. Try to find the sweet spot of the bass growl. Move the mic across the cone and in and out from the cone until you hear what you're looking for. Don't worry if the mic ends up in a place that looks wrong. Nearer to the edge of the speaker will give you more boom. Nearer to the cone will give you more color. Somewhere in between you will find the sweet spot that will best fit in the mix.

7. For that Paul McCartney/Beatles sound, place the amp in the middle of the studio (it helps if you have a large room) and place a large-diaphragm condenser 3 to 10 feet away. The large-diaphragm C 12 was also augmented with an STC 4038 for more of a darker sound, since it's a ribbon mic.

8. Another McCartney trick was to use a guitar amp with a 2×12 cabinet for bass with the mic placed about a foot away and between the speakers. Many Beatles songs from 1966 to 1968 used this setup.

Bassoon

The bassoon is a relatively modern instrument, coming to its present form in the 1800s. Due to its complicated fingering and problem with reeds, it's a very difficult instrument to learn and to play.

CONSIDERATIONS

As with all woodwinds, the sound from a bassoon emanates along the entire body of the instrument, with some coming from the top.

PLACEMENT

1. Place the mic in front of the instrument at eye level, about 3 to 4 feet away.

2. Place a mic at bell height about 45 degrees from the player's right side of the instrument.

3. Consider miking your woodwinds from above and in front. Start at least a couple feet above and a couple feet in front, wherever it sounds best to the ear (which depends on the room).

4. There are two common places to mount a pickup on the bassoon—the F# trill key hole on the wing and/or the bocal (the thin tube that goes from the reed to the bassoon). Most bassoonists will not let you clip anything to their bocal since these are typically very expensive, and good ones are hard to come by.

5. Try three microphones. Place a mic at the top, another near the middle near the bocal, and one more near the bottom.

Bongos

Usually thought of as a Cuban instrument, bongos actually originated in Africa. Although not thought of as an orchestral instrument, bongos are sometimes used in that setting played on a stand.

CONSIDERATIONS
▶ Bongos are made of two drums, the *macho* (smaller drum) and the *hembra* (larger drum).

▶ Tuning can be anywhere between a fourth and an octave between drums, depending upon the music.

▶ Always detune the smaller drum after use, since the head will either stretch or break because it's tuned so tightly (if it's tuned correctly).

PLACEMENT
1. Place a large-diaphragm condenser mic from 18 to 24 inches directly above and slightly favoring the smaller drum. If pointed directly in the middle of the two, the larger drum will sound louder because it's larger and has more output.

2. Sometimes a dynamic mic, such as an SM57, helps the bongos stand out in the mix due to its midrange emphasis.

3. If the player is sitting, try miking the bongos from underneath. Use a dynamic mic at a distance of at least 6 inches, again slightly aiming toward the smaller drum.

Bouzouki

Although one immediately thinks of Greek music upon mention of the bouzouki, it can be found all over Europe and especially in the Celtic music scene. Used in the music of Jackson Browne, Tom Petty, and other rock acts, it can be found in bands from Scandinavia, France, and Turkey.

CONSIDERATIONS
▶ Bouzoukis have almost no low end and can sound very thin and metallic if miked carelessly. The desired tone is usually quite rich in lower mids with a clear but clean treble.

▶ As with most other acoustic instruments, the quality of the player and instrument are crucial.

▶ Many older bouzoukis are "three course" (three sets of two strings), while more modern instruments are "four course" (four sets of two strings).

▶ The Irish bouzouki has four courses and a flatter back.

PLACEMENT
1. Place a small-diaphragm condenser mic 8 to 12 inches away, aimed at a spot between the bridge and the sound hole. If more low end is needed, move the mic more toward the sound hole.

2. The same mics and techniques used for acoustic guitar can work for bouzouki. Move the mics closer to the instrument and to the sound hole than you might with an acoustic guitar in order to increase the low-frequency response.

3. To augment the low end, tape a lavaliere mic near the sound hole.

STEVE ALBINI: *If you have an instrument that's really stringy and thin-sounding, a ribbon mic up close tends to make it sound a bit heftier.*

Brass

AL SCHMITT: *I've been using a lot of 67s. On the trumpets I use a 67 with the pad in, and I keep them in omnidirectional. I get them back about 3 or 4 feet off the brass.*

133

JERRY HEY: *Yes, directly on-axis. I'm of the feeling that if you play off-axis it sounds off-axis. I know that when you play right at somebody it's much more present than if you turn even a few degrees away, so that same thing translates directly with the microphone.*

CONSIDERATIONS

▶ With the mic aimed directly at the bell from a close distance, every bit of spit, excess tongue noise, air leak, and all the other nasties that every brass player occasionally produces is much more apparent. Pointing the mic a little off-axis of the bell can hide the majority of these unwanted extraneous noises without compromising the natural tonal color of the instrument too much.

▶ What are the differences between a trumpet, cornet, and flugelhorn?

   ▶ Trumpet is one-third flared tubing and two-thirds straight.

   ▶ Cornet is half and half.

   ▶ Flugelhorn is two-thirds flared tubing and one-third straight. A flugelhorn is really a soprano tuba.

▶ If the brass instrument itself is shrill, try putting a sock in the horn (which the player probably won't like), lower the mics, or point them slightly off-axis.

PLACEMENT

1. Place the mic 3 to 4 feet away, but above the bell and aimed toward the mouthpiece. (See Figure 8.4.)

2. Place the mic about 4 feet directly in front of the instrument.

3. For a section, place the players in a circle around a Blumlein pair (crossed figure-8s). Be sure that each player is on the lobe of the pattern and not in the null point.

4. If a stereo spread is not needed, try something as simple as an omni condenser in the middle of a circle of players. Balance the section by moving the softer horns closer to the mic and the louder ones farther away.

5. Try hanging an omni condenser about 4 feet directly over the horn group as an additional mic.

Figure 8.4
Arturo Sandoval playing into a
Royer R-121.

TROMBONE

1. If you are going for a more mellow jazz type of sound, place the mic about 20 to 30 degrees off-axis of the bell at a distance of about 2 feet. If you want a more aggressive sound that will cut through a dense mix, mic directly on-axis of the bell and move the mic in to about 12 to 18 inches in front of the bell.

2. Ribbon mics are great for trombones at a distance of about 6 to 12 inches from the bell.

TUBA

Position the mic about 2 feet over the top of the bell at about 15 degrees off-axis of center. If things sound too "blatty," aim the mic more off-axis (about 60 degrees).

FRENCH HORN

1. Place a mic from 2 to 4 feet behind the bell at a height that matches the top edge of the bell but aimed toward the center.

2. Add a microphone 2 to 4 feet in front of the player to fill out the sound.

3. Place a mic about 4 feet over the player's head and pointed straight down.

Choir or Ensemble (Vocal, Saxophone, or Other)

It takes a great choir to get a great choir recording. Singers need to not only blend well with each other, but to sing in tune and control their volume. This applies to ensembles of instruments as well.

CONSIDERATIONS

▶ Ten people is considered a small choir. Up to 25 is considered a medium-size choir. More than that number is considered a large choir.

▶ Choirs are always arranged in SATB sections, meaning sopranos, altos, tenors, and basses.

PLACEMENT

1. Place an ORTF pair about 3 feet above the conductor and aimed at the center of the choir as a starting point. A coincident or near-coincident technique will likely be far more preferable than a widely spaced omni technique. This is because with a choir you generally want to hear the interplay of vocal lines as they move about the sections of the choir, and spaced omnis won't necessarily give you that.

2. For a big but somewhat swimmy choral sound, try a pair of spaced omnis.

3. Try the legendary Bruce Swedien's method, which is a Blumlein pair (crossed figure-8s) with the choir placed in a circle around the mics.

4. Record the choir in sections to have more control over the balance during the mix. Place a mic 6 to 8 feet away from each section. The farther back the section mic is placed, the better the blend will get, but the more the other sections will bleed into the section mic (which defeats the purpose). You also won't have a true stereo recording, which might not give you that "you are there" listening experience.

Clarinet

Clarinets have been made from a variety of materials, including wood, plastic, hard rubber, metal, and ivory, but the vast majority of quality instruments are made from African hardwood. Although more closely identified with Dixieland, classical, and swing music, the clarinet has been used prominently on a few rock hits, such as the Beatles' "When I'm Sixty-Four" and Sly and the Family Stone's "Dance to the Music."

CONSIDERATIONS

▶ It's difficult to close-mike a clarinet effectively with just one mic. If you place the mic at the top, the bottom notes are weak. Unlike the sax, most of the sound comes straight out the bell at the lowest overblown note.

▶ On the other hand, miking the bell results in a weakness in the bridge notes between the fundamental and the first overblown range. Clarinetists spend years working on their tone through this area, so you need to support it when miking.

PLACEMENT

1. Place a mic pointing down at the small "A" key with a second mic off the bell.

2. If only one mic is available, use an omni placed about 2 feet away from the bell and 2 feet above the instrument, pointed down.

Claves

Claves are very important in Afro-Cuban music, since they're frequently used to play repeating rhythms. Most modern claves are no longer made of wood and instead use plastic or fiberglass because of their durability. The clave is also the name of a basic rhythmic pattern as well.

CONSIDERATIONS

▶ Claves are very loud and sometime require baffling to control the room reflections.

▶ There's not much body or decay from a clave, so the room your recording in is very important.

PLACEMENT

Place a dynamic mic about 10 feet away at about shoulder height of the player but pointed toward the claves.

Conga

Congas come from Cuba, although their origin can be traced back to Africa. Modern congas have a staved wooden or fiberglass shell with a screw-tensioned drum head.

CONSIDERATIONS

▶ For congas, a hard floor in a fairly large room is essential to getting a good "natural" sound. A hardwood floor is the best, but linoleum or some kind of tile will do.

▶ A small room is a bad idea for hand drums of any kind, except perhaps a talking drum, which has a very soft tone and doesn't rely so much on room tone.

▶ Congas sometimes sound better when placed directly on the floor than they do on a stand.

▶ The traditional tuning of the conga was much lower than what's used today on most records.

PLACEMENT

1. Place a small-diaphragm condenser or dynamic mic about 1 to 2 inches in from the outer rim, and hovering about 12 inches above each drum. (See Figure 8.5.)

Figure 8.5
AKG 452 over conga.

Variation: Add a room mic positioned about 6 feet from the drums and 6 feet high.

2. Using a single mic, place it 12 to 18 inches between the drums but slightly aimed toward the one that's higher tuned.

3. Place the mics so they are a few inches below the rim under the congas, angled up and aiming at the player's eyes. (See Figure 8.6.)

Figure 8.6
AKG 452 under conga looking up.

4. Add a dynamic mic below the congas, sitting on the floor and facing up between the drums, to fill the sound out.

Cowbell

The cowbell actually had its origins as a way for a herdsman to identify his freely roaming animals.

CONSIDERATIONS

▶ Cowbells project a high-frequency transient from the closed end as well as fundamental from the open end.

▶ The high end of the cowbell easily cuts through the mix, but the low frequencies sometimes get lost.

139

▶ Cowbell players sometimes move around when they play, so be sure that the mic is far enough away so they don't move off-mic.

PLACEMENT

Place a small-diaphragm condenser about 12 to 18 inches away, placed below the mouth of the bell and angled upward.

Didgeridoo

The didgeridoo is a wind instrument of the indigenous Aboriginals in Australia. The traditional instrument is made from dried bamboo or eucalyptus and has a single pitch.

CONSIDERATIONS

▶ Be aware that the instrument generates a lot of subsonic frequencies, so a hi-pass filter might prove useful.

▶ The didjeribone is a modern, professional version of this ancient instrument. It has the advantage of being able to slide between 10 keys. See didjeribone.net for more info.

PLACEMENT

1. Place the dynamic or a small-diaphragm condenser mic about 4 to 6 inches from the bell of the didj. This is the ideal distance in that it gives the best balance of low end and clarity.

2. Mount a small clip-on omni condenser on the end of the bell of the didj.

3. The Facebass is an alternative to using microphones for recording a didj. Like a headset-mounted microphone, it captures sounds from within the didj itself.

Djembe

A djembe is a skin-covered West African drum that's played with the bare hands. Because of its shape, density of wood, and the head material, it's capable of a wide variety of sounds, especially a very deep bass note.

CONSIDERATIONS

▶ The heads on most djembes are fairly wide (14 inches or so), and some of the bass sound comes from the bottom and not off the head.

▶ There really isn't a single spot close to the drum where the mic can capture the full djembe sound, so some distance is required in placement.

PLACEMENT

1. In a good-sounding room, the drum should be miked from 6 to 10 feet away. (See Figure 8.7.)

Figure 8.7
Mic over djembe.

2. For close-miking, a single mic placed 4 to 6 inches above the rim and angled across the drum head works well.

3. To capture the extra low frequencies, place a mic underneath the drum aimed at the opening.

Dobro

Dobro is actually a brand name of a resonator guitar, although the name and the guitar have become synonymous. National is the other company noted for the resonator. A resonator guitar is the same as an acoustic guitar except that a resonator is put in place of a sound hole. This was an attempt to acoustically amplify the guitar. There are two types: round necks, which are played like a normal guitar, and square necks, which are played on their backs facing up at the player.

CONSIDERATIONS

▶ The sound of the dobro really depends upon who's playing more than on most other instruments.

▶ The sweet spot is usually between the treble-side screen and the cover plate toward the bottom of the instrument.

► The screen area has mostly low end, and the sound gets brighter as you go into the cover plate.

PLACEMENT

1. Place a large-diaphragm condenser mic about 4 to 6 inches away from the screen area and a small-diaphragm mic at the cover plate, aimed at the screen area.

2. Place a mic about 6 inches off the resonator and another approximately 6 inches off the treble-side hole.

The Drum Kit

The drum kit usually gets the most attention in the majority of sessions because just about all modern pop and rock music is rhythm oriented and highly dependent upon the drums for movement. Indeed, in this type of music a wimpy-sounding drum kit means a wimpy track!

It's a fallacy to believe that the only way to achieve a big rockin' drum sound is by miking every drum and cymbal, though. In fact, there are many tried-and-true methods of drum miking that have been the source of hit records for decades that use anywhere from only one to three mics.

WYN DAVIS: *I feel that the drums are sort of like an orchestra in the sense that there are a lot of instruments, so I don't make any attempt to isolate drums from one another or to do anything that would take away from the overall sound. For instance, if you hit the snare, the whole drum kit rings and vibrates. In my opinion, that's a part of the sound of the set that you want to keep. So I don't make any attempt to narrowly focus mics or baffle things off or anything like that.*

Whichever method you choose, try looking at the drum kit as just a single instrument. Also realize that multiple miking isn't much different than if you were trying to record only the E string on a guitar while chords were being strummed.

And don't forget that the drums have to sound great by themselves first in order for them to sound great when recorded. (A great drummer doesn't hurt either.)

As a general starting point: Try placing a single mic 8 to 10 feet in front of the kit at about the same height as the drummer's head. A large-diaphragm cardioid will work nicely for this. Record the set for a minute or two. Listen to the playback. Is the set balanced or do one or two drums/cymbals stick out? If so, then it is most likely a player issue. If not, then set up your mics and start recording.

MARK LINETT: *The simple answer is that I've never heard a good drummer sound bad, and I've never heard a bad drummer sound particularly good. It's one of those instruments where the technique of the player really matters, like most acoustic instruments. When you get electric, it gets less important because the variables are much less.*

CONSIDERATIONS

▶ Try to keep all mics as parallel as possible to keep the acoustic phase shift to a minimum.

▶ Try to keep any mics underneath the drums at a 90-degree angle to keep the acoustic phase shift to a minimum.

▶ Most mics placed underneath the drums will be out of phase with the top mics. Switch the polarity on your preamp, console, or DAW and choose the position that has the most bottom end.

▶ Microphones aimed at the center of the drum will provide the most attack. For more body or ring, aim the mic more toward the rim.

▶ The best way to hear exactly what the drum sounds like when doing a mic check is to have the drummer hit about once per second so there's enough time between hits to hear how long the ring is.

SINGLE-MIC SETUP

1. Visualize an equilateral triangle with the base of the triangle being the overall width of the kit, then position a large-diaphragm condenser at the apex of the triangle, directly above the snare, with the pattern set to hypercardioid. In other words, the height of the mic is the same as the width of the kit.

2. Position a mic 3 feet in front of the kit, about 3 feet high, looking between the toms and the cymbals toward the snare. If you need more kick, lower the mic. If you need less, move it higher and away from the kick.

3. Same as #2, but use a stereo mic.

4. Place a mic about 3 feet in front of the drums, with the mic high enough to point down at the snare (the center of the kit) at about a 45-degree angle. If you need more kick, lower the mic. If you need less, raise it (see Figure 8.8).

Figure 8.8
Mic in front of drum kit pointed
down at 45-degree angle.

5. Place a mic 5 feet off the ground and 8 feet directly in front of the kit. (See Figure 8.9.)

Figure 8.9
Royer R-121 in front of drum kit.

6. Place a large-diaphragm condenser over the drummer's head, angled at the whole kit in such a way as to get coverage of the toms without too much cymbals.

7. Place a large-diaphragm condenser on a mic stand over the drummer's right shoulder, angled down into the center of the kit.

TWO-MIC SETUP

1. If you have two mics available, try placing one in front of the bass drum, about 6 inches away from the front head on a short stand, and positioning the other mic up about 8 feet high, looking down at the middle of the kit as an overhead. While the drummer is playing, have someone move the overhead mic around until the kit sounds balanced through the speakers. If you're not getting enough snare, for example, move it a little more toward the snare, or if you're getting too much, move it the other way. You may want to add a little equalization at 12 kHz to give the kit a little more clarity and crispness.

2. Producer Brendan O'Brien's two-mic drum technique:

   ► Good-sounding drums

   ► Good drummer

   ► AKG D 30 on kick

   ► Telefunken U 47 tube about 5 feet high and 3 feet in front of drums

3. Looking at the drums, place a large-diaphragm condenser on the ride cymbal side and a different-model large-diaphragm condenser on the hi-hat side, both about 4 to 5 feet away. The dissimilar mics give a really nice character spread from side to side, and when placed properly, provide the character of both mics in a mono playback. (See Figure 8.10.)

4. A version of #2 above, place a mic over the center of the kit, looking down at the snare drum from a height of about the top of the drummer's head. Add a kick drum mic as per the kick drum section. Move the overhead mic away from the snare if you need less in the mix (see Figure 8.11).

Figure 8.10
U 47 and M 149 in two-mic
configuration in front of the drums.

Figure 8.11
Two-mic configuration using
overhead and kick drum mics.

THREE-MIC SETUP

FRANK FILIPETTI: *As a drummer, I know that the sound at the snare is not exactly what I want to hear on the track. There's a lot of bloom around the snare and around the bass drum as well that I feel is essential to capturing the reality and the dynamics of the snare and bass drum in particular. So my overhead technique is to capture the overall sound of the kit and not just the cymbals. I tend to want to mic the kit so that I do get leakage of the snare, bass drum, everything into the overall sound. I want to be able to put up the overheads along with the bass drum mic and get a pretty nice sound on the kit. So my tendency is to mic a little further away from direct impact of the cymbals.*

1. Add a snare drum mic to any of the two mic positions mentioned above (see Figure 8.12).

Figure 8.12
Three-mic configuration using overhead, snare, and kick drum mics.

2. Place a mic about 6 inches in front of the kick drum. Place a mic about 30 inches over the left and right sides of the kit, pointing straight down at the floor at about a 90-degree angle. Move the mics around to get the perfect balance and stereo image.

3. Place the first mic about 6 feet away and 18 to 24 inches off the ground in front of the kick drum. The object of this mic is usually to pick up not only a good bass drum sound, but also the bottom of the toms and a bit of snare as well as some of the cymbals.

   Place the control room monitors in mono and put up a second mic, which will go anywhere from directly over the snare to over the drummer's right shoulder at a distance of 6 feet. Move until it aligns with the front mic for clear snare, foot, and open tom sound. The majority of your hat sound will be here, as well as the left-side crash cymbal.

   The key here is to add that mic so you get the snare, hat, top of the toms, and cymbals without the cymbals being out of balance with the rest of the kit. Listen in mono to be sure that it's in phase with the front mic.

The third mic is placed about 6 feet from where the drummer actually hits the snare drum, aimed so it's just peeking over the floor tom at the snare. This mic will net you the depth of the foot, a third dimension on the snare, as well as added depth on the racks. (See Figure 8.13.)

Figure 8.13
Three-mic setup: M 149 on left, U 47 in front, and Royer R-121 overhead.

Please note: All mics are about the same distance away, which makes everything somewhat phase coherent. If 6-foot distances are too ambient, move all the mics closer but make sure they are all about the same distance.

Variation: Also place another room mic 6 feet in front of the kick at the height of the top of the rim of the kick.

The early Led Zeppelin stereo recordings engineered by Glyn Johns used just three mics on the drums in most cases. Two U 67s—one over Bonham's head pointed at the snare and rack tom and one near the floor tom (to Bonham's right) pointed across the tom at the snare—were panned hard left and right. A kick mic was placed in front of the head, often an AKG D 20, and was mixed into the stereo drum mix.

4. Place a large-diaphragm condenser on the snare side of the kit at the apex of an almost equilateral triangle of the mic, the snare, and kick, about 6 inches off the floor looking upward. (See Figure 8.14.)

Figure 8.14
Large-diaphragm in front of drum kit.

Place a second mic on the floor tom side, about 2 feet behind the drummer, with the drummer's body blocking access to the hats and the snare. This mic should be placed just higher than the rim of the floor tom.

Place the third mic looking mostly at the hat and snare, again from about 2 feet behind the drummer. (See Figure 8.15.)

Figure 8.15
Small-diaphragm condenser behind the drummer, pointed at snare and hat.

5. Place a dynamic mic anywhere from 1 to 4 feet in front of the kick drum. Place a pair of small-diaphragm condensers in an X/Y array about 4 to 5 feet over the dynamic mic, aimed at either the outer side of the rack toms (assuming there are two) or the cymbals.

> **Variation:** Try one of the small-diaphragm condensers over the drummer's right shoulder. If more snare is required, add an SM57 a foot or two off the side of the drum.

6. Place a stereo mic about 5 to 6 feet over the snare drum with a large-diaphragm condenser 5 to 6 feet in front of the bass drum.

FOUR-MIC SETUP

1. Use three-mic setups #2, 5, or 6 and add a snare mic.

2. Close-mike the kick drum from a distance of about 1 to 2 feet in front. Close-mike the snare/hat from about 1 to 2 feet on the side, looking in. Add a large-diaphragm condenser 3 feet over the rack toms and a second condenser about 3 feet over the floor tom. The mic over the floor tom should be aimed at the floor tom from a foot or so behind the kit. This way you get a good image on the rest of the kit as well.

3. In this technique, the kick and snare mics stay the same, but the overheads are placed in a crossing ORTF configuration. Place them about 6 or 7 feet above the kit, directly in the middle. (See Figure 8.16.)

Figure 8.16
Four-mic technique with ORTF overheads.

Kick (Bass Drum)

The secret to a great-sounding kick recording is simple: Get a great-sounding kick! While many engineers struggle with the sound of the kick drum, remember that the drum must sound great by itself even before the mics are placed.

CONSIDERATIONS

▶ A really large kick can have fundamentals lower than what the room can support, so you end up hearing octaves of the fundamental instead of the fundamental itself. This puts the drum's perceived low end higher in pitch than what you'd hear with a smaller drum.

▶ Shredded newspaper works very well as damping material.

▶ A folded pillowcase or bath towels tucked in the drum in front of the pedal are great for damping. One- or 2-inch SONEX lining the shell can also be used for damping.

▶ A felt strip in with the head can be pulled tight or loose to vary the amount of head damping. If it rings too much, try putting a small pillow inside, but not touching the beater side.

▶ The best way to get a hole into the front head of the kick drum is to heat up a saucepan lid until it's red-hot, then drop it onto the head. This burns through cleanly and doesn't leave any rough edges that can split.

▶ Be aware that when using condenser microphones too close to the kick, you risk overloading the diaphragm or the mic's internal preamp. This will give you a sound reminiscent of a blown speaker.

▶ For more attack, add a few dB at 8 kHz. For a larger-sounding kick, add a little between 50 and 100 Hz. Attenuate at 1.5 kHz to decrease the "honkiness." Attenuate between 160 Hz and 400 Hz to eliminate the "beach ball" sound.

▶ A limiter can smooth out the peaks, but use it sparingly when tracking. A dB or two with a 2:1 ratio, a very fast release, and a 3- to 7-ms attack time is all you need.

ROSS GARFIELD,
THE DRUM DOCTOR:

What I would recommend is to take a down pillow and set it up so that it's sitting inside the drum, touching both heads. From there you can experiment, so if you want a deader, drier sound, then you push more pillow against the batter head, and if you want it livelier, then you push it against the front head. That's one way to go.

Another way to go is to take three or four bath towels and fold one of them so it's touching both heads. If that's not enough, then put another one in against both heads on top of the first one. If that's not enough, then put another one in. Just fold it neatly so that they're touching both heads. That's a good place to start, then experiment from there.

PLACEMENT

1. If the kick has a hole, place the mic just at the edge, angled at 30 to 45 degrees off-axis, aimed at the beater. (See Figure 8.17.)

Figure 8.17
AKG D 112 just inside the hole.

Variation: To get a tighter, more compact bass drum sound, place a folded packing blanket or a pillow against the bottom of the drum shell, lightly touching the head.

2. If the kick has no hole in the front head, place the mic about 3 to 4 inches in front of the drum, halfway up and off center. (See Figure 8.18.)

Figure 8.18
AKG D 112 just outside the head.

3. Put your hand in front of the bass drum while the drummer hits quarter notes. If there's no hole in the front head, you will feel a shockwave projecting from the head of the drum. Move your hand until the shockwave almost disappears. Put the mic at the edge of the shockwave, aimed at the center of the drum. (See Figure 8.19.) This can also be used to add a second kick mic (sometimes called an "out" mic) to capture the fundamental of the kick drum that the closely positioned mic misses. This mic might require a tunnel (see the upcoming "Kick Tunnel" section) in order to isolate the sound of the kick from the rest of the kit.

Figure 8.19
Finding kick shockwave.

4. Place the mic 3 to 4 inches inside the outer head, off center from the beater. (See Figure 8.20.)

Figure 8.20
Mic just inside kick.

5. Angle the mic at a 30- to 45-degree angle toward the corner of the drum, usually away from the floor tom, but away from the snare if it's louder. Start at a distance of 6 inches, then adjust to taste. (See Figure 8.21.)

Figure 8.21
Mic angled inside kick.

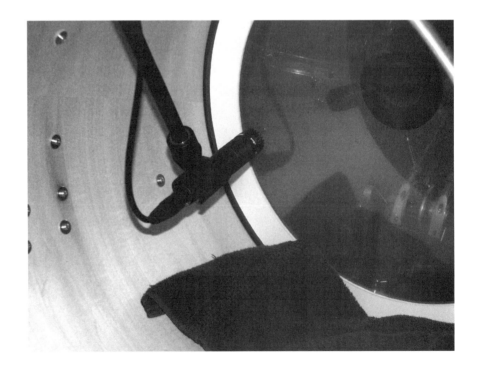

6. For a very aggressive kick sound, tape a large coin to the drum head so that the beater strikes the coin and not the head. (Make sure you consult the drummer first!)

7. Place a D 112 aiming 3 inches below the beater. This gives it just enough attack without getting too "clicky." For more click, aim closer to the beater.

8. Place a ribbon mic 1 to 6 feet from the outside of the kick drum. Point the diaphragm at a 45-degree angle aimed at the floor (see Figure 8.22). *Important:* If you don't use the 45-degree angle, you'll likely damage the ribbon due to the air blast from the kick.

Figure 8.22
Royer R-121 at a 45-degree angle outside the kick.

9. Put a speaker cabinet in front of the kick drum with one speaker lined up with the actual drum, and connect the output to a DI. (See the upcoming "Subkick" section.)

CHUCK AINLAY: *It's not straight in the middle; it's usually off center a little bit. Outside of the bass drum I'll place an FET 47. (That varies a lot, but usually about 8 inches.) Usually drummers have a hole cut in their front head, and I prefer that rather than no front head at all. It gives you a bit of that almost double-headed bass drum sound. I'll put the outside mic off center once again, away from where the hole would be cut. Then it's just a matter of time spent dampening the drum with some soft materials to try to get however much deadness you want out of the drum.*

ED CHERNEY: *On the kick I've been using a 421 inside fairly close for snap and an FET 47 about 2 or 3 feet out.*

STEVE ALBINI: *On bass drum it would depend on whether there was a hole in the front head, or no front head at all, or a closed front head. I normally mike both sides of the bass drum. I'll use either a small lavaliere or a clip-on condenser to mike the beater side of the bass drum. I've used a Crown GLM-100, Shure SM98, or a small dynamic microphone like a Beyer 201 on a little stand by the beater side of the drum. Then if it's a closed front head, I'll use either a large-diaphragm condenser mic like a 414 or an FET 47. Normally I'd use a dynamic mic like a Beyer M88, AKG D 112, or a really bassy microphone like a Beyer 380 for really murky, deep, rumbly sound.*

If there's a hole in the front head and there's a lot of air coming out of that hole, you have to be careful about where the mic is positioned. I don't have great results with the mic sticking inside the bass drum, but sometimes it sounds quite good with the microphone positioned slightly in off center in front of that hole. There I might use an RE20 or a D 112, or a Beyer M88, or occasionally a 421. If there's no front head at all, and it's a very short, dead, thumping kind of sound, then I would put the mic inside the mouth of the bass drum but very close to the beater, and I would probably use either an RE20 or a D 112. I have used other mics like a Shure SM7, for example.

The idea is that you want to record the bass drum so when you hear it on the speakers in the control room, it sounds like a bass drum. There are quite a few people who opt for a more stylized bass drum sound, where the bass drum doesn't sound like a bass drum but instead sounds like some archetype of a recorded bass drum. I've never had much luck with that. Trying to make it sound like something else always sounds funny to me. I want it to sound pretty much as it does in the room.

The nice thing about having a mic on the beater side as well as the front side is that you can get more attack out of the beater if you need it by balancing that mic against the front mic without having to screw the sound up with EQ. In order to get it to bite more, you don't have to add more high-frequency energy, which can also really exaggerate the spillage from the cymbals and stuff.

What it should sound like is determined by a conversation with the drummer. Different mics have different character to them. The RE20 has a quite midrangy sort of popping sound if you're going for a percussive bass drum sound. The D 112 has sort of a hollowed-out sound and doesn't have as much midrange. It has more attack and deep bass. The M88 doesn't have quite as much low energy as the D 112, but it doesn't have as much midrange energy as the RE20, so it's sort of a middle ground between those two. The 421 is much harder sounding and more pointed. It has reasonable bass response, but it's a more aggressive sound. The condenser mics tend to get used when the bass drum is being played quite softly because you want to pick up the character of the resonance and the character of the front skin.

WYN DAVIS: *I usually have the mics about midway into the kick. Generally I don't say anything to the drummer about making the bass drum sound good. If the drummer comes in, and he has a front head with no hole in it, I have a cable that I've made that I can slip in through one of the ports. I have a sort of shock mount that I'll mount inside and then we'll put the head back on. The most important thing is for the guy to feel comfortable and have the response from the drums that he's used to getting. If you change that, then his performance suffers, and you don't get what you're after to begin with.*

I have used a 47 FET before, but because the characteristics of every kick drum are different, it really depends on how much fundamental is in it and how empty the shell is. Some people fill their shells up with pillows, and some keep their front head on. Some people have a giant hole cut in the head, while some people have one just big enough to put your fist through. It really depends on the drum. In my opinion, there are few magic-sounding kick drums out there that have everything you want.

So you basically have to tailor the mic to the kick drum and figure out which mic is going to represent the best part of the kick drum for what you're after. I'm usually after something that will be at the bottom of the track fundamentally.

Kick Tunnel

A kick tunnel is constructed when additional isolation of the kick drum mic is required. This usually occurs when the room that the drums are being recording in is too live.

CONSIDERATIONS

▶ In order to get more isolation for the outside kick microphone, a "tunnel" is sometimes constructed around it. This can be made of anything from packing blankets draped over chairs and mic stands (#1 in the following "Placement" section) to something more formal (#2 in the following "Placement" section).

▶ The tunnel can be helpful in other ways as well. If you have a small room where you're getting as much reflected sound from the kick in the overheads and spot mics as direct sound, the tunnel can help. Also, a tunnel can stop the kick from exciting a not-so-great-sounding room.

▶ One side effect is a slight lowering of the resonant frequency of the drum, since the tunnel will acoustically couple with it, so the drum may have to be retuned up just a little to compensate. The tone is widely variable simply by adjusting the distance between the drum and the opening of the tube.

PLACEMENT

1. A makeshift tunnel can be constructed using chairs, mic stands, and packing blankets. The upside of this is that the outside leakage will be reduced somewhat into the outside kick mic. The downside is that you won't be able to take advantage of the resonant qualities of a more permanent tunnel, as described below.

2. From an industrial paper tube manufacturer or cardboard concrete form tubing, obtain sections 24 inches in diameter and 3/4-inch round. Line with 2-inch Auralex foam and cap off the end with a 1/8-inch circle of Luan, which is also covered inside with Auralex. The foam makes the tube extremely dead inside and also lowers the resonant frequency. The tube should be about 6 feet long. A packing pad is used to close the gap between the kick drum and the tunnel.

CHUCK AINLAY: *Usually then I'll put either some mic stands or chairs or something that I can drape with some double-thick packing blankets so that it makes sort of a tunnel around the bass drum and helps seal off some of the leakage into that outside microphone.*

Subkick

The subkick phenomenon started due to the desire to get more bottom end from the kick without having to increase the low-end EQ. The unit is only capturing 20 to 40 Hz, which is something that you feel more than you hear.

CONSIDERATIONS

▶ It became popular to take the woofer from a Yamaha NS-10M and use the magnet to attach it to a mic stand in order to construct a subkick (see Figure 8.23).

▶ Get your main kick drum sound first, then add only about 10 percent of the subkick to the kick, or just until you feel it. Of course, if your speakers won't reproduce anything as low as 30 to 40 Hz, then you probably shouldn't even try this because you'll just be guessing at how loud the subkick actually should be, and if you add too much it will sound too woofy and will lack definition.

▶ The subkick can be used on other instruments as well. Try it on a bass amp or even a trombone.

Figure 8.23
A homemade subkick.

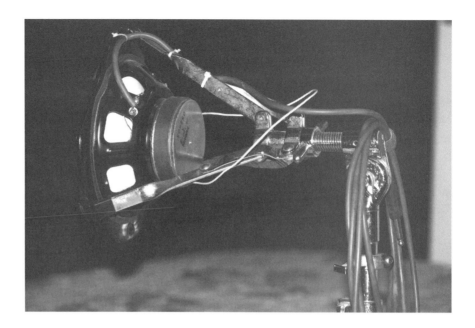

PLACEMENT

Place the subkick about 2 inches directly behind the main kick mic (see Figure 8.24).

Figure 8.24
Subkick setup.

Snare

The snare is the most important drum in the drum kit because it's the backbeat of most popular music, playing every second and fourth beat. Therefore, it's important to pay extra attention to its sound.

159

CONSIDERATIONS

▶ The Shure SM57 has been the standard snare microphone for years and shows no signs of being replaced. It's one of the few mics that maintains its punch and sound regardless of how hard the drummer is playing.

▶ The "crack" of the snare doesn't necessarily come from the close top mic. For more crack from the snare, use a well-placed room mic. If there's too much cymbals and kick on it, key it from the snare track.

▶ Add a dB or two at 10 to 12 kHz for a more crisp sound.

▶ To smooth out the peaks when tracking, consider using a slight bit of compression (just a dB or so) with a 2:1 ratio with the fastest possible attack and release times.

STEVE ALBINI: *The first step is to listen to the snare drum in place for a while and try to discern what the drummer's intent is. Ask him pointed questions: Do you like a ringing sound or a short one? Do you like a lot of stick sound and top head, or do you like a lot of the snare wires and crispy ghost strokes? Do you usually play with a rimshot or only occasionally? Have you done anything special to the snare drum that is new to you? What are some of your favorite records? Will you be using brushes? After a little listening and conversation, you should know where to go.*

If you hear something (good or bad) about the snare sound that strikes you as exceptional (rattle, strong note, or after-ring, unusual tightness or looseness), draw the drummer's attention to it, and ask if he likes it or not. What you think is an irritation may be the drummer's favorite thing about his snare drum. Don't suggest making any changes to the snare drum unless the drummer agrees that something is wrong. I like to think that the sound of a drummer's kit is an extension of his playing style, and changing things on him is as weird as asking a guitar player to play ukulele—it should only be done for cause.

CHUCK AINLAY: *So then on the snare drum I like to put it to where the rear of the mic is rejecting the hi-hat as much as possible, but it isn't in the way of the drummer. The main thing with miking drums is for the drummer to never think about hitting a mic while he's playing. The mic usually comes in somewhere between the hi tom and the hi-hat, but I like to somehow get the rear of the mic towards the hat for the most rejection. It usually is pointing down at sort of a 45-degree angle. I find that the more I angle it across the drum, the better side-stick sound I'm going to get. If it's pointed down too straight at the drum, then the side stick becomes too much of a high-frequency click rather than a nice woody sound. So if there's a lot of side stick, then I might have to position the microphone more for that instead of rejection of the hi-hat. Once again, all this stuff varies from session to session.*

STEVE ALBINI: *Doing anything (like recording a drum of any kind) is never a one-solution-for-many-problems scenario. I'll give you a few specific things I've tried with success (and failure—that's just as important) in the past:*

Because I often have to bus several mics to a single channel, and because I hate making the session more complicated than necessary, I almost always use the console preamps and routing for the close mics on a drum set. I'm happy with the console mic amps here at Electrical [Neotek Series II and Elite/custom], but because I try to avoid a convoluted signal path when I can, I'll stick with console preamps even if I'm working on an SSL, MCI, Amek, or the like. If the desk is a real piece of junk, then it's unlikely there is anything better in the rack anyway.

For a cracking, attack-strong sound, lately I've been using an Altec 175 or 165 with a 29a or 29b capsule. A good substitute for this is a mic I'm trying out [as a prototype] from Shure—it doesn't have a name yet, but I'm sure you'll hear all about it when they're ready to sell. I have had mixed (occasionally good) results with AKG C 28, C 60, and 451 mics, but they're not usually the first thing I try. I have, in a pinch, used Shure SM98s by themselves.

For a thicker sound, especially in a dead room with a dampened snare, I'll use a Sony C-37P or a combination of a Beyer 201 with a Shure SM98 taped to the side of it—align the diaphragms, or the high end sounds funny. I used this setup almost exclusively for years because most other things I tried didn't sound as good. Lately I've found a few more.

I often have a bottom mic in place, but I don't always find a need for it.

For brushwork, I really love the Manley/VTL/Langevin CR-3A and the Audio-Technica 4051, and I have had good results with AKG 414s and the Schoeps 221B.

If the room sounds good, I always try to record the ambient sound as well. The ambient sound can be a big part of the sound of the kit, but not necessarily—don't force the issue. If the room sounds good, then the drums will sound good with the room signal, but if the room sounds bad, then settle for good-sounding drums with little room sound.

I don't compress or gate the drums to tape, but in mixing I'll occasionally use 3 dB or so of an expander—Valley Dynamite or Kepex II, dbx 172—to tame the hi-hat, and occasionally use a peak limiter if there is a specific reason to do so.

Honestly, I've used so many different things, as the case requires, over the years that I don't think there is a single answer to recording anything—even something as simple as a snare drum.

ROSS GARFIELD: *The way I look at that is to get the snare drum where you want it first because it's way more important than the way the toms are tuned. You hear that snare on at least every two and four. The kick and snare are the two most important drums, and I tune the toms around that and make sure that the rack toms aren't being set off by the snare. For me, the snare is probably the most important drum in the set because for me it's the voice of the song.*

PLACEMENT

1. Place an SM57 on a boom stand and position it about 1 inch, or about 2 of your fingers, above the rim. The silver "ring" of where the mic head meets the body should be placed just over the rim of the drum. Make sure there's a slight angle so the mic front is pointed toward the center of the drum head (see Figure 8.25). In order to get some isolation from the other drums and cymbals, try to get the snare mic pointing away from the hi-hats, but make sure it's not in the way where the drummer will hit it. A good place is directly between the rack tom and the hi-hats, if it's out of the way of the drummer.

Figure 8.25
Standard SM57 snare setup.

2. A variation on #1, place the mic at the rim of the snare near the hat, elevated about 2 inches. Place the mic so that it looks across the head, aiming for the far edge. Adjust outward for more shell or inward for more impact. (See Figure 8.26.)

Figure 8.26
SM57 across the snare top.

3. Position a mic 4 to 8 inches away from the snare and aim it at the shell. Move it closer to the bottom head for more snare sound, or closer to the top head for more attack and less buzz. (See Figure 8.27.)

Figure 8.27
SM57 at snare side.

Variation: Aim the mic at the port from an angle on the side of the drum. Miking the port will give you a good, solid transient with both heads in phase. Be sure to mic the port at an angle, or you might record a wind blast.

4. Along with the top mic, place a mic about an inch from the bottom head and right under the snares. Remember to flip phase on the bottom and see if it has more low end when blended with the top. Also try to keep the bottom mic at about a 45-degree angle from the top mic. Mix the bottom mic in for presence. Cut 50 to 100 Hz from the bottom mic or use the roll-off on the mic if the kick is leaking into it. (See Figure 8.28.)

Figure 8.28
Sennheiser 441 under snare.

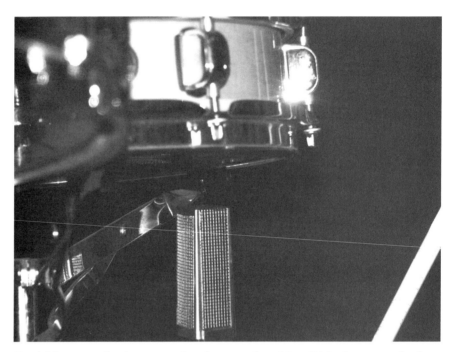

5. Add a second mic, not under the snare but 18 to 24 inches away, looking in from the side. Use a hypercardioid pattern if available.

6. Use a condenser with the pad on and the hi-pass pass filter switched on. Place it in the room at a point where the snare sounds great and print it to another track, compressed just a little. Then, during the mix, put a gate on that track with a key function triggered by the original snare signal so that it only opens up when the snare hits, and adjust the parameters to taste.

7. For better isolation from the hat, cut off the top of a plastic milk jug or bottle down to the end of the handle. Slip the snare mic backward into the hole, then into the mic clip (an SM57 fits just right). Be aware that this will most likely change the sound of the microphone, but you'll get a lot of isolation. (See Figure 8.29.)

Figure 8.29
Isolated snare mic.

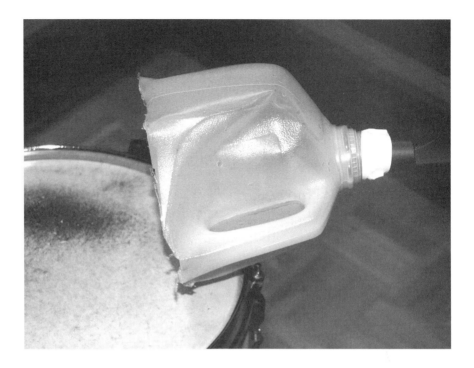

Variation: Use a Styrofoam drinking cup instead of the plastic jug or bottle. (See Figure 8.30.)

Figure 8.30
Isolated snare mic 2.

8. Tape a small-diaphragm condenser to an SM57, lining up the elements to ensure phase correctness. The condenser will give you top, and the 57 will give you body.

9. Take a contact mic, such as a Barcus-Berry, Korg, or Cold Gold (contactmicrophones.com), and tape it to the snare drum, out of the way of the drummer. Connect it to a mic pre and then to the key input of a gate. If you use a gate with a filter section, you will be able to remove all other frequencies from the key input. The gate will open on every snare hit as or before the sound gets to the mic and will be extremely consistent. If for any reason the drummer misses a snare hit, it will be much easier to fly in a sample this way.

STEVE ALBINI: *You want it somewhere where it's out of the drummer's way. You don't want it to interfere with what he's doing, and you don't want the drummer to be preoccupied with not hitting the microphone. Every drummer's set is slightly different, so you try to find a place where it's not going to pick up too much of the hi-hat and it's not going to be in the way of the drummer.*

It's nice if you can get a few inches of distance between the snare drum mic and the snare drum, but you have to put it where it will go rather than making the drummer work around it.

Brushes

They're not used very much, so brushes usually don't end up sounding as good as they can because most engineers aren't sure what they're supposed to sound like. Although many of the following suggestions may be counter-intuitive, they'll help you get a great brush sound quickly.

CONSIDERATIONS
▶ The brush sound is partly the attack of the individual bristles, which you want to sound crisp, partly the ring of the rim and shell, and partly the ambient sound from around the kit.

▶ Getting a good brush sound comes from how you mic the entire kit, not just the snare. Close-miking the snare doesn't seem to work for this application, so don't think in terms of one mic, but in terms of the sound of the entire kit.

▶ Part of the trick is to give the drum kit more space than what you normally would. The overheads provide the depth.

▶ Coated heads are recommended.

PLACEMENT
1. Tape a piece of cardboard to the top of the snare and play the brushes on that. It can sound more like a snare than a real snare.

> **Variation:** Play with brushes only on a cardboard box.

2. Move the overheads in closer.

3. Place a dynamic mic about an inch from the rim, pointed at the center of the drum but placed so that half of the capsule is below the rim and half is above. Mix with the overheads.

Hi-Hat

The hi-hat often gets the least attention of all the pieces in the drum kit, but it's actually the main timekeeper and propels the song forward. Plus, many drummers consider their hi-hat work their drumming signature.

CONSIDERATIONS

▶ Heavy hi-hat cymbals that sound great for live work tend to have a lot of low overtones that cause frequency interaction with some of the drums when recording. Lighter hats tend to record better as a result.

▶ Placement too close to the end of the cymbal might pick up the air noise. Too close to the bell might sound too thick.

▶ A condenser mic is usually used to mike the hi-hat to best capture the transients.

▶ Be sure to use a −10-dB pad if it's available, since hi-hats put out a lot of level.

▶ Make sure that the mic is placed toward the rear of the kit, as far away from the crash cymbal as possible for maximum rejection.

▶ Add a dB or two at 10 to 12 kHz to give the hat sizzle.

▶ Sometimes it's best to filter out everything below 160 kHz using the hi-pass filter on the console or preamp. These frequencies won't be missed and will tend to clean up the sound when the rest of the drums and cymbals are placed in the mix.

▶ If the hi-hats sound too thick or heavy, attenuate 1.2 kHz by 2 or 3 dB or move the mic away and more toward the edge of the top cymbal.

PLACEMENT

1. Place a small-diaphragm condenser pointing straight down at the cymbal about halfway from the center to the rim but placed toward the back of the hat. Dynamics or ribbons can also work. Depending upon the mic, this is good for isolation from the rest of the kit. Move the mic closer to the bell for a thicker sound and more toward the edge for a thinner sound (see Figure 8.31).

Figure 8.31
Mic on outside of hi-hat.

2. Position the mic about 4 to 6 inches above the hat and angle it toward the place where the drummer hits the hat. This is where you get the most clarity of the part. If you need more air and sizzle, move the mic higher up and aim it straight down toward the cymbal. (See Figure 8.32.)

3. Place a mic looking down the post of the hi-hat for an extra thick sound.

CHUCK AINLAY: *I position the mic so that it's pointing away from the rest of the kit. It's hard to explain, but basically the mic is poised over the hat and points at a 45-degree angle down toward the side of the hat farthest from the snare. I have never had a problem getting a good sound doing this, and obviously the iso is better than if the mic were pointed toward the rest of the kit.*

Hi-hat I vary between a 452 and a KM 184. It depends on what kind of sound I want. If I want a chunky-sounding hat, the mic will usually be over the hat, pointing out across the hat somewhat away from the snare drum, so if you're the drummer it would be on the other side from where you're hitting it. But if I want an airier sound, I'll move the mic more and more off to the side of the hat to where it's not even over the hat to get that paper-thin sort of sound. The only thing that you have to be aware of is the wind blast that might happen when he pumps it.

Figure 8.32
AKG 452 on inside of hat.

Toms

For better or worse, the sound of the toms often defines the sound of a record. If they sound big, the record sounds big, but if they take up too much space, it's hard to fit them into the track with the other instruments. As with the other drums, the toms should sound great acoustically before the mics are placed in order to get the best sound.

CONSIDERATIONS

▶ You'll get more of an attack and less of a thump with a condenser mic than with a dynamic.

▶ When miking multiple toms, keep all the tom mics facing in the same direction as much as possible to eliminate any possible phase issues between them. If you're looking down from the ceiling from behind the drum kit, they would all be pointing to the 6 o'clock position.

▶ Listen to all the tom mics in mono. Flip the phase switch on the pre-amp, console, DAW, or interface for the fullest sound.

▶ With most toms, adding a little (1 or 2 dB) EQ at 5 kHz will emphasize the attack, and 8 kHz will emphasize the presence. Attenuating 1.5 kHz will decrease the thickness. Attenuating 400 to 500 Hz will decrease the "boxiness."

▶ Top and bottom miking may be a good overall approach, but it can be very phase sensitive and generally lacks the clarity of a single top mic.

► On a large kit, miking each pair of toms may work better than miking each tom individually.

► Use some tape to add a bit of tension to the head to break up and/or damp out a resonance without ruining too much of the snap of the drum. Tape it about 3/4-inch from the edge of the batter head, pull it a bit and then stick it down over the hoop on the outside of the drum. Done right, it should stick onto the batter head for only about 1/2-inch of the tape's length. The tape trick is best done using only a small bit of tape (1 inch by 3 inches). "Deadringers" (1/2–inch-wide rings of thin plastic that go over the periphery of the batter head) do a similar job but can eat up too much of the drum's tone.

► The "under" tom approach (with the mic actually inside the drum) may only be helpful on top head–only toms where the leakage is a problem.

► The two heads on the drum can usually be tuned to give the drum much more fat and power than one head alone.

► Gates can be used to diminish the ring from a tom that you can't tame with tape, padding, or tuning, but use them only during mixing, not during recording. But remember, your tom mikes are also your snare mikes. If you gate them, you might destroy your snare sound, too.

PLACEMENT

1. The classic method: Place the mic 2 to 3 inches off the head above the rim at a 45-degree angle, looking down at the center of the head, to get the most attack. (See Figure 8.33.) For more ring and less attack, point it closer to the rim.

Figure 8.33
Sennheiser MD421 over rack tom.

2. Instead of miking the toms from above, try the mics a few feet in front of the set and very close to the floor (being careful to avoid reflections).

STEVE ALBINI: *As a technical note, I usually have the top mic 4 or so inches above the head and the bottom mic the same or an inch closer. I've wondered about this myself…. Why does this work? Then I realized that I had visualized the resonant system incorrectly. The initial transient moment of the attack does take a millisecond or so to get to the bottom mic, but once the system of the drum head and air volume and shell and bottom head starts vibrating, it is vibrating as a whole, and the top and bottom heads behave as a single membrane.*

This means that without flipping the electrical polarity of one of the mics, you'll have some cancellation, more in that frequency range than elsewhere. And isn't that a range where you often start out EQing toms by dipping a little out? Flip the polarity, and you'll reinforce that frequency range. If you normally goose up that frequency range, then I've just proved that the practice of reversing polarity of one mic is valid. But if what works is cutting a bit in that range, then perhaps not reversing polarity is more effective.

I never thought about that, but being a foot or so apart, it doesn't seem too likely. They'll probably reject room reflections (leaving the room sound available for a properly placed distant mic) since they're far enough away so that the arrival time from a wall to the two mics will be pretty close, but it's unlikely that they'll reject another drum in the kit.

The drum kit is still present in the tom mics, but the low-frequency room rumble, bleed from the bass guitar, et cetera are attenuated dramatically. This is a double benefit, since adding low-frequency EQ to the tom track (in an attempt to bring out the resonance of the drum) would otherwise accentuate these muddy noise components.

It is important—really, it is important; don't believe what some ex-club-sound hack tells you—to use good mics on the drums. There will always be spillage, especially from cymbals and other drums, and using mics with clean high end and good overall response allows this spillage to be used as an element of the sound, rather than being a problem that has to be eliminated.

CHUCK AINLAY: *For toms, the microphone choice there varies the most of anything. It will vary from a 57 or a 421, although I've been using these Audio-Technica ATM25s a lot lately. Sometimes if I want a beefier, warm sound I'll go to a condenser microphone, which can go from a 414 to an 87 if I want a sort of fat '70s sound, to Sony C-37s if they're available and working [laughs]. Once again, Audio-Technica makes a clip-on condenser, the 8532, that I've had a lot of success with. It has a lot of isolation and doesn't have that huge proximity effect that you get from a lot of other condenser mics. It also works great on acoustic guitars. Between that and an AT4033, I get an amazing acoustic sound.*

Also on toms, I always put gates on the inserts of the tom channels. What I do is use these little contact mics that were intended to be trigger microphones for triggering sound modules for drums and plug them into the key side of the gates for the toms. Whether or not I turn on the insert depends on whether I want the leakage on the toms or not. Toms add so much to the warmness of your snare drum and bass drum, but this way I have a really solid trigger on the gates and I don't miss the nuance-type fills. I don't necessarily always use it, but it works so good when I need it. Usually when I do gate toms, it will only be 6 to 10 dB of reduction. I don't gate them to nothing. I usually use the console mic amps so I can do this.

I normally place the mic between lugs of the tom. If you get over one of the tuning lugs, you get too much of the flap from the drums. Drummers usually don't tune their toms perfectly, so they don't ring on forever. They'll intentionally detune them slightly so they sort of bend away and stop ringing quicker, so if you split the lugs it sounds better.

Also, I try to not get too close to the head. You're compromising between leakage and tone, but if you get too close you're just going to get attack and no warmth out of the tom. It's usually somewhere between 2 1/2 to 4 inches; probably closer to 3 inches. If I take my three fingers and put it between the mic and the head, that's usually a good starting place. Sometimes I'll mic underneath as well, but that's rare.

3. On floor tom, place a dynamic or large-diaphragm condenser pointing about 45 degrees, aimed at the center of the head and about 2 inches high, at about the 1:30 position, looking at the drum from behind the kit. If there's not enough bottom end after doing everything possible with heads and tuning, put a large-diaphragm condenser mic or any mic with a strong low end under the drum with the phase reversed. This mic will pick up only the low-frequency information, but will have a noticeable time delay compared to the top mic. (See Figure 8.34.)

Figure 8.34
MD421 on floor tom.

4. You can sometimes get the greatest rejection of the kit from the floor tom mic by placing it underneath the ride cymbal, again about 3 inches above the rim pointed at the center of the head (see Figure 8.35).

Figure 8.35
Floor tom miked from under the ride cymbal.

Overheads

Depending upon the sound you're going for (which is dependent upon the song, artist, and player), the overheads either can be used to capture the sound of the entire kit or can be used primarily as cymbal mics.

CONSIDERATIONS

FRANK FILIPETTI: *As a drummer, I know that the sound at the snare is not exactly what I want to hear on the track. There's a lot of bloom around the snare and around the bass drum as well that I feel is essential to capturing the reality and the dynamics of the snare and bass drum in particular. So my overhead technique is to capture the overall sound of the kit and not just the cymbals. I tend to want to mic the kit so that I do get leakage of the snare, bass drum, everything into the overall sound. I want to be able to put up the overheads along with the bass drum mic and get a pretty nice sound on the kit. So my tendency is to mic a little further away from direct impact of the cymbals.*

▶ Generally speaking, with an X/Y overhead configuration the image is better and there are fewer phasing issues.

▶ If you have a room that's too live, move the overheads closer to the kit to reduce the amount of room being picked up.

▶ Make sure that you switch in the −10-dB pad either on the mic or on the console/DAW interface since the cymbals will cause the mics to have a high output.

▶ Sometimes you can clarify the sound of the cymbals and clean up the ambient sound by engaging the hi-pass filter either on the mic or on the console.

▶ Make sure the kit sounds balanced when listening to only the overheads. The snare should be just right of center, the same way you're looking at the kit (if you're mixing the kit from the audience perspective).

▶ If using the overheads only as cymbal mics, check the cymbal balances. Move the mic away from a cymbal if it's too loud and closer to it if it's too soft.

AL SCHMITT: *It's usually the sound of the kit. I'll start out with the mics that I normally use and just go from there. If it's a jazz date, then I might use the Royers, and if it's more of a rock date, then I'll use something else.*

ED CHERNEY: *It depends. If it's a gentle song and the drums are being atmospheric, I'm going to spot mic cymbals and rides and swells. But with a rock kit, I'll try to get a pretty good balance with the overheads, yet still get the cymbals without them ripping your head off.*

WYN DAVIS: *I use the overheads to capture the whole kit, but with an emphasis to the top end of the set, meaning all the cymbals, hi-hat, and accent cymbals. I basically use C 12s almost over the toms and not directly facing the cymbals. I put them off-axis from each other a bit, so that the two C 12s are looking in the opposite directions a little bit. They're sort of close together, maybe a foot or 18 inches apart, looking in two different directions back toward the mic stands.*

If the intention is for the drum sound to be real ambient, which is the case in a lot of rock situations, I usually put the overheads about 2 feet above the cymbals so they're capturing a fairly wide angle.

FRANK FILIPETTI: *One of the things that I do, because I know that my overheads are going to be so important in the overall sound, is to make sure that the distance from the snare to each overhead capsule is identical. I want to hear the snare in the center when you just listen to the overheads. When you just mic the cymbals and you solo those mics, the snare tends to shift depending upon your perspective. So I make those mics identical in distance from the snare, as well as identical in distance from the cymbals that they're miking, so no mic gets a signal prior to the other one. With just the overheads up I want you to get a good idea of the kit, but with the snare in the center, which is not really how the kit is since the snare is always placed slightly on one side. The bass drum is in the center, so in the best of all possible worlds, I try to make the snare right above the bass drum and I mike it accordingly.*

PLACEMENT

STEVE ALBINI: *If the drums are being recorded in a live room with a lot of ambient sound, I tend to think that the cymbals sound better that way than with mics right up close to them. I do have overheads up over the drum kit, generally just to correct balance problems with the cymbals. Like if the crash cymbal isn't loud enough, it's nice if there's an overhead mic to bring it up, but I generally prefer the sound of the cymbals at a distance. Of course, it depends what the band is after. There's sort of a '70s characteristic sound where the cymbals are thin and sustaining, but there's no real ambience to the sound. It's a dry recording, but there's a lot of sustain on the cymbals. If we're shooting for that sound, it does require you to use close mics rather than ambient mics, and in some cases even use a peak limiter on the overheads so that the snare and toms don't overwhelm the cymbals.*

CHUCK AINLAY: *That varies a lot, but it's either 414s, or what I've been using most recently is the stereo Royer microphone, the SF-12. Ever since I started using that thing, my drums have sounded so much more real. I can sort of rely on that for the drum sound and then fill it in with the close mics rather than the other way around.*

Well, it depends on whether I'm using a stereo overhead mic like that, which then you can use it for the main kit sound. If you're using spaced pairs where you're just miking cymbals, then it doesn't work at all. It depends on the intent and if you want this really in-your-face closed mic thing or if you want the drums to be more set back and more real-sounding. If you're going for that '70s/'80s tighter sound, then you'd put the mics over the cymbal. If you want them more real-sounding, then you'd go for the stereo mic.

1. Position an ORTF pair just behind the drummer's head, pointed out into the room at about a 45-degree angle. This provides more distance and a realistic spatial image of the kit. (See Figure 8.36.) Aim the mics out toward the room for more ambience.

*Figure 8.36
ORTF overheads.*

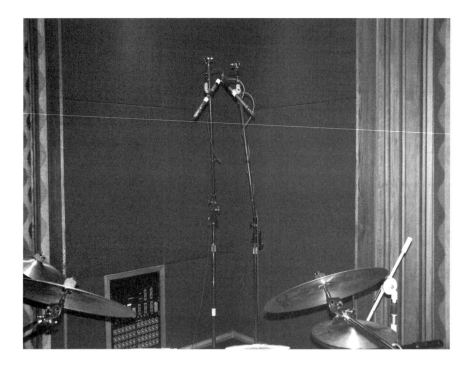

Variation: Try a stereo mic instead of an ORTF pair. (See Figure 8.37.)

Figure 8.37
Royer SF-12 as stereo overhead.

2. For cymbal miking, position the mic over the side of the cymbal away from the snare. (See Figure 8.38.)

Figure 8.38
Royer R-121s over cymbals.

Variation: If #2 results in a lot of "swishing" from the cymbal movement, place a condenser mic 12 to 16 inches off the bell of the cymbals.

3. For really old-school overhead placement, place a single ribbon mic up off to the right of the top of the drummer's head. (See Figure 8.39.)

Figure 8.39
Royer R-121 as single mono overhead.

4. Place an X/Y configuration at least 12 inches off the ceiling aimed toward the outside of the cymbals. Aim them at the bell of the cymbals for a little fuller tom tone and a little less wide stereo separation overall.

Variation: In order to tame a damped low ceiling, use two figure-8s instead of cardioids in configurations 1 through 4.

5. If the ride cymbal is too quiet compared to the other cymbals, place a mic about 6 inches underneath the ride pointed at the bell. Make sure you reverse the phase!

6. Place an omni overhead on the hi-hat-snare-ride and a cardioid small-diaphragm condenser on the other cymbal and toms, angled slightly out toward the room.

FRANK FILIPETTI: *I've experimented with a lot of different positions, and I've come up with a placement that works best for me. Most engineers seem to come in with the mics coming from the front of the kit looking back toward the drummer. I put my overheads in the back near the drummer, looking ahead toward the kit. I just found after years of experimentation that's where the best sound for me is. Just above the snare looking out toward the cymbals gives me the depth and the impact that I'm looking for.*

The microphones are probably a foot or so above the drummer's head. I don't want him banging his head or hitting them with his sticks. They're far enough back that if he raises his sticks to hit a cymbal, his sticks might hit a mic in front of him but not one slightly behind him. Not only is it great for the snare and the cymbals, but it's great for the toms as well. What I end up generally having to do because of that is to also mike the ride cymbal separately because the ride sometimes needs that little extra "ping" that you can't get from further away.

Room

To many engineers, the room sound is a major part of their drum sound, while for others it's a mere afterthought. It's worth it to spend a little time capturing the room sound, however, since it can add that extra bit of "glue" that can't be achieved any other way.

CONSIDERATIONS

▶ A figure-8 pattern might work better as a room mic in a small room. This is because the mic picks up the end-to-end reflections, but not the side/side or floor/ceiling reflections. Even if the mike is angled, it will still pick up fewer of these reflections than any other pattern. As a result, where a small room reveals itself unpleasantly when recorded with omnis or cardioids, it may sound perfectly acceptable with a figure-8.

▶ Consider what you're trying to achieve by recording the room. If the goal is more ambience, then a single mic pointing away from the drums might work well. If the goal is to get a bigger drum sound, then mics placed even with the drums at the point where the kit seems most balanced should work.

▶ Generally speaking, the fewer close drum mics that are used, the more effective the room mics will be.

▶ Two or 3 dB at 12 or 14 kHz can open up the room and give it a little "air."

FRANK FILIPETTI: *The sound of the room and how much metal the guy plays determines the position. Some guys are splashy cymbal players, and other guys aren't. If there's a lot of cymbal activity and a lot of splashy metal work going on, my tendency is to go lower to the floor to get things warmer. It's one of those things determined by the amount of time there is to play around.*

PLACEMENT

CHUCK AINLAY: *I usually put them about 4 feet out in front of the snare drum. [See Figure 8.40.] Not the kick drum but the snare drum. I'm sort of splitting the positioning between the hat and the bass drum with what I call a mid-field mic. I'll usually put up one of the mono Royer mics [R-121] and use some severe limiting on it with an 1176, and that becomes my 'meat' microphone. It just sort of brings in the drums as an overall picture, and it really adds a lot of meat to them. Then about 12 feet away—sometimes less—in front of the drums, I'll put up a pair of 149s or a pair of these Joe Meek microphones, the JM47s.*

Figure 8.40
Royer R-121 as room mic.

ED CHERNEY: *I'll put up an 87 in omni about 10 feet in front of the drums and maybe about 6 feet high as a room mic, just to have a listen to things to get it going.*

WYN DAVIS: *In my drum room I'll Velcro a couple of PZMs to the wall that the drums face and use those as room mics sometimes.*

1. Place a mic at each side of the kit, pointed directly at the outer edge of the furthest cymbal at a distance of 6 to 10 feet. The mics should be at the same height and be exactly parallel to each other (see Figure 8.41).

Figure 8.41
Parallel room mics.

2. Place a stereo mic 6 to 8 feet in front of the kit at about 7 feet high. The mic should be at about a 45-degree angle, facing down at the kit.

3. Turn the room mics away from the drums to pick up more of the slap from the walls.

4. Have the drummer hit only the snare and find a point in the room where it really takes on the character of the "CRACK." Mic that place and then during mixdown, gate that track using the close-miked snare to trigger for the gate. Adding compression changes the character of the sound.

5. Keep the room mics down low, in front of the kit, 3 feet or so off the floor, pointed upward. (See Figure 8.42.)

Figure 8.42
U 47 as drum kit room mic.

1960s Beatles Sound

The Beatles' drum sound changed quite a bit through their eight years of recording. Ringo's kit used mostly minimal miking in the beginning and gradually evolved to a setup similar to what we normally use today (with a mic on every drum and stereo overheads) on the very last song the band recorded (appropriately titled "The End").

CONSIDERATIONS

▶ The drum sound on later Beatles' records and on songs such as "Hey, Jude" and "Come Together" utilized "tea" towels (thin towels similar to cloth napkins) covering the heads of all the drums. The sound is enhanced by the use of a Fairchild 660 limiter.

▶ Regardless of the number of microphones used on the drum kit, the drums were always recorded in mono to only a single track. The only exception was on the previously aforementioned "The End," which was recorded in stereo on two tracks.

PLACEMENT

1. For the early Beatles drum sound, place a cardioid mic (an AKG D 19 was originally used) over the center of the kit, anywhere from 6 inches high to the top of the drummer's head. Move closer to the snare if more snare sound is needed. Place a large-diaphragm cardioid mic (an AKG D 20 was used originally) about 3 to 6 inches from the kick drum, raised to about the level of the top of the rim and pointed downward at a 45-degree angle.

2. For the later Beatles drum sound, augment the above with a cardioid mic under the snare from about 6 inches away from the edge of the drum and pointed up at a 45-degree angle. Do the same for the rack tom. For the floor tom, place an identical mic 6 to 9 inches away from the top head. Don't forget the towels over the heads.

1970s Drum Sound

The late '60s/early '70s drum sound was the sound of deadened drums, which was mostly the result of the influence of the Beatles' drum sound from that period.

CONSIDERATIONS

▶ There are many ways to achieve the '70s deadened drum sound, but a common mistake is to deaden the drums too much.

▶ The reason for the damping was to kill sympathetic resonances so that you would mostly just hear the drum that had been hit rather than the ringing of the whole kit.

PLACEMENT

1. Place a small towel on the snare. This will deaden the drum considerably (but that's the sound you want).

2. Cut the rim off a snare head and then put the remaining part on the drum head to deaden it.

> **Variation:** Cut off the rim and the inside of the old head, which essentially gives you a "dead ringer." Make sure that you use a little tape to hold it in place since the stick tends to get caught up in the ringer.

3. Use half of a sanitary napkin taped on one side so it flaps up on the attack then settles back on top of the drumhead. A pad can also be applied to the bottom head if the ring is too long.

4. Remove the batter head and rim of the drum and place a strip of felt or cloth 2 to 3 inches wide completely across the drum. This is the classic way that drummers were taught to damp drums.

5. Tape a piece of cloth to one edge of the snare with a flap about 3 to 4 inches over the top head.

Have the drummer put his wallet under the flap. (See Figure 8.43.)

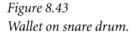

Figure 8.43
Wallet on snare drum.

6. For that old Motown disco hi-hat sound, mike the top cymbal by pointing a mic directly at the bell from about an inch away (see Figure 8.44).

Figure 8.44
A mic aimed at the hi-hat bell.

The Reggae Drum Sound

Looking for that Bob Marley sound? Here are some things to try:

▶ Dead heads (usually old clear pinstripe or Evans-type hydraulic heads) and boxy-sounding toms are the norm if you want that old-school Lee "Scratch" Perry dub sound. Try a timbale tuned up really high and place it where the floor tom would normally be.

▶ Wailers' drummer Carlton Barrett's snare was a vintage Ludwig 5-1/2×14 with a coated head tuned up until the snare began to choke itself. This gave a timbale-like effect when struck on the edges of the head (slightly ringy but controlled) with the advantage of having a loud and snappy cross-rim shot. The tighter the head, the snappier the rim-shot sound.

Dulcimer

There are two kinds of dulcimer. The Appalachian dulcimer is a fretted instrument with drone strings, while the hammered dulcimer uses small mallet hammers to strike each set of strings. Like many other stringed instruments, the hammered dulcimer uses sets of strings to increase the volume.

CONSIDERATIONS

▶ The sound of the pick (or the quill, as is more traditionally used) is very much part of the sound of a dulcimer, but it should not be overbearing.

▶ Try moving the mics a little closer to the noter (the left hand) to capture some of the resonant sound without getting so much pick. There are sound holes near both the bridge and the headstock that produce some of the resonant sound. Unlike acoustic guitars, mountain dulcimers generally do not get boomy at the sound hole.

▶ The key is to get some distance (at least 2 to 4 feet) so that you don't pick up the low-frequency "thump" sounds that frequently occur.

▶ Also, it helps if the player knows that he or she doesn't have to play the instrument as hard as might be required in a live gig. If a lighter touch is used, the tuning might last a little longer.

PLACEMENT

1. Place a pair of omnis spaced about 1 to 2 feet apart at a height of 2 to 3 feet above the instrument.

2. Place an X/Y configuration of small-diaphragm condensers at about 3 feet away from the center of the instrument.

Fiddle

Basically, the only difference between a fiddle and a violin is the type of music that's being played. Fiddle music the world over is mainly dance music, while violins are more associated with classical and orchestral music.

CONSIDERATIONS

▶ Put a finger in your ear and walk around the instrument, listening with the other ear. You will find the sound changes dramatically with position because the radiation pattern is so uneven, and it's different with every instrument. Find the place where you like the sound and place the mic there.

▶ Get farther back from the fiddle than you think you need to be because you need to get the mic far enough away so that the sound can project out of the instrument. If you still have a hard time getting a good sound, you might try pointing the mic slightly off-axis. This will roll off some of the harshness.

▶ Bow noise and grit are sometimes referred to as *rosin noise*. However, rosin is the stuff that is put on the bow hair to make it grab the string better, and it doesn't produce any noise of its own.

PLACEMENT

1. Place a mic pointed at where the bow hits the strings but tilted a bit toward the neck at a distance of about 8 to 12 inches.

2. Place a mic slightly above and about 6 feet in front of the fiddle to capture the full body of the sound without catching too much of the bow effects (scratchy sounds).

3. Place a ribbon mic over the player's left shoulder for close-miking.

4. Position a mic *underneath* the violin in addition to the top mic.

5. Position the mic behind the violinist so the head and body of the violinist are partially obstructing the direct path between the mic and the instrument. This is a great way of reducing the ratio of direct-to-ambient sound without pulling far away from the instrument.

6. Place the violinist in the corner of the room with the mic about 3 feet away and 2 feet above the instrument.

Flute

Flute is one of the least demanding instruments to record accurately. Its pure tone is easily captured by most microphones. The words *transient* and *flute* almost never appear together, except when the music calls for accents.

CONSIDERATIONS

▶ The higher notes will be closer to the flute head, with the lower notes spread more toward the bottom of the instrument.

▶ Miking too close will pick up a lot of key clicking.

▶ The flute side (normally the right side) of the player can have more coloration effects than the other side. The flute side also has more key noise. The other side may have more mouth sounds.

▶ If you mic near the blow hole, you'll end up with an airy sound. If you mic farther down the instrument, you'll end up with a smoother, less bright sound.

PLACEMENT

1. Pick your spot by ear (usually in front or above). *Do not* record from the open end of the flute. It doesn't sound like a flute there.

2. As a starting point, place the microphone several feet away from the flute, above the flute's embouchure and somewhat off to the side. (Try both sides.)

3. Jazz flute is best recorded very close (6 inches from the mouthpiece to catch all the breath sounds). Classical flute is best from 4 to 6 feet or even more, depending upon the room.

French Horn

See the "Brass" section.

Acoustic Guitar

CHUCK AINLAY: *In Nashville we tend to make pretty-sounding acoustic recordings. I guess it's an AT4033 if I want that bright Nashville sound. That mic works nicely. Or a 452. If I want more of a richer sound, I'll use either a KM 84 or KM 56 or one of the new 184s. In all instances the mic is pointed at where the neck joins the body and then out about 5 or so inches. I usually use a second microphone that moves around a lot. It's usually a large-diaphragm mic that's placed away from the guitar. That varies so much. A 67 is probably my preferred mic for that, but an Audio-Technica 4033 or 4050 works well, too.*

I'll start out straight in front of the sound hole. If that's too boomy, I'll move either towards the bridge or lower or sometimes above the sound hole above the cutout. Sometimes off the shoulder near the right ear of the player works. I might just put on a pair of headphones and move the mic until it sounds great. That's about the only way that you can mike an acoustic guitar. You just have to listen.

STEVE ALBINI: *With acoustic guitars it depends on whether there's going to be singing simultaneously with the acoustics. If there is, then you have to try to make the mics not favor the vocal. If there's no singing, then you can record the instrument at a distance and pick up some room sound, and that's nice. Normally, I try to have a stereo image either from the audience perspective or the player's perspective. The Neumann SM 2 is a great acoustic mic. Schoeps 221s are great. I've used the AT4051 at a distance. They get a bit brittle if you get too close.*

If you have an instrument that's really stringy and thin-sounding, a ribbon mic up close tends to make it sound a bit heftier. The same basic thing holds true for things like mandolin and banjo. With banjo you have to be careful because it's a brittle instrument and you have to use a darker microphone.

CONSIDERATIONS

▶ Generally speaking, the least desirable sound from an acoustic guitar comes from close-miking the sound hole. The sound is much more tonally balanced in the vicinity of the bridge or at the joint of the neck and the body.

▶ Anything closer than a foot is going to result in a big proximity boost of the low end if you're using a directional mic. Either switch to an omni or back the mics off.

▶ Since many of the successful miking methods utilize two or more microphones, be sure to check the phase and listen in mono.

PLACEMENT

1. Place a mic about 8 inches away from and pointing at the point where the fret board meets the body. (See Figure 8.45.)

Figure 8.45
AKG 452 on acoustic guitar.

Variation: Position a second mic pointing at the body about halfway between the bridge and the end of the guitar at a distance of 10 inches. This should not sound boomy, and when the two mics are printed to different channels and panned apart, it can sound spacious and lush.

2. Place an omni mic near the sound hole. There is no increased low end due to proximity effect since it is an omni.

3. Use a stereo mic about 8 to 12 inches away with one capsule aimed toward the bridge and the other aimed toward the headstock.

4. Place one dynamic mic aimed at the body of the guitar and one condenser over the guitarist's shoulder at about ear height and roughly even with the front edge of the guitar, pointing at the neck. You get two different tones that can be combined in different ways in the mix depending on what the song calls for (see Figure 8.46).

Figure 8.46
AKG 452 over shoulder acoustic guitar.

5. For a guitar-only recording, try two small-diaphragm condensers in an X/Y configuration. Aim one at the body below the bridge and the other at about the twelfth fret.

6. For great rhythm guitar sound, start with a small-diaphragm condenser 12 inches from the twelfth fret, aiming at the twelfth fret. Don't let the guitar player move to face the mic in the sound hole of the guitar. Engage the hi-pass filter on the mic and on the preamp.

Compress at a 6:1 ratio with a slow attack, which should make the attack blend nicely with the hi-hat and rhythm percussion. Compress with a fast attack if you want to hear less pick. If you double the part and hard pan them, it leaves a nice hole in the middle for your main instruments.

GUITAR TRICKS

1. To decrease string squeak, try a fine grade of steel wool rubbed lightly over the strings. Keep it away from the frets and finish on the neck. (A piece of notebook paper or thin cardboard slipped between the strings and the frets beforehand will assuage the fears of even the most finicky owners of vintage instruments if there is any question.)

2. Try recording using a High 6 (Nashville 6) tuning. You'll get a great guitar track that'll sit nicely in almost any mix. For this trick you must restring your guitar with the high strings from a 12-string guitar set. Depending on how light a gauge you like, the gauges would be something like:

   E = .008 – .011 (Tuned to normal pitch)

   B = .011 – .015 (Tuned to normal pitch)

   G = .008 – .010 (Tuned to one octave higher than normal pitch)

   D = .011 – .015 (Tuned to one octave higher than normal pitch)

   A = .016 – .022 (Tuned to one octave higher than normal pitch)

   E = .022 – .028 (Tuned to one octave higher than normal pitch)

   Sometimes just using the third or fourth string up an octave can be very effective as well.

3. One of the best ways to record vocals and acoustic at the same time is with two figure-8 patterned mics. Aim one at the guitar and make sure the null side is pointing toward the vocalist's mouth, and then take another one for the vocal and make sure its null is pointing toward the acoustic.

Nylon- or Gut-String Guitar

Everything that applies to acoustic guitar also applies to a nylon-string guitar, plus the following considerations.

CONSIDERATIONS

▶ With a nylon-string guitar, much of the sound is projected toward the floor from the right side of the guitar if the guitarist sits in the traditional position with a footrest.

▶ Consider putting a small carpet of some sort under the mics to minimize floor reflections.

PLACEMENT

1. If the guitarist is right handed, place a mic 2 to 3 feet to his right and close to the floor, pointing up toward the guitar. Place a second mic 2 to 3 feet away, just a little up the neck from the sound hole, on the guitarist's left side. If you get too close, you will emphasize the fret noise. This should work in stereo or mono providing the phase relationship between the mics is correct.

2. Place a small-diaphragm condenser about a foot to the left of the player's left ear, looking down on the twelfth fret. Add a large-diaphragm condenser about 12 inches from the strap peg at the same height.

3. Place a small-diaphragm mic 6 to 8 inches from the sound hole but pointed either at bridge or where the bridge meets the body. Move closer to the sound hole for more low end.

4. Place two mics on a stereo bar in an ORTF-type configuration slightly below the guitar, facing slightly up. The mics in this configuration will be about 24 to 30 inches out from the player.

5. As a spot mic in an ensemble, a large-diaphragm condenser 8 to 18 inches above the instrument can sound really nice.

Electric Guitar

Unless you're going direct, the sound of the electric guitar is really the combination of the guitar, the amplifier, and the effects signal chain. But the biggest contributor to the actual guitar sound is the one that's sometimes overlooked, and that's the player himself. If the player doesn't have it, then no guitar, amp, pedal, or mic will get you there.

CONSIDERATIONS

▶ An amplifier or speaker cabinet usually sounds better if it's raised up off the floor. Raise it into the air by putting it on a road case, table, or chair.

▶ There are different tones you can get by simply moving the mic more toward the speaker's dust cap or toward the surround (the edge of the speaker where it meets the metal basket). Different angles, different mics, and different distances from the cabinet will all alter the tonal quality.

► The guitarist's signal chain can be a huge help or a big hindrance. You'll get a warmer yet aggressive guitar sound by decreasing the amount of distortion from pedals, but turning up the amp's volume instead to obtain the sustain/distortion from the amp and speaker.

► Typically, it's best for a player new to the studio to keep the signal chain more on the simple side without lots of processing happening at the amp. That being said, some effects are integral to a player's sound.

EDDIE KRAMER: *If I hear a sound that I like, then it goes to tape. If it's a guitar, then I'll print the reverb as well on a separate track, so the sound is there and locked in. I usually have an idea of what it's going to sound like in the final analysis, so the EQ and compression are done right then and there. I think if you bugger around with it afterwards, you have too many choices.*

WYN DAVIS: *Recording guitar is not easy. Unfortunately, there is no foolproof recipe for getting a good guitar sound. First of all, so much of it is 'in the fingers.' Second, guitar sounds are so subjective. One person's totally awesome golden tone is pure torture to the ears of another. If you cannot afford an 'expert engineer,' then I suggest you experiment with a fairly close mic, be patient, and have someone with ear protection move the mic around a bit while you listen. That'll get you started.*

So here goes a dumb story. I had a session with George Harrison once. He was in town, and the artist I was working with wanted to get him on a track. He didn't have any of his 'stuff' with him. My client asked me to line up some equipment for him to play through. I rented this awesome refrigerator rack from one of the session guys I know around town. When George came in, he looked at all the stuff and said, 'I'll just go direct.' I said, 'Really?! Okay, cool.' I played the track and for a while I was sweating it. The guitar didn't sound very good; I thought I was blowing it. George just fiddled around with the song for about half an hour and finally said, 'Okay, I'm ready.' I was completely dumbfounded when all of a sudden, the guitar sounded perfect. He played a couple of passes, doubled it, and when it was done, it sounded exactly like George Harrison. So like I said, barring some complete intrusion by the engineer trying to impose something entirely inappropriate on the performance, it's in the fingers.

MICHAEL BEINHORN: *The reality of the situation is that harmonically there are immense similarities between a symphony orchestra and a band that uses multitracked, multilayered distorted guitars. Really, from a harmonic standpoint, there's no difference at all between the functions that these types of things serve. They're essentially operating in the same general frequency range. Guitars and string sections, it's all the same. I believe you get the same psychological effect that you get from a group of violins that have been miked closely to pick up the grit as you do on the electric guitar. The electric guitar is a very complex sound.*

How the distortion works and what you do with it are key to being able to understand it. Distortion is a very important thing in modern recording. Things like how it's dealt with, what function it serves, where it sits in the mix, and how you get separation are all important.

▶ On the typical 4×12 speaker cabinet (like the standard Marshall 1960 model), the four speakers usually become additive at a distance of 15 to 24 inches from the cabinet center.

▶ When doubling or adding more guitars, it's best to have a variety of instruments and amplifiers available. Two guitars (a Les Paul and a Strat, for instance) and two amplifiers (a Fender and a Marshall is the classic combination) combined with different pickup settings will allow a multitude of guitar tracks to more effectively live in the mix together.

▶ In an odd paradox, smaller amps and speakers tend to sound bigger than large amps/speakers when recording.

PLACEMENT

1. The classic setup: Place an SM57 about 1 inch away from the best-sounding speaker in the cabinet. Place the mic about three quarters of the way between the edge of the speaker and the voice coil (away from the voice coil). Move toward the voice coil for more high end. Move toward the edge of the speaker for more body. Make sure that the mic does not touch the speaker cone during the loudest passages (and longest speaker excursion) played. (See Figure 8.47.)

Figure 8.47
SM57 on guitar cabinet.

FRANK FILIPETTI: *The first thing I'll do is try to choose the best speaker on the amp. Usually we're using a four-speaker cabinet like a Marshall, and generally the speakers don't all sound the same. I try not to mike from too far away because you start to introduce phase anomalies from the different speakers coming from the cab. I tend to get as close as I can with whatever my miking scheme is.*

2. Another classic setup: Place the SM57 as above. Now add an MD421 at the same position to the right of the 57, at a 45-degree angle pointing toward the voice coil. Many sounds can be achieved from this setup by summing the mics at different levels and by flipping the phase on one. (See Figure 8.48.)

Figure 8.48
SM57 And Sennheiser MD421 on guitar cabinet.

3. After finding the correct position as shown above, bundle an SM57, a 421, and a Beyer M160 (or other ribbon mic, such as a Royer R-121) together. All three mics are aimed directly at the speaker. Add together to taste. The 57 will provide the bite, the 421 the mids, and the 160 the body. (See Figures 8.49 and 8.50.)

4. Along with any of the methods mentioned earlier, place a ribbon mic 2 inches off one of the rear corners of a Marshall cabinet in order to capture the low end of the cabinet. This only works with Marshall cabinets due to the wood used and construction unique to Marshall (but it works really well!). (See Figure 8.51.)

Figure 8.49
SM57, Beyer M160, and
Sennheiser 421 on guitar cabinet.

Figure 8.50
Sennheiser 421, Royer R-121, and
SM57 on guitar cabinet.

Figure 8.51
Beyer M160 on Marshall cabinet
corner.

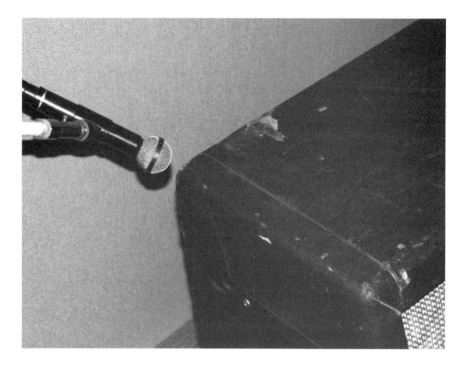

5. Position a single mic 10 to 20 inches from the cabinet, dead center to all four speakers or, if a Marshall cabinet, aiming for the logo plate. (See Figure 8.52.)

Figure 8.52
Sennheiser 421 placed where
speakers converge.

6. With an open-back amplifier (like a typical Fender), place a mic in the rear of the amp, off center from one of the speakers. If used in conjunction with a mic in the front of the amp, flip the phase and use the position that works best.

7. Though a little dated, the archetype for that "LA clean rhythm guitar sound" popular in the '80s is a DI'ed guitar, compressed about 6 dB, with a 25-ms delay on the left side and a 50-ms delay on the right.

8. For distorted guitar, place a dynamic mic up close, two-thirds of the distance from the center to the edge of the speaker about 8 inches away, pointed toward the nearest corner of the cabinet. For ambience, place a large-diaphragm condenser in figure-8 mode in the same position as the first mic, but at a right angle to the amp to create a side channel for later decoding with an M-S decoder.

9. Add to the above an additional mic (often a large-diaphragm condenser) at the spot where the sound of the speakers converge 18 to 24 inches away. This distance might be increased to as much as 6 feet depending upon the size and sound of the room.

10. For more ambience, add a third mic facing a hard wall in the room. The three mics can be mixed together in various proportions to create many different tonal effects.

STEVE ALBINI: *Electric guitar mics tend to be farther away from the cabinet because if you're really close to the speaker, then the acoustic interactions with the cabinet are more localized. If you pull the mic farther away, then you get a more coherent sound from the cabinet as a whole.*

11. Use a tiny battery-powered amp, such as one of the Marshall Minis or Fender Mini Twins. Close-mike the speaker. The result is a surprisingly large sound. (See Figure 8.53.)

Figure 8.53
SM57 on Marshall Mini.

MACK: *I prefer small amps to big ones. The big stuff never really does it. For guitar amps, Marshalls are pretty standard, but with everything else, smaller is better.*

12. Another one that usually only works well with clean guitars is to tune an acoustic to the key that the song is in (using an open tuning) and place it on a stand near the amp. The amp will make the strings resonate. Position a mic on the body, pointing toward the sound hole. The sympathetic vibrations of the strings give you an instant tuned reverb chamber.

13. For a clean sound, place the amplifier or speaker cabinet under a piano. Put a brick on the sustain pedal and have someone hold down every key on the piano tuned to the song so the piano strings will ring out sympathetically. For example, if the song is in the key of E (major or minor), then hold down all E and B keys. Mic the piano as in the "Piano" section.

MACK: *Just leave enough distance from the amp so you get a bit of room reflection to it. I used to do the thing where you crank the amp so it's noisy, then put on headphones and move the mic around until you find the sweet spot. I usually use two mics (which is sort of contrary to my beliefs because you get a lot of phase stuff) because you get a natural EQ if you move the second one around. If you can remember what the hiss sounded like when you had a good guitar sound, then half the battle is won.*

WYN DAVIS: *I usually end up asking the guitar players to turn whatever treble control they have on their guitars back a hair. It takes just little bit of the edge off. It really warms things up a lot if you just crack that tone control back a couple of numbers. It makes it sound a little bigger, especially if you're layering three or four guitars on top of one another.*

Glockenspiel (Also Known As Glock or Orchestral Bells)

The glock is a smaller, higher-pitched version of vibes. Glocks have become quite fashionable in popular music, popping up in almost all genres from hip-hop to jazz. (Check out Bruce Springsteen's "Born to Run" for a good example in rock.)

CONSIDERATIONS

▶ The glock projects a lot of high-frequency information. A darker mic, such as a ribbon, sometimes does a good job in capturing it.

▶ For less attack, use rubber mallets.

PLACEMENT

1. Place a pair of dynamic mics at either end of the instrument, about 6 inches above the bars.

2. If there are too many transients, place the same mics at the same distance from underneath the glock.

Gong

There are three types of gongs: suspended gongs; bossed gongs, which are flat with a raised center; and bowl gongs, which rest upon cushions. Suspended gongs that are played with a mallet are the ones most used in modern music.

CONSIDERATIONS

A gong has a thunderous low end, so a cardioid mic with proximity effect will make it sound muddy. Try an omni instead.

PLACEMENT

1. Place a small-diaphragm omni mic about 2 feet from the center.

2. Place a dynamic mic low to the floor at about 4 feet away to capture the low end, and a small-diaphragm omni condenser about 18 inches away near the top of the gong to capture the harmonics.

Hand Claps

Claps are best done in a group, and the more clappers, the better. Claps are often augmented with foot stomps, boards, or electronic claps to achieve the proper effect.

CONSIDERATIONS

▶ Use a fairly live room, back the mic away from the clappers, and use a compressor that has variable attack and release times. Compress heavily (10 to 20 dB) and adjust the attack time so that there's not too much attack. Set the release time fairly fast.

▶ Gating (but not too tightly) will help keep the track clean. If you need an "ultra tight to the snare" sound, key the gate from the snare drum.

▶ Double-tracking the claps makes them sound far bigger. Expect to do a number of punches to avoid flamming.

▶ As with other percussion instruments, the peaks are always 10 to 15 dB greater than what a typical VU meter is reading (if you happen to be using one). Therefore, it's best to record the signal at about –20VU or so.

▶ Try having the clappers sit and slap their thighs; you get twice as many claps and a somewhat darker, more full-bodied timbre. You don't get as much edge or definition, however.

▶ Space the clappers a couple of feet apart distance-wise from the mic. Five people works well. Have the folks nearest the mic clap more on top of the beat and the folks farther away clap more laid back. Split the claps between two styles: sharp slap-clap done by slapping the fingers of one hand into the palm, and a deeper, more standard palm clap done by clapping both palms together. The distance and timing variation give a nice, thick, cascading effect.

PLACEMENT

1. Claps need distance to develop, so start with a dynamic mic at least 3 feet away. Use a mic with a figure-8 pattern to avoid any slap echo from the floor or ceiling.

> **Variation:** Use a ribbon mic (automatic figure-8 pattern) to smooth out the transients.

2. Mix in someone clapping two pieces of wood together (instead of their hands) with the real hand claps (a classic old-school trick).

Harmonica

Miking a harmonica acoustically is different from miking a blues harp (where you're miking an amplifier like a guitar).

CONSIDERATIONS

▶ The harmonica is typically on the shrill side, so a darker mic, such as a ribbon, can smooth some of that out.

▶ Open-ear headphones or using just one phone helps the player stay in tune.

▶ The higher the key, the shriller the instrument will become.

PLACEMENT

1. Place the mic about a foot away, but underneath the hands and pointing up at the harmonica. This will reduce any mouth noises present.

2. Some players get great results simply playing into an SM58 cupped in their hands, like on stage.

3. A combination of both of the above can be very effective.

Harp

The concert harp seen in orchestras has either 46 or 47 strings and 7 pedals that are used to change their pitch. The lowest strings are copper or steel wound with nylon, the middle are gut, and the highest are nylon.

CONSIDERATIONS

▶ When miking an orchestral harp (not to be confused with a Celtic harp), the main thing to remember is that the sound comes from the soundboard, not from the strings.

▶ Generally, the major problem in miking the instrument is isolation from other instruments.

▶ For a more natural sound, back the mic up a few feet and let the room support the sound of this very resonant instrument. Transient response is less important from a distance (3 feet away or more), but absolute level drops quickly, so you'll need a quiet room and a low-noise mic and preamp. Close-miking requires a mic with good dynamic range to handle the pluck and the ringing. (It's like recording a piano, just quieter.)

PLACEMENT

1. The classic harp miking calls for a mic placed about 2 feet to one side, about a foot forward of the harpist and about 4 feet off the floor. This prevents pedal noise and gets a percussive attack from the fingers.

2. In orchestral situations, place a figure-8 mic pointed at the middle of the soundboard. Point the null of the mic toward the loudest interfering sounds.

3. In orchestral situations, clip a small lavaliere mic into one of the sound holes along the musician side of the instrument. Gain before feedback and ambient noise are never a problem with this setup.

4. Place a small-diaphragm condenser aimed two-thirds of the way up the soundboard from about a foot away.

5. Aim a small-diaphragm condenser slightly above the instrument and to the right, pointed down toward the higher strings.

> **Trick:** For overdubs against an orchestra, place a mic where the harp will sit later. Send a mix minus (all music *minus* the mic sound that was picked up by the harp mic) out of a speaker in the room after the string section leaves and reverse the phase of the mic for the harp overdub. The harpist now does not have to wear headphones and can play more accurately as a result.

Indian Instruments

I've put the traditional Indian instruments—sitar, tabla, tambura, and santur—into a single category because when they're not recorded together, the approach to recording each one is similar.

CONSIDERATIONS

▶ Tabla is a pair of drums. It consists of a small right-hand drum called *dayan* and a larger metal one called *bayan*.

▶ Indian musicians don't seem to think of the tambura as a real instrument, since it's there for drone ambience and pitch reference for the vocalists.

▶ Remember that the room is half the sound in the case of Indian instruments.

▶ Sitars produce little sound pressure, and the sound tends to emanate from the whole instrument and not a localized area, like with a flat-top guitar.

▶ When recording sitar, consider that the sympathetic strings are heard from far away. Close-miking may destroy this effect because the close sound is very different from the distant sound.

▶ The sitar has a very odd radiation pattern, so if you close-mike it, you'll need multiple mikes.

PLACEMENT

1. For sitar, use a pair of omnis at a distance of 4 to 12 feet. Mic positioning can generally be from floor level to standing height for consistently natural sound. Greater heights will be more unpredictable in overall effect.

2. For close-miking a sitar, place a dynamic in close to the bowl and a small-diaphragm aimed at the neck to get a thicker sound.

3. In a pure solo or traditional ensemble context, a stereo pair of large-diaphragm microphones in X/Y placed 3 to 4 feet in front and slightly above the performer, angled toward the instrument, will produce a larger-than-life sound.

4. Place an omni behind the performer, almost looking over his shoulders, and a cardioid a couple of feet in front of and angled back toward the picking hand.

5. A stereo pair in any configuration 3 to 6 feet in front of the instrument provides a good representation of what it sounds like to audience members.

6. For tambura, place a small-diaphragm condenser about 18 inches away from the body. You don't want to hear the individual plucking of the strings, just the resulting drone.

7. Santur is a hammered dulcimer. Mic with an X/Y pair overhead at a distance of 1 to 2 feet. Sound emanates from the whole length of the neck as well as the body.

Koto

The koto, the national instrument of Japan, is traditionally a 13-string instrument, although some may have as many as 25. Although it is thought of as a distinctly Japanese sound, it has been used in popular Western music by David Bowie, Queen, Dr. Dre, and the jazz-rock band Hiroshima. The player uses three finger picks (thumb, forefinger, and middle finger) to pluck the strings.

CONSIDERATIONS

▶ The koto has a lot of high-frequency energy, so a darker mic, such as a ribbon, works well.

▶ The tuning is adjusted by moving the bridges before playing.

PLACEMENT

1. Place a single small-diaphragm condenser (or two in ORTF or X/Y for stereo) directly over the instrument, aiming down from a height of about a foot above the player's head.

2. Place a lav or contact mic inside and a mic on the koto's sound hole. This works especially well in a live situation.

Leslie Speaker

The sound of the Hammond organ (and many other organs, for that matter), the Leslie is a set of rotating speakers that employ acoustic Doppler shift to obtain their effect. The high-frequency horn provides frequency modulation (Doppler shift). The rotating low-frequency section provides amplitude modulation.

CONSIDERATIONS

▶ The farther from the speakers, the less you'll hear the grit, whir, and noise of the Leslie.

▶ The Leslie rotating effect is much more dramatic when the louvers are miked, rather than the horn opening. (See Figures 8.54 and 8.55.)

Figure 8.54
SM57 placed on Leslie top louver.

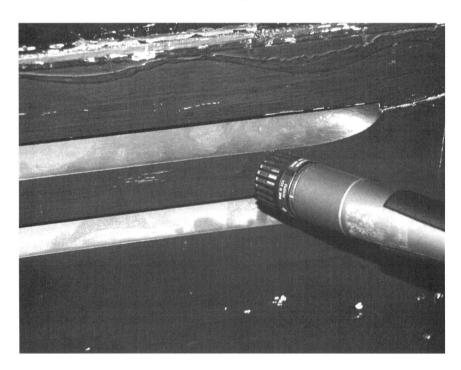

Figure 8.55
AKG D 112 placed on Leslie
bottom rotor.

PLACEMENT

1. The classic stereo method: Place two mics at opposite sides of the cabinet against the top louvers and put a single large-diaphragm condenser on the bottom louver. Since the two mics on top are out of phase (in a good way), you hear the moving Doppler effect when they're panned in different places.

> **Variation:** For mono, place as above but use just a single top mic on the same side as the mic on the bottom rotor.

2. As above, but place the upper mics at 90 degrees (one on the front louver and one on the side). Be careful if this will go to mono. (See Figure 8.56.)

3. Place a large diaphragm condenser for mono or a stereo mic about 5 feet away and aimed about halfway down the cabinet.

4. Place an omni directly on the top of the Leslie cabinet, using small, folded pieces of a matchbook or a masking-tape reel to isolate the mic from vibration. This requires a moderately reflective room. (See Figure 8.57.)

Figure 8.56
Leslie top and bottom rotors miked.

Figure 8.57
Neumann KM 83 on Leslie top.

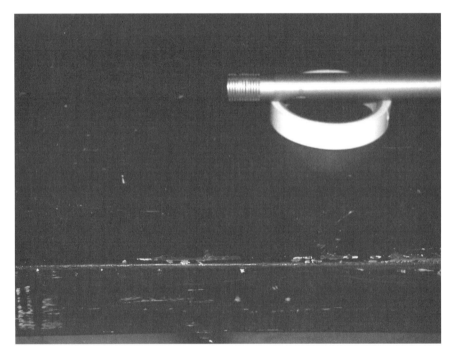

5. To the traditional setup in #1, add a distant mic approximately 4 to 6 feet away, aimed at the top rotor. The bottom mic is panned center, the top close mic is panned to 11:00, and the distant mic is panned to 3:00, mixed at least 6 dB lower in level than the close mic. To make it even larger-sounding, send a bit from an aux to a stereo plate reverb whose returns are panned fully left and right. Bus all the above to two tracks.

6. Place an M-S array about 4 to 5 feet away with a diffused wall 2 feet opposite the Leslie and wood gobos, tightening the sides.

7. Place a pair of small-diaphragm condensers 8 to 10 inches off the corners, about at the middle of the Leslie and pointed slightly up. Place the tip of an omni an inch or so directly into the low port on the back. Use just enough of the low mic to balance the image.

Mandolin

Mandolin is basically a soprano lute. It has four courses (double strings) that are tuned the same as a violin and the opposite of a bass (GDAE).

CONSIDERATIONS

Watch the hand movements of the player so the picking hand doesn't obscure the mic.

PLACEMENT

1. Use one mic pointed down at the top string from about 6 inches away and a second mic pointed up at the sound hole from underneath, again at a distance of about 6 inches.

2. Place a mic between where the picking hand and the neck meet, at a distance of between 12 and 18 inches. Place a second mic near the lower f-hole for fullness.

3. For stereo, place a mic on each f-hole, keeping them about 6 inches apart.

Marimba

See the "Vibes" section.

Mouth Harp (Also Called Jew's Harp or Jaw Harp)

Said to be one of the oldest instruments in the world, the mouth harp has a metal or bamboo tongue reed attached to a frame.

CONSIDERATIONS

▶ It's possible to modify the pitch of a mouth harp by varying the shape of the mouth.

▶ The instrument is very quiet and requires much more amplification than other instruments, so the level of noise of both the mic and the preamp becomes a factor.

PLACEMENT

Place a mic (a dynamic works fine) from 12 to 18 inches from the nose of the player, pointed at the harp.

Piano

STEVE ALBINI: *I've had really good luck with the Neumann SM 2 stereo mic over the piano. AKG C 12s and C 24s sound great, too. Those Audio-Technica 4051s are great piano mics. I'll usually place them perpendicular to the harp, one on the long strings and one on the short strings. You have to shuffle them in and out until the stereo image sounds normal. The SM 2 I'll put in front of the piano with the lid open, sort of looking in on the strings. Same with the C 24.*

AL SCHMITT: *Piano is a difficult instrument, and to get a great sound is probably one of the more difficult things for me. I've been using the M 149s along with these old Studer valve preamps on piano, so I'm pretty happy with it lately. I try to keep them up as far away from the hammers as I can inside the piano. Usually one captures the low end and the other the high end, and then I move them so it comes out as even as possible.*

CONSIDERATIONS

▶ Microphones inside the instrument will pick up unwanted pedal and hammer sounds in addition to the music, but they'll capture a brighter, closer sound.

▶ Microphones outside but near the side of the instrument "looking in" can also hear reflections from the top. That can be good or bad depending on the sound you want.

▶ Microphones away from the instrument will record the piano and the room. If your room sounds good and you don't need a very close sound, this is a safe method for recording a balanced piano, as the sound of the instrument doesn't really exist properly until you get some distance from it.

▶ Miking from the side usually means that the higher notes will be captured at a higher level. Miking inside the case will tend to emphasize the middle octaves, which could be good for some music styles and not for others.

▶ To make the piano brighter, add a few dB at 10 kHz. For more definition, add a little at 3 kHz. If the piano sounds thin, adding a few dB at 100 Hz helps.

PLACEMENT

1. For orchestral or solo piano, place a spaced pair of mics aimed at the middle of the "rounded" part of the piano, 6 feet away from the piano and at an angle equidistant between the keys and lid. If there's not enough ambience from this technique, move the pair back and up but keep the angle. Place the high piano mic pointing at the hammers and the low mic pointing at the low strings. (See Figure 8.58.)

Figure 8.58
Small-diaphragm microphones in X/Y outside of piano.

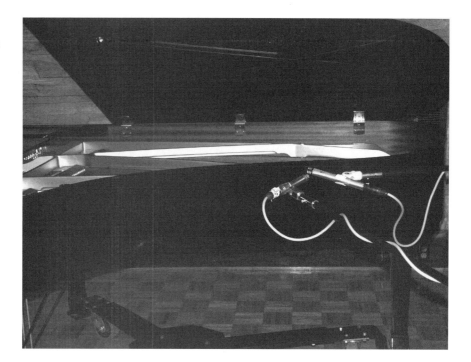

2. Place one mic by the upper-mid hammers and one by the extreme back end over the lower strings. (See Figure 8.59.)

3. Sometimes recording from above and behind the pianist works well—especially with a stereo pair. Point the mic toward the soundboard about an octave below middle C. You don't get much attack on the strings, but it's good fill and it sits well in the mix.

Variation: Place the mic just above the music stand, directly in the center.

Figure 8.59
Small-diaphragm microphones
inside piano.

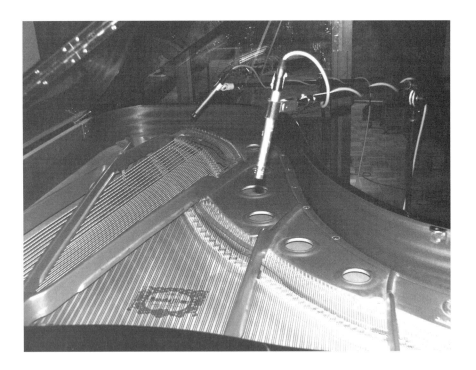

4. Have the pianist play scales. Stick your finger in one ear and walk around to find the point in the room where the hall ambience and the direct piano sound are balanced. When you find that place, walk back and forth along the piano and listen to how the bass changes. Find a place that has the right tonality and the right balance. Place an ORTF pair there.

5. With the piano lid at full stick, place a pair of X/Y cardioids at the edge of the body aimed in and down more toward the higher strings. (The lower end of the piano is omnidirectional and will be picked up as well.) Move as needed to balance the sound.

6. Place a pair of small-diaphragm condensers spaced about 4 feet apart and positioned about 6 feet away from the piano and about 8 to 9 feet high. Angle them to aim at the edge of the lid when on full stick.

7. For more of a rock-and-roll sound, place a mic about two-thirds of the way up the bass strings, 12 to 18 inches over the strings and another aimed at the label (under the high strings) from a similar height. To balance between the high and low strings, put the monitors in mono and move the mics around until it sounds balanced, then record on two tracks.

Variation: For more body, add a single mic in one of the classical positions (outside the piano in the room). Again, listen in mono for correct balance and phase.

8. Also, a classic rock-and-roll setup and a variation on the above, place an X/Y or near-coincident pair within 2 feet of the center of the harp, where the high and low strings cross. (See Figure 8.60.)

Figure 8.60
Small-diaphragm microphones in X/Y inside piano.

9. For a classical recording, place a pair of figure-8 ribbons in a Blumlein configuration 8 or 10 feet outside the piano. Aim them where the hammer hits the string at about C above middle C.

Upright Piano

1. Place an ORTF or X/Y stereo pair about 3 feet away from the back soundboard.

2. Take the panel off underneath the keyboard. Place an omni 12 inches away from the point where the low and high strings cross. Put a ribbon right above the separation, pointed toward the high keys.

3. Open up the top of the piano and place a mic on the bass side and another on the treble side facing down, just over the lip of the piano.

Piccolo

The smallest of the flutes, the piccolo can be constructed of wood, metal, gold, plastic, or any combination.

CONSIDERATIONS

Because the piccolo's sound is in such a high register, it has the tendency to be shrill. Therefore, a darker mic, such as a ribbon, can be very effective in capturing its true sound.

PLACEMENT

The piccolo has a very high output in the high frequencies, so it's best to use a ribbon or large-diaphragm condenser mic about 10 feet away and pointed at the middle of the instrument. It also helps to compress the signal 2 to 4 dB at about a 4:1 ratio to smooth out the variations in level between notes.

Recorder

The recorder is a whistle-like woodwind instrument that was the precursor to the flute. It has been revived in the 20th century to keep performances historically accurate and as a simple instrument for teaching music.

CONSIDERATIONS

The sound of the recorder is very pure and has a distinct lack of upper harmonics.

PLACEMENT

Similar to a flute, place a mic from 1 to 2 feet over the middle of the instrument, looking down.

Saxophone

The sax is another relatively new instrument, invented in the 1840s as a means for woodwinds to get the projection and volume of brass instruments.

CONSIDERATIONS

▶ The sound of a saxophone comes from every hole and from the body of the instrument at the same time and in totally different proportions for every note. The bell gives you honk on the highs and some of the low-frequency components, with only the lowest note coming exclusively out of the bell.

▶ The notes at the top of the instrument range come out of the upper body's left-hand side. Altissimo notes (higher again), typically high-pitched screams, come out the front upper and middle tone holes but are usually much louder than most other notes.

▶ The bell sound is generally quite focused but disproportionately edgy and harsh. The side pads of the saxes generally radiate a "woody" sort of tone, which by itself can sound like the reed is soggy.

▶ When they're warming up, sax players will inevitably find the spot in the room (usually a couple of feet from a wall) where the horn sounds best to them. This may be the best place to put the player or the mic.

PLACEMENT

1. A large-diaphragm condenser directly in front of the sax at a distance of 12 to 16 inches captures a sound that's very authentic.

2. Add a side mic to the front mic, as discussed above, for more fundamentals on the low notes. Start at about a foot away and adjust the distance so as not to get too much valve click. Try switching phase/polarity and use the fatter setting.

3. Place a ribbon mic about halfway up the keys, aimed down at the bell. (See Figure 8.61.)

Figure 8.61
Royer R-122 on sax.

4. Place a ribbon mic about neck or face high to the player, aiming down on the horn.

5. Position the mic about 3 feet away, slightly above head height and about 30 degrees to the left of the player, aimed toward the middle of the horn.

6. Place a mic between 18 and 24 inches away at an angle, pointing at the left hand of the player.

7. For soprano sax, place the mic above the sax at about the midpoint, aimed straight down.

Shaker

Shakers have become a vital part of the rhythm section in popular music. Sometimes cutting through the track and sometimes subtly adding motion, many drummers and percussionists use a wide variety of shakers, both store-bought and homemade.

CONSIDERATIONS

▶ There are many different types of shakers, and they all sound different. However, the technique for capturing their sound remains the same.

▶ Sometimes some salt in a Styrofoam drinking cup will sit better in the track than a real shaker.

▶ As in miking a tambourine, the mic placement has to be far enough away to account for the movements of the player.

▶ Most shakers have high-frequency transients that place extra strain on the microphone preamp. Try several (if you have them) to find the combination of mic and preamp that sounds the best.

PLACEMENT

1. Place a condenser mic or an omni 5 or 6 feet away at about head level.

2. As above, only using a ribbon mic instead.

3. Place a dynamic mic behind the player and from 1 to 2 feet over his head, pointed down at the shaker.

Steel Drums (Also Known As Steel Pans or Pan Drums)

Originally made from 55-gallon oil drums (now machined to precise specifications), steel pan drums are chromatic and have 13 members in the pan family. The most commonly used is the double tenor.

CONSIDERATIONS

▶ Steel drums are very much like fiddles in that their radiation pattern changes with every note played. There is no single place in the near field where you can mike them and have all the notes captured evenly.

▶ A close-miked steel drum can sound more clanky than melodic.

▶ Have the player rewrap his pan sticks (or replace the surgical tubing on the end, if they're constructed that way) for the recording. Having fresh mallets to work with makes a huge difference.

▶ Dynamic mics often work better than condensers because of the transients involved.

PLACEMENT

1. Place a ribbon mic directly over the player's shoulder.

2. Place an omni about 6 feet away from the pans and about 2 feet above.

3. Place an omni from under the rim of the steel pan pointing up at the center.

4. Place a dynamic mic about 8 feet above the pans to allow the transients some space to dissipate.

Stick (Chapman Stick)

The Stick (sometimes known as the *Chapman Stick* after its inventor, Emmett Chapman) is a 10-stringed instrument (although versions with 8 or 12 also exist) played by tapping both hands on the fret board. It gives a player the ability to play chord inversions not possible on a regular guitar and an instrumentalist the ability to play both bass and chords/lead at the same time.

CONSIDERATIONS

▶ The Stick is an electric instrument with two outputs: one for the high strings and one for low strings.

▶ The strings on the bass side vary in volume as you move up the neck, so a bit of compression is useful to match the level of all notes.

PLACEMENT

1. Use two DIs for the outputs.

2. Connect the high string output to a guitar amp and the low string output to a bass amp (or DI) and proceed as if miking a normal guitar and bass amp.

String Section

Since the majority of people who read this book won't ever get the chance to record a large symphony orchestra (and probably aren't interested, either), I won't go into it much in this book. There's plenty of information available in the many books published strictly on this subject. Plus, you can read the interviews with Bruce Botnick, Michael Bishop, and Eddie Kramer, which outline the two major approaches. However, recording a small string section is within the realm of possibility for most engineers, so here are some techniques.

AL SCHMITT: *The major trick in all of this—and I learned it from both Tommy and Bob—was that you go out in the studio, stand next to the conductor, and listen to what's going on. You're job is to go in and capture exactly what he wants to hear out there.*

AL SCHMITT: *On some of the dates I'll just use the room mics up over the conductor's head. I'll have a couple of M 150s or M 50s or even M 149s set to omnidirectional. I'll have some spot mics out there, but lots of times I don't even use those. It works if you have a conductor that knows how to bring something like the celli up when it needs to be louder, so I'll just try to capture what he's hearing out there.*

CONSIDERATIONS

▶ All string instruments radiate omnidirectionally, but the brilliance of the tone comes from the top of the instrument. Violins and viola (known as the *chin strings*), project up and over the performer's right shoulder. The celli and basses project more forward and lower.

▶ You can record a bowed string instrument from any angle, but the results are usually better if the mic can "see" the top of the instrument.

▶ Walk around, listen to the ensemble, find where the group sounds best, and put the mics where your head was.

▶ Go with closer miking (but not too close) in a small room since the distant approach may show how small the room is.

▶ Although you may not use them, spot mics are okay to use. It's always easier not to use a mic during the mix than not to have the control you need.

▶ The lush sound that the composer expects comes from the front mics, but the clarity of the inner voices comes from the spots.

BRUCE BOTNICK: *If you listen to your overalls and then open up your sweeteners into it, you can control the amount of presence that you want from that distant pickup.*

▶ A good room is a necessary ingredient for a good string sound. A low ceiling with acoustic tile will murder your string sound (and every other sound, too).

▶ Strings do not sound beautiful when close-miked. The sound is usually harsh and shrill. Strings need space for the sound to develop.

BRUCE BOTNICK: *On a rock-and-roll date, there's more close-miking than in orchestral recording, which uses mostly distance microphones.*

EDDIE KRAMER: *In regard to mic techniques, what I adapted was this classical idea of recording—i.e., the distance of the microphones to the instruments should not be too close if you wanted to get anything with tremendous depth. Obviously, I used close-miking techniques as well, but it started with the concept that 'distance makes depth' that Bob Auger taught me. Generally, the basic philosophy of getting the mics up in the air and getting some room sound and some air around the instrument was what we used. Then you'd fill in with the close mics.*

PLACEMENT

1. Place an ORTF or X/Y pair about 4 feet behind the conductor and as high as you can get them.

2. Use a spaced pair about 20 feet apart at head height or higher (at least), pointing down at about 30 degrees.

3. For string quartets, place a small-diaphragm condenser on each player about 3 feet away, but more out front than overhead. Supplement these with an ORTF pair of large-diaphragm condensers up about 7 feet high and about 3 or 4 feet behind the line between the first violin and cello.

MICHAEL BISHOP: *At that time, when I first started here, Jack was typically recording with three omnis across the front of an orchestra and perhaps two omnis out in the hall, and that was it. So I followed along in that tradition until I came up with something of my own to contribute. I changed it from the three omnis across the front to four omnis across the front with the two center mics being 24 inches apart, so it was a little like half of a Decca Tree in the middle, but the positioning was very different.*

Synthesizer (Or Any Kind of Electric Keyboard)

While it may seem that the best approach with electric keyboards is to record them direct (which is the first instinct of most engineers), sometimes an amplified and miked keyboard can sound much more realistic and fit into the track better. It may take more time to record an instrument this way, but the addition it makes to the sound can be well worth the extra hassle.

CONSIDERATIONS

▶ The reason why electronic keyboards don't sound "real" is that they don't have a first reflection of the ambient sound field that all acoustic instruments have.

▶ Many so-called "stereo" instruments achieve their stereo spread by modulating one of the outputs. This can cause phase problems when summed into mono. You're better off using only the output labeled "mono" and achieving the stereo spread another way.

PLACEMENT

1. The traditional method is to take the outputs directly into the console or DAW through direct boxes.

2. A better way is to feed the mono signal back out into the studio (by either the playback speakers or an amplifier) and mike the room from a distance of about 6 to 10 feet with a stereo mic or X/Y or ORTF pair. This accomplishes two things. It adds the needed first reflections to make the instrument sound more real, and it provides a nice stereo spread that sounds a lot more natural and sums to mono well. Add this to the direct sound.

Tambourine

Tambourines come in many sizes and shapes and are made out of a variety of materials. The classic instrument has a drumhead, but most modern varieties used in pop music do not.

CONSIDERATIONS

▶ Place your tambourine player in the livest, brightest part of your recording room.

▶ Keep in mind that since a tambourine must be moved when playing, close-miking usually won't work.

▶ If you're using a console, don't record very hot. A good level is –20, as a tambourine has peaks that can be a full 15 dB over what a VU meter is reading.

▶ Sometimes a really dark-sounding mike (something with a rolled-off high-frequency response) works best.

PLACEMENT

1. Place a condenser mic with an omni pattern 5 or 6 feet away at about head level.

2. Place a ribbon mic as above. (See Figure 8.62.)

Figure 8.62
Royer R-121 on tambourine.

Timbale

Typically, a set of timbales consists of two single-headed drums, a wood block, and two cowbells mounted between the drums. A small cymbal is mounted off to the side.

CONSIDERATIONS

▶ Timbale miking can change considerably if the timbale is used in a Latin style, since the cowbell will be attached and can easily drown out any mics aimed at the top of the instrument.

▶ Also, if the music is salsa, the player may play on the side of the drum, which can only be captured well from below.

PLACEMENT

1. Place a dynamic mic (a 57 or a 421 works nicely) under each drum, about 6 to 12 inches away, angled at the head.

2. To capture the entire timbale kit, add a small-diaphragm condenser mic to the under mics at a distance of 1 to 2 feet. Position the mic for the best balance between wood block, cowbells, and cymbal.

3. An ORTF or X/Y pair about 1 to 2 feet over the timbale kit will provide a nice stereo picture. Move the mics as needed to get the best balance.

4. For just a mono recording of the kit, place a large-diaphragm condenser from 1 to 2 feet away as above.

Variation: Replace the condenser with a ribbon mic. The figure-8 pattern will give you more room sound (assuming the room sounds good).

Timpani (Also Known As Kettle Drum)

Although primarily an orchestral instrument, timpani has been used in modern music by everyone from Elvin Jones to the Beatles, Led Zeppelin, Queen, and the Beach Boys.

CONSIDERATIONS

▶ Unlike most drums, timpani produce a definite pitch when struck.

▶ The shape of the bowl determines the sound of the drum. Parabolic bowls are usually brighter than hemispheric bowls.

PLACEMENT

1. Place a large-diaphragm condenser about 6 feet directly over the drum, looking down (see Figure 8.63).

2. Place a dynamic mic (an RE20 works great) about a foot away and a foot underneath the drum. Point the mic up so that about a third of it peeks just over the head. Add a large-diaphragm condenser about 6 feet directly of the drum, looking down as in #1.

Figure 8.63
Mic 6 feet over timpani.

Triangle

A triangle is usually made of steel and left open at one end so that it doesn't have a true pitch.

CONSIDERATIONS

▶ The triangle has a lot of transients, a lot of harmonics, and a lot of high-frequency energy, which makes it one of the hardest instruments to record. You can really tell the difference between preamps as a result. (Some use a triangle as a test before buying.) Try different preamps to see which sounds best.

▶ Microphones can be really stressed to their limits when recording a triangle. A dynamic mic sometimes works well because it softens the transients.

▶ Make sure to engage the hi-pass filter either on the mic or the DAW/console in order to decrease the low harmonics and any unwanted low-frequency noise or rumble.

PLACEMENT

Place the small-diaphragm condenser mic in omni at least 3 to 4 feet away, slightly above the triangle and aiming down. Move the mic back until any low-frequency harmonics or microphone distortion disappear.

Trombone

See the "Brass" section.

Trumpet

See the "Brass" section.

Tuba

See the "Brass" section.

Vibes (or Vibraphone)

The vibraphone is similar in appearance to the xylophone and marimba, but it uses aluminum instead of wooden bars and has a sustain pedal similar to that used on a piano. The pedal works the opposite of a piano's pedal; when the pedal is up, the bars are all damped, and the sound of each bar is short, but with the pedal down, they continue to sustain.

CONSIDERATIONS

▶ If the player isn't using the motor to get a tremolo effect, make sure that the rotor fans in the resonators are set to the same angle for each set of resonators for consistency across the range of the instrument and between the upper and lower manuals.

▶ Experiment with the position of the fans. Setting them vertically will increase the volume of the resonators and decrease the sustain of the instrument; setting the rotors flat will decrease the volume of the resonators but increase the sustain.

▶ Be prepared to spend a few minutes getting rid of squeaks and rattles.

PLACEMENT

1. Place a spaced pair or an ORTF pair about 2 to 3 feet over the center, dividing the instrument equally.

> **Variation:** For a closer sound, add a large-diaphragm omni about 2 feet off the low F bar in the bass end.

2. Using three microphones, place a mic at each corner about 6 to 8 inches above the bars, just out of mallet reach, tilted slightly downward and aimed into the nearest third of the instrument. Place the center mic at the same height, but back just a little compared to the other two, and aimed at a slightly greater angle down and toward the middle of the instrument.

3. Place four mics with two splitting the middle and the outer two covering a bit less of the instrument.

4. For marimba, place two small-diaphragm condensers at a 45-degree angle about 18 inches from the keys.

5. For marimba in mono, place a large-diaphragm condenser 3 feet over the center of the instrument.

Vocals

CHUCK AINLAY: *I still base everything around the vocal. To me you have to find the microphone that fits the vocalist the best because if you get a great vocal sound, you're going to bring up everything to match that. If the vocal is so much bigger than everything else, then you are going to work on everything else until it's as good as the vocal. If the vocal sound sucks, then nothing is going to sound good because you don't want to overpower your vocal with the band.*

If it's someone that I've never worked with before, I will hopefully get an opportunity to work with the vocalist before the tracking date to find a mic that works. Or I may use what has been previously used if I thought that sounded good. If not, I have to go with what I think is going to work, but usually it's a large-diaphragm tube microphone. I won't stop there, though. I might try other things.

ED CHERNEY: *You know what to expect from a drum kit or a guitar amp or piano, but the human voice is so personal. Even if you have a microphone that works 90 percent of the time, you're always looking and you're always guessing. And it's the most dynamic instrument, too. So it's the most difficult instrument because it has the most variables.*

For rock vocals, I'll use dynamic mics a lot of times, like an RE20 or SM7. I just did Hootie and the Blowfish, and he sounded great on an SM7. A lot of times a C 12 sounds good for a female voice. Jagger loves it too, but he sounds about the same on any mic he uses. 47s usually sound good. I've used the Audio-Technica 4050, and I kinda like that. That's a pretty good place to start.

STEVE ALBINI: *There are as many vocal microphones and vocal styles as people singing. I know a lot of people just throw up a U 47 and call it quits. I have used a U 47 with good results, but I can't say that it's my number-one favorite vocal mic.*

If I have a number-one favorite vocal mic, it's probably the Josephson microphone called the 700. I've used that quite a bit. But even as great a microphone as it is and as much use as I get out of it, it's not appropriate for fully 75 percent of the people I work with. I end up using everything from RE20s to old tube mics to ribbon mics. It totally depends upon the singer and the delivery. This is one area that you really can go around in circles looking for something that sounds good.

If someone's voice is the center of attention in the music, I like to be able to just listen to that and have it be satisfying. If you're listening to the voice by itself, it should make you think, 'That sounds really great.' If that's the center of attention, then you want to make sure that it's a rewarding listen.

WYN DAVIS: *It depends on the vocalist, but I'll use any number of mics. It's almost always some kind of condenser mic and some kind of tube mic. There's a lot of really great vocal mics out there that do a great job; it just depends on who's singing. It can be any number of microphone preamps, depending upon who's singing and what kind of sound you're looking for. For tracking I use an LA-3A with a quick attack, slow release, letting that lightly catch anything jumping through.*

CONSIDERATIONS

▶ A singer who is experienced at working with microphones knows which consonants are tough to record, reacts to what he/she hears in the headphones, and knows how to balance the consonants against the vowels to get a good final result.

▶ With a good singer, many times you'll get the "sound" automatically just by putting him/her in front of the right microphone. On the other hand, given a bad singer (or even a good singer who just doesn't adjust well to the studio), no amount of high-priced microphones or processing may be able to get you there.

▶ Windscreens are actually of little use when recording a vocalist with bad technique. There are two different sorts of people in this category: the people who have never sung with sound reinforcement, and the people who have developed bad habits from PA mikes.

▶ Decoupling of the stand to the floor will help prevent unwanted rumbles. Place the stand on a couple of mouse pads or a rug for a cheap but efficient solution.

▶ A major part of the silky-smooth hit female vocal sound is singing softly and breathily very close to a large-diaphragm condenser mic. To get this effect, tell her to close her eyes and act like the mic is a baby's ear. This usually produces instant vocals that are very soft and natural.

▶ The best mic in the house doesn't necessarily get the best vocal sounds.

▶ An easy way to have a vocalist gauge the distance is by hand lengths. An open hand is approximately 8 inches, while a fist is about 4 inches. If you say, "Stay two fists away," the vocalist can easily judge his distance and usually doesn't forget. (See Figure 8.64.)

Figure 8.64
Setting vocal distance by hand.

▶ In general, vocals sound better when recorded in a tighter space. Vocal booths should be tight but not dead to the point where there is a loss of top end and air. Low-ceiling rooms can also be a problem with loud singers because they tend to ring at certain lower midrange frequencies.

To eliminate pops, lip smacks, and breath blasts:

▶ Place the mic above the lips so the singer's breath is right below the capsule (see Figure 8.65).

Figure 8.65
Vocal mic placement using a large-diaphragm condenser mic.

▶ Move the mic up 3 or 4 inches above the singer's mouth and point it down at the mouth. This also cleans up mouth noises and the nasal sound that some singers have a problem with. (See Figure 8.66.)

Figure 8.66
Alternate vocal mic placement using a large-diaphragm condenser mic.

▶ If popping continues, move the mic higher and/or farther away.

▶ If popping continues, turn the mic slightly off-axis.

▶ Change the mic's directional pattern to omni.

BOB OLHSSON, FORMER
MOTOWN (DETROIT)
ENGINEER:

Provided that you use a fabric pop screen, my experience has been that small-diaphragm condensers are no more difficult to use, and if you have a well-isolated, uncolored studio, they have the advantage of allowing the singer to back off, which tames the unwanted dynamics created by moving around. They are also lots easier to shock mount.

RCA, Motown, and, from what I understand, EMI all used KM 86s for vocals from the time they came out in the late '60s through the '70s, when most label-owned facilities went away. The indie studios generally bought U 87s because they looked more impressive to clients, were more difficult to walk off with, and didn't cost any more. The standard of the industry for dialogue and opera singers has been the Schoeps line for many years. An awful lot of famous vocal recordings have been made using the finest small-diaphragm mics while U 47s, 67s, and 251s sat in the mic closet.

As for shock mounting, the best way I've ever found is to shock mount both the stand and the mic. Lighter-weight mics make this much more practical. The Shure donuts are far more effective than most. I've been using them on KM 84s and 86s for over 30 years.

THE HANGING MICROPHONE

Everyone has seen the photos of the vintage large-diaphragm tube mic hanging upside down in front of the vocalist (see Figure 8.67), but there really are several good reasons for this. Here are just a few things to consider:

▶ The rationale behind hanging a mic upside down comes from tube mics. The heat rising from the tube can cause the diaphragm to change temperature over time, which will change the sound of the mic. Placing the tube above the capsule will let the heat rise without passing over the diaphragm.

▶ Another good thing that happens when singing slightly upward into a mic is that it forces the airway open and encourages a full-bodied voice. Take a deep breath and sing a low note; start with your chin to your chest and slowly lift your head until your chin has about a 15-degree lift. Hear any difference?

▶ Maybe even more important, the mic can be positioned so the singer is less likely to direct popping air blasts into the mic.

▶ It's easier for the singer to read any music or lyrics since the mic is out of the way.

Figure 8.67
Hanging tube condenser
microphone.

PLACEMENT

1. Place the mic with the capsule just about even with the singer's nose. You get very little blasting from breath that causes pops. If popping continues, turn the mic slightly off-axis. The distance will vary widely depending on the singer, the type of sound you're trying to get, and the SPL-handling capability of the mic. Somewhere between 4 and 12 inches should work for most things. (See Figure 8.64.) For a whisperer, get even closer than 4 inches.

2. To get a cool stereo vocal sound, place two condenser mics 1 foot in front of the singer at shoulder height and 2 or 3 feet apart and pointing up toward the mouth. This will yield a kind of wide, thick sound that is very cool if the mix is sparse, but will not do well in a dense mix as it will tend to sound dark and full. Many singers have trouble with this, so you might have to put up a close dummy mic for them to sing into.

3. Using a stereo mic, run one capsule with 10 dB more gain on the mic pre than the other. Put a compressor on this one. The one with 10 dB more gain should register about 12 dB of compression when the singer gets loud. This turns down the capsule with more gain on it more than the capsule with less gain on it. The net result is that as the singer changes volume, the capsule with the best gain for the application will take precedence.

4. If a vocalist has trouble staying in the right place or wants to eat the mic, use the mic as a decoy and put a second mic up a couple of feet

behind it. Although the sound might be a little more distant, it will also be a lot more consistent.

5. Many vocalists are just more comfortable with a handheld mic like they use on stage. Don't be afraid to give them an SM58 if it makes their performance more comfortable and easy.

6. Position a mic 4 to 6 inches below the vocalist's mouth and then aim the mic up at the mouth to fill out a thin-sounding voice. You'll pick up some low end from the chest cavity, but you might pick up more extraneous noises.

Background Vocals

Although sometimes dismissed as an afterthought, the processes of performing and recording background vocals are not as easy as they are sometimes perceived. Both require at least the same amount of attention as every other instrument.

CONSIDERATIONS

▶ Since background vocals are invariably stacked, layered, or at the very least doubled, try the following to make them bigger and to make them have a greater sense of space. For every subsequent overdub after the first recording, have the singers take a step backwards, but increase the mic preamp gain so that the track's level is equal to the first layer. In essence you want to "fill up the meters" so the level on the meter is the same regardless of where the singers stand.

▶ If the singers have trouble blending or singing in tune, ask them to remove one side of the headphones or at least put it slightly back on the ear. Sometimes this helps them sing in tune because they can then hear the blend acoustically.

▶ The best background blends usually come from having multiple singers positioned around a single mic or stereo pair.

▶ Large-diaphragm cardioid condensers are usually used because they combine a proximity effect and slight midrange scoop along with a slight lift in the upper frequency ranges. This accentuates the "air" portion of the sound (or conversely, scoops out the "non-air" portion), which helps the background vocals sit better in the mix.

▶ The microphone does not always have to be a large-diaphragm condenser. Sometimes the natural compression of both volume and transients offered by a dynamic can make it sound better and will keep the vocal much more under control than a condenser.

▶ The better the singer is as a lead vocalist, usually the harder it is for him or her to do background vocals that blend well because the voice is recognizable.

▶ If the lead singer is singing the background parts or part of the background vocal ensemble, try not to use the same mic that the lead vocals were recorded on. This will cause a buildup of any peaks in the singer's voice, mic, or the room.

▶ Always try to do something a little different on each track. A different mic, mic preamp, room, singer, or distance from the mic will help to make the sound bigger.

▶ A trick to help things blend better is to record the background vocals, then play them back through the studio monitors and record the playback. The distance of the mic placement depends upon the sound of the room. Walk around and find the place where the playback sounds the best and place the mic there. Mix this in low, underneath the original background vocal tracks.

▶ For a performance in which the singers will sing a live harmony, use a cardioid pattern with three people on the mic. On the first pass, one person is on-axis and the other two are off-axis by 90 degrees (facing each other). On the next pass, have the person singing the next note trade places with the on-axis singer. Do a third track the same way until all three singers have an on-axis track and all three notes are on-axis. If it's only two notes, then double each note using the same method.

▶ Another variation of the above technique is to have all three people sing the same note at the same time using the same mic technique, then proceed as above.

PLACEMENT

1. Try a large-diaphragm condenser in omni about 3 feet away from the vocalists.

2. The standard jingle production technique: Stack the overdubs with three vocalists on a pair of mics in X/Y or a stereo mic. Have them sing each part in unison, then change position and double. Do the same for all parts.

3. For extra-thick background vocals (a la Def Leppard), cut four tracks of the root, two tracks of the harmony, then one or two "whisper tracks" of each part. Compress the whisper tracks heavily. They'll add the "air" of 100 overdubs.

4. Many of the techniques used for recording a choir also work for background vocals (such as the Blumlein pair).

Voiceovers

To most music engineers, voiceover recording seems easier than it actually is. There is a tried-and-true technique that produces the results you hear every day on radio, television, and movies, which is a great place to start.

CONSIDERATIONS

► The worst thing that can happen on a voiceover is a pop, and therefore it must be avoided at all costs.

► Room requirements for VO work are in some ways less demanding than for a music recording space. The room should be acoustically dead (not too dead, though) and, most important, really quiet. Nothing will ruin a spot or story quicker than small-room reverberation on the VO.

► Even among professional voices, there are some whose voices will sound good on almost anything, while others need a specific mic to get the right sound. If you're recording the average person, the variances increase.

► Your mic selection, amount of EQ, and compression used are totally dependent on the voice you are recording.

PLACEMENT

1. The classic way of recording VOs: Place the mic 3 to 4 inches from the talent and off-axis about 45 degrees to prevent popping. Compress about 9 to 12 dB at a 4:1 ratio with attack and release as fast as possible. (See Figure 8.68.)

Figure 8.68
Voiceover with an RE20.

Whistling

Another item that fits in the "harder than it seems" category, whistling is one the most difficult things to record.

CONSIDERATIONS

▶ Whistling has a unique combination of wind and transients that constantly attack the mic.

▶ A foam windscreen or professional wind filter (as in Figure 1.17) can be very effective in cutting the whistling wind noise.

PLACEMENT

1. Place the microphone by the side of the whistler's head so the mic hears what the whistler hears.

2. Get the mic off-axis as much as possible and try a dynamic, such as an SM57. The key is to find the right spot.

CHAPTER 9

The Recording Session

It's all well and good to know the technical part of recording, but the intangibles that go into a session really make or break it. This chapter will provide some tips and observations that go beyond simple technique and get down to the nitty gritty of what ultimately is more important: the interpersonal aspects of a session.

Preparing for the Session (By Al Schmitt)

The first important element of recording for me is the planning process prior to the actual recording session. The better this is done, the smoother the recording sessions are going to go.

At the outset, I'll talk to the producer and determine what he is trying to do and what it is he's after. Is this music to be part of an album or is it for a single? Is it going to be done in layers, meaning recording rhythm, then maybe the vocals and background parts, then overdubbing the strings, brass, guitars, et cetera? We discuss how we're going to record this music—whether we're going to use Pro Tools or analog (some producers have strong allegiance to one or the other), and if analog, whether we're going to use Dolby SR.

Depending on the type of music to be recorded, we'll decide the type of tape we're going to use, and at what levels we're going to record. If I'm recording non-Dolby, we will record at plus 6 over 185. If I'm recording Dolby SR, we'll record at plus 3 over 185.

After making these basic determinations, I talk to the contractor and find out how many musicians are going to be on the date and who they are. This is important to me because, having worked with so many of them for so long, I often know how they play and what their sounds are like. For example, I may know how many toms they have on their drums (whether it's two, three, or five), and this helps me plan my mic setup. I'll contact the studio and get a list of their microphones, and I own a large complement of mics as well. Together, I usually have what we'll need, but I determine up front if we'll need to rent anything.

Then, I begin visualizing how I'm going to set up the studio and what microphones I'm going to use. I'll plan how I'm going to lay out the board as far as what mics are going to go in what positions on the board. I usually start by putting the bass first, then the drums, then the keyboards, and then the guitars. So all the rhythm section would be first. Percussion might be next. If there is brass, I'll set up the saxophones, the trombones, and the trumpets. Then I'll have the ambience mics for the brass. If there are strings, I'll put the harp first (if there is one), then the violins, the violas, the celli, and the upright basses.

Once the board is set up, I'll think of how I'll take these instruments and put them to tape. For example, if I have a direct pickup and a microphone on the bass, I will combine them to Track 1. Then drums will be next. I will put the kick to Track 2, the snare to Track 3, the hi-hat to Track 4, and then depending on what there is, I might put the toms next and then the overheads, or I might combine the toms and overheads together. This will depend on how many tracks I have available and on how big the session is.

Next I will put the keyboards, whether they are acoustic pianos, Rhodes, or synths. All the keyboards will be together or close to each other on the tracks. Then, I'll put the guitars, then perhaps the vocals, the ambience mics, the saxophones, the trombones, and then the trumpets. Then it'll be the strings and, depending on how many tracks I have left, I will determine how I lay out the strings. I may use two tracks for the violins, one for the viola, and I may use just one track for the cello and basses. Again, the layout of the strings depends on what my options are as far as number of tracks remaining.

So, that's how I lay out the board. I'll also set up all my echoes, which are merely for monitoring purposes at this point. If I'm doing a live date, the chances are I will have enough space on the board to use two or maybe three echoes. I'll set up an echo for the vocal, maybe an EMT 250. I'll set up an echo for the strings, and then the brass.

If I'm working at a studio like Capitol, I'll use a live chamber. I'll use a separate chamber for the drums and for the brass and saxes. I'll use these merely for monitoring purposes. They will not go to tape. I'll print everything dry.

Echoes will be added during the mixing. I'll get a setup sheet from the studio and then discuss it with my assistant, Bill Smith. We'll talk with the studio assistants—one or two, depending on how big the session is going to be—and discuss what we're going to be doing, how we're going to lay out earphones, where the instruments are going, what mics we're using with what instruments, and where the mics are going to go. This sets everyone on the same page before we even begin. Then, about three hours before the downbeat, we set up the room.

WYN DAVIS: *The art of being prepared for the studio, along with a lot of the engineering arts, is being lost in all the cut and pasting. I've found that the preparation that people have before coming into the studio has diminished over the last few years by an astounding amount. People will come in and work hard to get something on the first chorus and then say, 'Okay, can't you just paste that everywhere now?' When people used to play these performances from top to bottom, there was a synergy with the track that happened. Something would evolve as the track went on. You definitely lose that if you're just using a hard-disc recorder as a glorified musical word processor.*

Headphones and the Cue Mix

Perhaps the greatest detriment to a session running smoothly is the inability for players to hear themselves comfortably in the headphones. This is one of the reasons why veteran engineers pay so much time and attention to the cue mix and the phones themselves. In fact, a sure sign of a studio neophyte is treating the headphones and cue mix as an afterthought, instead of spending as much time as required to make them sound great. While it's true that a veteran studio player can shrug off a bad or distorted phone mix and still deliver a fine performance, good "cans" make a session go faster and easier and take a variable that is quite possibly the biggest detriment to a session out of the equation.

TIPS FOR GREAT HEADPHONES

1. Long before the session begins, test every headphone to make sure there's no distortion and that they're working correctly. (Test them with actual music.)

2. Make sure there's plenty of cable available so the musicians can move around as needed. Use extenders as necessary.

3. Check to make sure the cables are not intermittent. (Nothing stops a session as quickly as a crackling phone.)

4. Send some of the stereo monitor mix (the one that you're listening to) to the phones first. Add a little of the individual instruments as needed ("more me"). This is a lot easier than building up individual mixes (unless they're required).

WYN DAVIS: *In a tracking situation, aside from your responsibility of getting something decently recorded, the most important thing is to get good headphone mixes for these guys. In fact, to get the best one possible. Amazingly bad things happen to even the best players when the headphone mix is all screwed up. I don't think you can pay enough attention to that part of it because if the guys are hearing something that feels good, it moves the session from sort of a technical exercise for the musicians to a real inspiring and fun thing. It's really amazing how no matter what tools you're using, if people aren't having a good time, it's just not going to work.*

ED CHERNEY: *It's critical. I'm really concerned with it so I do it myself. What I typically do is feed what I'm hearing (the stereo buss) to the headphones, and if I'm lucky enough to have a headphone mixer, I'll add some kick, snare, and bass and vocal, and whoever else needs more "me." A lot of times I'll even add the stereo buss to the stereo cue mix so I can be additive. So I'll have the stereo buss coming up, and on the console I'll also add some kick and snare, because you have to get it up over the sound that's in the room. So I'll sweeten the drums, and that's where I'll usually start. The idea is to be making music quickly with everybody hearing themselves. If I'm hearing them, then they're hearing it. I just don't want to spend any more time getting sounds than I have to before people are playing together with the red lights on.*

TRICKS FOR LOUD HEADPHONES

So you want really loud and clean headphones, just like the major studios have? Here's how they do it using a power amplifier:

▶ Use the largest power amp (at least 200 watts or more per channel) you can.

▶ Put a 40- to 50-Hz hi-pass filter on the input. (Those frequencies aren't needed for headphones, as they just contribute to the distortion and headphone failure.)

▶ Use a limiter at a minimum of a 10:1 ratio with a fast attack and a medium to long release. (This is not required, but helpful.)

▶ Use a pair of 10-watt 100-ohm resistors in series with each output, or...

▶ For best results, use a pair of 600-ohm transformers to keep the system at a constant impedance.

▶ Also, to lessen ear fatigue, EQ the headphone send by attenuating some of the presence frequencies (2 to 5k). If their ears are tired from the volume, they'll want it louder and louder as the session goes on.

See www.headwize.com and www.jensen-transformers.com for more information.

These days it's easy and inexpensive to buy a unit that works great and is specifically designed for headphones from any number of manufacturers. Companies like Behringer, Furman, PreSonus, Rolls, and Aphex all make units that will work better and be a lot cheaper than the traditional method of a large power amp and resistors. (See Figure 9.1.)

Figure 9.1
Behringer PowerPlay Pro-XL.
Courtesy of Behringer.

Personal Headphone Mixes

Perhaps the best thing to come along in recent years has been the introduction of the relatively inexpensive "more me" personal headphone systems. These systems allow the musician to control the headphone mix by supplying him with up to 8 channels to control. Each headphone mixer/box also contains a headphone amplifier that can (depending upon the product) provide earsplitting level. Manufacturers include Furman, Oz Audio, Aviom, and Hear Technologies (see Figure 9.2). As above, it's best to provide a stereo monitor mix (what you're listening to) as well as kick, snare, vocal, and whatever other instruments are pertinent.

Figure 9.2
Hear Back headphone system.
Courtesy of Hear Technologies.

The Click Track

The click track, or recording to a metronome, has become a fact of life in most recording. Not only does playing at an even tempo sound better, but it makes possible cut-and-paste editing between performances in a DAW. Playing to a click can present a number of problems, however, such as leakage of the click into the mics and the fact that some people just can't play on time to save their lives. We'll cover these shortly.

MAKING THE CLICK CUT THROUGH THE MIX

Many times just providing a metronome in the phones isn't enough. What good is a click if you can't hear it or, worse yet, groove to it? Here are some tricks to make the click not only listenable, but cut through the densest mixes and seem like another instrument in the track, too.

▶ Pick the right sound. Something that's more musical than an electronic click is better to groove to. Try a cowbell, a sidestick, or even a conga slap. Needless to say, when you pick a sound to replace the click, it should fit with the context of the song. Many drummers like two sounds for the click: something like a high go-go bell for the downbeat and a low go-go bell for the other beats.

▶ Pick the right number of clicks per bar. Some players like quarter notes while others play a lot better with eighths. Whichever it is, it will work better if there's more emphasis on the downbeat (Beat 1) than on the others.

▶ Make it groove. By adding a little delay to the sound, you can make it swing a bit. Now it won't sound so stiff and will be easier for players who normally have trouble playing to a click. As a side benefit, this can help make any bleed that does occur less offensive because it will seem like part of the song.

PREVENTING CLICK BLEED

Okay, now it cuts through the mix, but it does it so well that it's bleeding into the mics. Try the following:

▶ Change your headphones. Try a pair that has a better seal. The Sony 7506 phones provide a fairly good seal, but Metrophones Studio Kans (see Figure 9.3), Vic Firth S1H1s, or even RadioShack Racing Headphones (they're mono, though) will all isolate a click from bleeding into nearby mics.

Figure 9.3
Metrophones Studio Kans.

▶ Run the click through an equalizer and roll off the high end just enough to cut down on the bleed.

▶ Have the players use one-eared headphones. Many times players will leave the phones loose so they can hear what's going on in the room. If they can have click in one ear (in the headphone sealed closely to the head), then they get the live room sound in their free ear.

JERRY HEY: *We always use one-sided headphones because it's very difficult to expect the engineer to get your balance good enough with the rhythm section and also balance the horn section the way it should be in order to play in tune with double-side phones. That puts another cog in the link of recording when you have to make the engineer work that hard. Also, with one headphone we can hear everyone in the room which helps keep the time and phrasing the same.*

▶ Run the click to just one person (such as the drummer or the conductor) and let him/her communicate the click to the band/orchestra.

If all else fails, try this method. It might even provide the loosest feel and the best groove, too.

1. Put one mic in the room.

2. Play the song three times with the click and *record it on a single track only!*

3. Choose the best version.

4. Instead of a click, use the track for the drummer to play against.

5. Record all your overdubs.

Using this method, the drummer can hear the rest of the band and play along through headphones so that there should be very little bleed. Once the drums are printed, the session can progress as normal.

WHEN A CLICK WON'T WORK

Let's face it, not many people like to play to a click. It's unnatural and doesn't breathe like real players do. But in this world of drum machines, sequencers, and DAWs, most musicians have grown used to playing with a metronome.

But there are those times and those players (and it's usually the drummer) when a click just won't work. The performance suffers so much that you get something that's not worth recording. No problem. Don't get obsessed with the click or the fact that the tempo fluctuates without it. Many, many great hits have been recorded without a click and with wavering tempos. Remember, feel and vibe are what make the track, not perfection.

EDDIE KRAMER: *But the track has to move and breathe. Listen to all the great songs and albums that have been recorded in the last 30 years. The ones that really stand out are the ones that breathe and move. With human beings, their tempo varies. I do admire what can be done in Pro Tools, but if there's something that wrong, you should have done another take and maybe chopped things together.*

MACK: *But if it's a good band, then you do notice the difference. Stuff that has been layered in parts is just not the same. The little accelerations and decelerations are so together that it just makes things come to life. I'd rather leave the little flaws in or repair them later. You don't notice a lot of them anyway. It's the performance that counts.*

Getting the Most from a Vocalist

One of the hardest things to record can be a vocalist who is uncomfortable. Even a seasoned pro sometimes can't do his or her best unless the conditions are right. Consider some of these suggestions before and during a vocal session.

▶ Make sure the lighting is correct. Most vocalists prefer the lights lower when singing.

▶ A touch of reverb or delay in the headphones can be helpful.

▶ If you need to have the singer sing harder, louder, or more aggressively, turn down the vocal track in the phones or turn up the backing tracks.

▶ If you need to have the singer sing softer or more intimately, turn up the singer's track in the phones or turn down the backing tracks.

▶ Keep talking with the artist between takes. Leave the talkback on if possible. Long periods of silence from the control room are a mood killer.

▶ Try turning off the lights in the control room so the singer can't see you. Some people think that you're in there judging them when you might be talking about something completely different.

▶ If the take wasn't good for whatever reason, explain what was wrong in a kind and gentle way. Something like, "That was really good, but I think you can do it even better. The pitch was off a little." This goes for just about any overdub, since players generally like to know what was wrong with the take rather than be given a "Do it again" blanket statement.

▶ Keep smiling.

Recording Basic Tracks

While many modern recordings are made with as few players as possible playing at once, most recording veterans prefer to have as many players as possible during the basic tracking date. The reasons? The vibe and the sound. Although such a session can be rather nerve-wracking in complexity, it can be a lot of fun as well.

STEVE ALBINI: *Given a three-piece rock band, for example, I would prefer to have them try to play live, although not necessarily all in the same room, so that they're interacting with each other and can accommodate each other's little changes in emphasis and timing. Given a larger ensemble, I've always found that you get better results if it's possible to set everybody up to play live. I've done sessions with as many as 12 or 14 band members playing simultaneously. If it's possible to have everybody play at once, that's the best way to do it.*

CHUCK AINLAY: *Many times the musicians will play it down the first time and that will be the take. We're not just talking about a small section. We're talking about bass, drums, two guitars (one may be acoustic), fiddle, steel, two keyboards (piano and organ), and vocal. This all goes down live. So you have to be ready to get the first take because they'll have it ready by at least the third take. So when you ask how long it takes to get drum sounds, it's got to be fast. It's a blast to cut tracks in Nashville because you're so on fire.*

EDDIE KRAMER: *Obviously there are other ways to do it. You can do it in sections and pieces and overdubbing and recutting and that certainly works too, but to me there's nothing more exciting than having the band in the studio cutting live straight to tape, and that's the performance and that's what gets mixed. That's the essence of any great recording. I don't care if it's classical or rock or country, you've got to capture that performance, and the hell with the bloody leakage.*

BRUCE BOTNICK: *If I was doing rock and roll, I'd put it all up at the same time and balance it quickly. I know what I want to do on the drums from years of experience. Generally I'll just ask everyone to play at once and listen to the whole thing. Then I'll go in and tighten up anything afterwards. I might ask them to play a little by themselves and refine it. But there's something good about getting your sounds all together and defining what's happening as it's going down rather than making everything an individual sound and then putting them together and wondering why it doesn't work.*

WHERE TO PLACE THE PLAYERS IN THE ROOM

Regardless of how good the headphone system is, the players won't play their best unless they can see each other, so that becomes priority number one. Even if the players have a song down cold, they can't react to any nuances without clean sightlines to each other. Plus, many players (especially studio veterans) rely on looking at the drummer playing the snare in order to stay locked in time.

STEVE ALBINI: *One really revealing thing is to walk around a room and sort of stomp and clap and holler and hear where you're getting reinforcement from the room and hear where it sounds interesting. Wherever you find the place that you like the reflected sound is a good place to start.*

AL SCHMITT: *I try to set everybody, especially in the rhythm section, as close together as possible. I come from the school when I first started where there were no headphones. Everybody had to hear one another in the room. So I still set up everybody really close. Even though I'll isolate the drums, everybody will be so close that they can almost touch one another.*

STEVE ALBINI: *The most important thing is the band's comfort and their sightlines. There's no point in having one tiny little corner of the room where the drums sound good if the bass player can't see that far. So I tend to avoid the bad spots rather than finding the good spots.*

MACK: *I try to keep everyone pretty close so they can communicate outside the headphones. There's nothing worse than putting someone in a box out of his environment.*

How Long Should It Take?

Generally speaking, you should be recording within the first hour after the musicians arrive, providing that you were prepared in advance and didn't start your setup when the musicians did.

There was a time in the '70s when a few high-budget projects would take an entire week just to get the right (or so they thought) snare-drum sound. While they might've attained musical snare-drum nirvana, 99.99999 percent of sessions have to move faster than that, and they should. The more time you take before recording, the less time you'll actually spend recording, because the attention span of the players decreases proportionately. Although you want things to sound as good as possible, a poor-sounding track with a great vibe is a lot more usable than a well recorded but musically stale track.

ED CHERNEY: *About 10 minutes. I find that when I do it faster it works better. The idea is to be making music quickly with everybody hearing themselves. I just don't want to spend any more time getting sounds than I have to before people are playing together with the red lights on. I get the drummer to play a little time, but not wear him out, and if it's not right you know it right away. And sometimes if it's not right you go ahead and cut the song anyway. When you have a listen, good musicians will go, 'Oh yeah, my snare's too dark,' or something like that. I want to get the sounds to tape as quickly as possible, then play it back so you can talk about it. It's real at that point. It's easy to modify once you can hear it. I've been in places where you mess around a lot before you play any music, and the session doesn't move forward.*

CHUCK AINLAY: *I'm pretty fast. Maybe an hour at most, and that's for getting things situated in the room. But after that we might change the drums before each song, and it'll be 15 minutes. It's more about changing stuff out rather than tweaking things on my side. I certainly don't take two days like they did on the old Fleetwood Mac albums.*

MACK: *Probably anywhere from 20 minutes to an hour or so. I tend to work really fast. I don't want anything technical to get in the way of the music. You usually don't get a lot of time anyway because people are frequently wandering around and anxious to play. You start a session, and people are sort of playing around. I like to use that time to get the whole setup done when the players are pretty uninhibited. When we start taking, I don't want to interfere with the creative process and go, 'Can you give me that left tom again, and again, and again?'*

FRANK FILIPETTI: *There are two ways that I approach these things. On a setup that I have time to play, then all of the techniques that you and I have learned over the years and all of the stuff that we've read about all comes into play, so we get to try some things and experiment. That's why I really love those sessions. On the other hand, if you do a date where the tape has to be rolling in 15 minutes and you have 40 musicians sitting out there in the studio, you stick a mic in the most logical place and go.*

EDDIE KRAMER: *This isn't rocket science, it's music. Just record the thing the way you hear it! After all, it is the song that we're trying to get and the guy's emotion. We're becoming so anal and self-analytical and protracted with our views on recording, I think it's destructive and anti-creative. It's bad enough that we have to be locked into a bloody room with sweaty musicians [laughs].*

Recording without Headphones (By Fletcher)

1. The key to not using headphones in a spread-out recording situation is to keep the amps about 10 feet behind the players and get the players pretty close to the drums. The visual of everyone that close together helps, as well as minimizing the acoustic delay times that occur when you spread the players out too far. When live on stage, there are monitors to solve that very problem.

2. Sometimes a small speaker, like a 10- or a 12-inch as a satellite speaker placed in the null of the pickup pattern of the mics, will work wonders getting the drummer to lock with the bass player while you move the bass amp farther away from the drum kit. Gobos will often come in pretty handy, too.

3. A lot of my guitar reverb/ambience can be had by moving the guitar amp so the little bit of bleed in the drum mics makes it a cool ambience for the guitars. Be careful that this doesn't overpower the drum kit.

4. If there are two guitar players, set them up on opposite sides of the kit. This will provide a better stereo picture when you disengage the mono button.

5. Now that you have the whole band set up in a room…mic the room. You should get a reasonable balance of all the instruments. It should sound like a band in a room—fancy that! The mono button is still in until you're positive about the clarity of the bottom of the track.

6. Need more snare? A Shure 57 aimed about a foot off the side of the center of the shell of the snare drum usually will add all you need without complicating the rest of the balance.

7. I usually try to get soft things around the drum kit. I actually carry a soft [4-inch insulation, cloth-covered] booth that's 8 feet high, 20 feet wide [in the back], and 10 feet long [on the sides] that descends from 8 feet high in the back to 4 feet high in the front. Front gobos as needed—usually just a gobo between the amps, and the kit will work pretty well at helping you control the bleed.

This usually alleviates the bounce and splatter that will be caused by reflections off of hard walls. Depending on where you position the kit, these reflections will come back to haunt you as Haas effect garbage.

8. At times, a floor monitor, like at a bar gig, will work well for scratch vocal. Make sure you can EQ the monitor so the little bit of bleed you get from the scratch vocal track can be used as a vocal reverb when it's time to mix. Sometimes it's a way, way cool thing to have the reverb of the scratch track be the main vocal reverb. Not only are there always performance variations, but if you're trying to place the singer in the same room with the band, it works like a charm. Just like the guitar and bass amps, you may need to move it around for balance.

9. Most of the time the singer will actually gravitate to the spot in the room where the band's balance is best.

EDDIE KRAMER: *You put the mics up, place them correctly, and give the artist the room and the facility to work in and make sure it sounds cool, so when they walk into the control room they say, 'Oh, that sounds just like I was playing it out there.' That's the goal: To capture the essence of what the artist is actually doing in the studio.*

Leakage

Acoustic spill (known as *leakage*) from one instrument into another's mic is many times thought of as undesirable, but it can and should be used to enhance the sound instead of being avoided. Many recording novices are under the mistaken impression that during a tracking session with multiple instruments, every track recorded must contain only the instrument/source at which the mic was pointed. Since that's pretty hard to achieve, why not just use the leakage to embellish the tracks instead?

MICHAEL BISHOP: *I let leakage be my friend. Leakage is inevitable for the kind of recording that I'm doing because I like to keep the musicians together as a group in the studio rather than spreading them all out with isolation for everybody. I keep them together in as live a setting as is possible. That means that there's plenty of leakage, and I just deal with it. I don't have to have the isolation because typically I'm not doing overdubs and replacement of tracks. We fix things by doing new takes to cover the spots that we need to cover. They'll take a running start at it to cover the measures that they need, and we'll edit it later, which is very much a classical orchestra style of recording.*

WYN DAVIS: *In situations where the band wants to play and capture the rhythm section as a unit on the spot, I don't worry about leakage. I actually treat it as part of the overall sound and try not to have any glaring phase anomalies.*

AL SCHMITT: *Actually leakage is one of your best friends because that's what makes things sometimes sound so much bigger. The only time leakage is a problem is if you're using a lot of crap mics. If you get a lot of leakage into them, it's going to sound like crap leakage. But if you're using some really good microphones and you get some leakage, it's usually good because it makes things sound bigger.*

BRUCE BOTNICK: *I like leakage. If it's a good-sounding room, leakage is your friend. It's what makes it sound bigger. Let's say I've got 12 woodwinds and I'm using four microphones. In other words, one for the flutes, one for oboes, one for the bassoons, and one for the clarinets. They're going to be pretty tight, meaning about 5 or 6 feet over them. That's not rock-and-roll tight. That's orchestral tight. But if you open that microphone, you're going to pretty much hear what that mic is pointing at, and the leakage from the other microphones on the woodwinds make the size bigger on the instrument.*

CHUCK AINLAY: *If at all possible, I really like the sound of the bleed in the room. If I have a great bass player that I know I'm not going to move a lot of notes (which is most of the guys in town), I'll let them have the amp right next to them. The room mics for the drums pick it up, and you get this big bass sound that fills up the whole stereo image instead of something that's just right in the middle.*

MARK LINETT: *So a lot of what we end up doing with room mics sort of emulates what that sound would have been if all that leakage would have spilled into the other mics. One of the problems with multitrack recording is we get very concerned about being able to isolate every sound but yet have it sound really good when it's all pushed up together, and that gets really tricky. You start to understand where they got the sound on those old records. It might have been only on three-track, but it was pretty well soldered together using leakage to their benefit. Once headphones and multitracks came along, all that sort of went away because people wanted to have options. On a lot of great records they had the vocal slightly baffled out in the room, but they weren't planning on replacing them anyway.*

FRANK FILIPETTI: *Generally, I view leakage as a positive as opposed to a negative. My view is that leakage is your friend and what makes the sound real and live and wonderful. I like the way it makes things blend with each other and fills in a little as it would in a live situation. It's just like on the drums. I don't mike the overheads for the cymbals, but for the overall sound that comes from around the kit.*

Instead of trying to avoid the leakage, great attention should be paid to the kind of leakage being recorded, rather than trying to eliminate it. Leakage can be used as a sort of glue between instruments in much the same way that instruments magnify one another in a live situation.

So, when tracking with multiple instruments, keep in mind the following:

▶ Keep the players as close together as possible. Not only will it help the players communicate, but the leakage will be more direct sound than room reflections, which will sound better.

▶ Whenever possible, use omnidirectional pattern microphones. The leakage picked up by omnis tends to be a lot less colored than that picked up by directional microphones.

BRUCE BOTNICK: *I was always amazed how much things would change, especially if you changed microphones or patterns. I used to try a figure-8 next to a cardioid to try to avoid the phase shift.*

The Assistant Engineer

You may never work in a studio that has a second engineer, and if you own your own gear, you may never be one yourself, but it's good to find out what an assistant in a major facility like the Record Plant, Capitol, Ocean Way, or Avatar really needs to know. These tips from the legendary Al Schmitt (who's won more Grammys than any other engineer) will help you understand what's expected of an assistant and will help you run a professional session, regardless of the level you're at.

ATTRIBUTES OF A GREAT ASSISTANT ENGINEER (BY AL SCHMITT)

I'm always asked what I think the most important attributes are for being a great assistant engineer. For this article I polled some of my colleagues, and it's very interesting how consistently we all cite the same desirable qualities. Here are the top 12, though not necessarily in order of their importance:

1. An assistant should be well versed in the use of Pro Tools. This has become very important. Most studios today won't even hire assistants unless they are proficient with Pro Tools. It's almost mandatory.

2. Most of the good assistants we work with today are good musicians in their own right. They can read music. When we're punching in and have a score in front of us, it's easy to find the spots, and this saves time. We work with a lot of artists, and occasionally some temperamental ones, who don't want to be wasting time while an assistant is looking for the top of the second verse, Bar 84, or the third beat of Bar 22. This has to be done quickly, and it's up to the assistant to be able to find these spots fast so we can do the punches and fixes.

3. Good personal hygiene was cited by nearly everyone I spoke to. Very simply put, a good assistant smells good. I don't necessarily mean cologne. I mean no body odor, bad breath, dirty socks, et cetera. No one wants to be in a small control room for 10 or 12 hours with someone who smells like an old goat. Take a shower, wear clean clothes, and keep the breath mints handy.

4. One of my engineer colleagues used a word that best describes an important attribute of great assistants: transparent. When you really need them, they're there. The other times they're in the background, but they're always paying attention to what's going on and staying with the program. If the assistant sees a problem, he tells the engineer at the appropriate time, and it's the engineer's job to take care of it. A good assistant never displays a bad or negative attitude and always leaves his or her ego at the door.

5. Develop strong computer skills. With everything we use today being computerized, you'll need to be up to speed on Microsoft Office and all facets of the Internet.

6. If you make a mistake, admit it. Right away. You may have to take your lumps, but we'll fix it and move on. And once the mistake has been corrected, don't continue to dwell on it. If you're worrying about a mistake you just made, you're going to make another one right away. It's like golf; you learn from your last shot, but you've got to focus on your current one.

7. Keep a good, accurate, and legible track sheet. It's very important. Otherwise, you're looking at creating a lot of confusion and mistakes. We find many interns coming out of the schools who just don't have this skill down, and it's one of the most important things an assistant does. When noting the track sheet, make sure you talk to the engineer and find out whether it's a DNU ["do not use"] track or a TBE ["to be erased"] track. If it's supposed to be on Track 18, make sure it is on Track 18; if it's supposed to be on Track 6 or 7, make certain it is. The importance of this cannot be overstated.

8. If you are asked a question by the engineer or producer and you're not sure of the answer, don't guess. Be honest. Let them know you'll find out and do it. Today, with the Internet and the great maintenance crews, information is readily available. Get the right answer and give them the information.

9. An assistant needs to know how to align the tape machine. The ability to line up an analog two-track machine or a 24-track machine is a skill you should master. There isn't always going to be a maintenance guy around at the moment that it's required, and you should be able to do it well and accurately.

10. When I was starting out, I found this item very important and helpful. Keep a notebook with you during a session and make diagrams of all the setups. Note how the board is laid out and the names of the engineer and artist, what microphones are used, et cetera. Three months from now, if you're doing a follow up to the session, this information will be a big help to you (and to the engineer) because you'll be prepared and know what he needs. This notebook will also prove very important to you if you later find yourself thrown into a session on your own. You can refer back to the session in the notebook (assuming the recording sounded great) and see how the studio was physically set up, what mics were used on what instruments, and where they were placed. Believe me, this will prove a big help when starting out on your own. But in the near term, while you're an assistant, this will help you be more prepared and efficient.

11. On a light but nevertheless important note, keep food menus at hand and be sure to know where you can get a good pizza, or good chicken, good burgers, sandwiches, et cetera, and who delivers. You're at a studio where you're working all the time and people come in from out of town. They'll want to know where they can get good sushi or whatever. You should know where the good places are and who delivers, and have the menus available.

12. And last but not least, know how to make a good pot of coffee!

FRANK FILIPETTI: *To me the assistant has two main jobs. One is he's your liaison with the studio and the second is documentation. One of the things that is sorely missing is the need for proper documentation from studios. I'm amazed that studios don't require every assistant to write up a proper track sheet on a session. I don't care if it's recorded to Pro Tools or a DAW, I want to see a track sheet at the end of the day.*

CHAPTER 10

Surround Miking Techniques

With so much attention given to mixing in surround these days, it seems like there's much less time given to actual surround recording. Even though orchestral recordists have been recording in surround for some time, those of us in the areas known as rock, pop, R&B, and jazz have done little to exploit the possibilities. Since the aim of any recording is to capture the environment as well as the source, surround miking accomplishes this goal to an extent that we have never heard before. Any of the methods discussed in this chapter add a spaciousness that you simply can't even approximate with outboard processors or any other previously mentioned miking techniques.

Multi-Miking in Surround

Here are some different approaches to consider when miking in surround.

OCT SURROUND
Optimized Cardioid Triangle (OCT) is a modified Decca Tree that uses three cardioid microphones in a triangle, with the center mic about 3 inches from the center and the side mics (which face out toward the sides, 15 to 36 inches away from each other). For better bass response, omnis may be substituted. By adding two additional rear cardioids 15 inches back from the L and R and 8 inches farther outside the L and R and pointing to the rear, a surround version of OCT can be derived. (See Figure 10.1.)

Figure 10.1
OCT surround.

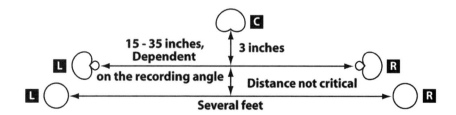

IRT CROSS

IRT stands for the German-based Institute of Radio Technology. This configuration is in essence a double-ORTF setup (see the section "Near-Coincident Pair" in Chapter 5) with four cardioids arranged in a perfect-square shape with an angle of 90 degrees to each other, respectively. To compensate for the narrower angle compared to ORTF (which is 110 degrees), the distance between the mics is greater (8 inches compared to 6 inches with ORTF). Strictly speaking, the IRT microphone cross is an array for ambience recording. Its prime characteristic is a transparent and spatial reproduction of the acoustic environment. It is the primary configuration used for NPR's spectacular "Radio Expeditions" recordings. See Figure 10.2.

Figure 10.2
IRT cross.

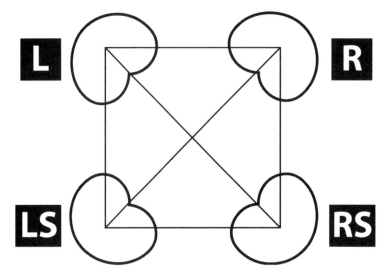

HAMASAKI SQUARE

The Hamasaki Square configuration is similar to the IRT cross except that figure-8s are used instead of cardioids. The length of each side is much wider, at about 6 feet, and the figure-8s have their nulls turned to the front so that this array is relatively insensitive to direct sound. (See Figure 10.3.)

Figure 10.3
The Hamasaki Square.

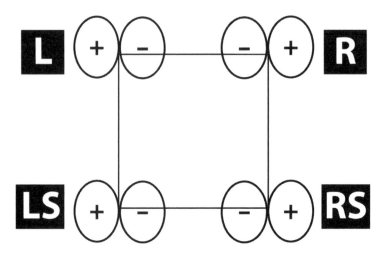

DOUBLE M-S

The method uses a standard M-S configuration with the addition of a rear-facing cardioid mic. (See Figure 10.4.)

Figure 10.4
Double M-S.

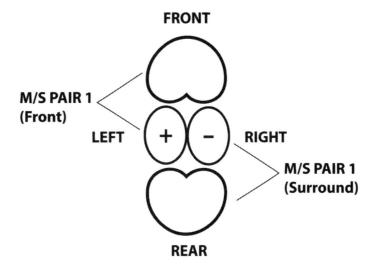

Drum Surround Multi-Miking

Since drums are the heart of most modern music with a backbeat, they also are ideal for recording in surround. Following are a couple of methods to try.

MULTI-MIC #1

This method augments what would normally be stereo room mics directly in front of the kit by adding a center mic and two rears (see Figure 10.5) along with the normal complement of close mics on the kit. The front mics should be placed between 5 and 6 feet away from the drums (or wherever the sweet spot might be), with the center mic directly in the center surround at about the height of the snare drum. The surround mics should be placed in approximately the same position in the rear. Each mic is bussed to the appropriate multichannel track. This setup of three mics in front of the drums and two behind gives the listener a surround soundstage from the drummer's perspective.

Figure 10.5
Drum surround mic #1.

ALTERNATE TO MULTI-MIC #1

Place the three front mics behind the drums and the surround mics in front of the kit. This will give you a soundstage from the listener's perspective. Also, try setting up the mics in more of a pentagram to spread things out a bit wider to really emphasize the spaciousness of the room.

MULTI-MIC #2

Another interesting approach is actually miking the room itself. That is, bring the room mics in close to the drums or source and turn them around to face the room and not the drums (see Figure 10.6). Surprisingly enough, this provides a much more usable, more clearly defined result. Whereas the mics looking in at the drums can sound washy and ambient, mics looking out hear the room directly instead of the reflections of the room.

Figure 10.6
Drum surround mic #2.

MULTI-MIC #3

Another method initially intended for stereo that can easily be adapted for surround uses a single shotgun mic 6 to 8 feet over the snare drum, a U 47 FET aimed at the kick but moved back from the drums until the sweet spot of the room is found, a U 47 on each side of the kit at 90-degree angles, and a stereo Schoeps for the rear directly behind the drummer.

A simple variation would be to keep the shotgun over the kit as a hard center channel, but put stereo mics at the sweet spot of the room both in front of and behind the drums.

Obviously, in a larger room you can move the mics back and forth to time the ambience to the track, but the techniques are equally valid (maybe even more so) to gain the added spatial dimension in a small room as well.

THE HALO

While the room-mic technique certainly provides a big, spacious sound, an array of five mics in a circle can yield very interesting results. Because the logistics of this aren't too easy to execute with even small-capsule microphones, DPA's tiny 4061 miniature microphones work perfectly in this application. The mics, which measure only 12.7×5.4 millimeters, weigh next to nothing, and have a surprising frequency response of 20 Hz to 20 kHz with a gentle rise from 8 to 20 kHz, are more likely to be seen on a news anchor than in a recording studio. The mics are mounted on a hoop suspended over the center of the kit. The mics are pointed outward in order to cover the entire kit. (See Figure 10.7.)

Figure 10.7
Drum halo.

CHAPTER 11

Surround Microphones

While using multiple mics for surround recording gives you great versatility, the labor required can sometimes be prohibitive. Luckily, there are several surround microphones that provide excellent results in a compact package.

The Holophone Surround Microphone System

The Holophone was designed and patented by musician/sound designer Mike Godfrey and was developed by Rising Sun Productions of Toronto and Canada's National Research Council. As with many groundbreaking developments, the unit was inspired by chance. The story goes that Godfrey, listening to Pink Floyd's "The Final Cut" on his Walkman via headphones, was fooled by the recording into thinking that someone was walking up behind him. Some time later, Godfrey discovered that what he had experienced was in fact a binaural recording, so he set out to re-create the effect. After a series of dummy-head binaural experiments, the inventor found that applying some of the techniques used in surround sound would re-create that same three-dimensional space he had experienced before, but now without the use of headphones. After he made his first prototype and it became apparent that the patent would issue, Canada's NRC joined in a collaborative research agreement to fine-tune the system and take the prototype to the next level.

The Holophone (see Figure 11.1) is actually an entire system rather than just a microphone. The focal part of the system features a 7.5×5.7-inch fiberglass epoxy ellipsoid that looks something like a giant teardrop. This ellipsoid holds eight omnidirectional microphone elements: five in the now-standard multichannel fashion with the front center element at the tip of the teardrop, plus one at the rear of the teardrop for the center rear channel, one on top for height, and an element internally mounted in the ellipsoid for the LFE channel. This setup makes it relatively easy for the sound designer to collect samples in the field; just point the mic, and the Holophone does the rest.

Figure 11.1
The Holophone H2-PRO. Courtesy of Rising Sun Productions.

With the success of the original unit and the H2-PRO, Holophone has added the lower-cost 5.1 H3-D, the H4 SuperMINI, and the PortaMic 5.1 for camera-mounted applications. For more information, contact the company via its website at www.holophone.com.

The Schoeps KFM 360

The Schoeps KFM 360 Surround Microphone System, designed by location recordist Jerry Bruck, utilizes a KFM 360 sphere microphone and a DSP-4 KFM 360 processor. (See Figure 11.2.)

Figure 11.2
Schoeps KFM 360 by Bruck.
Courtesy of Schoeps GmbH.

The central unit in this system is the sphere microphone KFM 360, which uses two pressure transducers and can also be used for stereo recording. To achieve surround capability, the unit uses two figure-8 microphones that are attached beneath the pressure transducers by an adjustable, detachable clamp system with bayonet-style connectors (SGC-KFM). These two microphones should be aimed forward.

The DSP-4 KFM 360 processor derives the four corner channels from the microphone signals with a center channel being created from the two front signals. An additional channel carries only the low frequencies up to 70 Hz. It is possible to lower the level of their channels, to delay them, and/or to set an upper limit on their frequency response.

The processor unit features both analog and digital inputs. In addition to providing gain, it offers a high-frequency emphasis for the built-in pressure transducers as well as a low-frequency boost for the figure-8s.

SoundField MKV Microphone and Model 451 5.1 Decoder

While the SoundField microphone has been around since the '70s in a stereo version, the microphone truly became a surround microphone when the MKV model and the model 451 surround processor were introduced. (See Figure 11.3.)

Figure 11.3
The SoundField MKV. Courtesy of SoundField.

The SoundField microphone employs a four-element array in a tetrahedral pattern that can be electronically controlled from the supplied pre-amp/controller, which is connected by a 55-foot multi-core cable. The mic is rather small and unobtrusive, considering the number of capsules employed, and can easily be placed in most miking situations, even in the supplied shock mount.

The SoundField controller is actually a multi-function processor that combines a microphone preamp and the appropriate electronics needed to control the various parameters of the Mark 5. The front panel has an input section that consists of a Master Gain control, which provides up to 30 dB of gain in 10-dB steps, and a Fine Gain control, which is detented at 0. This section also has solo switches for the individual capsules, as well as switches that compensate for microphone orientation if the mic is used in either an inverted or an end-fire position. There is also a stereo output section that consists of a Pattern control, which is variable from omni to figure-8; an Angle control, which electronically points the capsules either in the same direction (0°) or 180° opposing; and a headphone jack with gain control. There are also switches for a 40-Hz hi-pass filter and for M-S decoding, as well as a set of four LED bar graphs that can be switched to read either the B-format output (more on this in a moment) or the stereo output.

The heart of the processor lies within the SoundField controls, which offer some unfamiliar parameters usually not associated with a microphone. For instance, Azimuth provides for complete electronic rotation of the microphone, Elevation allows for plus or minus 45 degrees of continuous variation of the vertical alignment, and Dominance is a form of zoom control that gives the effect of the mic moving either closer to or farther away from the sound source. There is also In/Out control for the SoundField controls, as well as a B-format Input switch for using the controller with prerecorded B-format material.

B Format

While stereo defines the world of sound in just two dimensions, B Format defines it in three. B Format contains information to define front to back (one dimension), left to right (two dimensions), and up and down (three dimensions). Essentially B Format is a sphere with four elements: an X plane (front to back), a Y plane (left to right), and a Z plane (up and down), all with a central reference called W. SoundField uses B Format as its core technology for documenting and translating the four elements of real acoustical events so they can be recorded on a 4-channel audio recorder so that the microphone parameters can be manipulated later. Also, all options are based on the same reference information, so there are no phase difference issues to contend with.

The SoundField 451 5.1 Decoder

The SoundField 451 Surround Decoder (see Figure 11.4) enables the SoundField to become a true 5.1 microphone. The processor takes either the B-Format outputs from the Mark 5 processor or material that has been previously recorded and delivers full 5.1 surround via balanced XLR outputs.

Figure 11.4
SoundField 451 Decoder. Courtesy of SoundField.

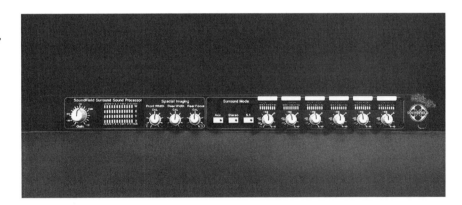

The 451 features a Master Gain control and individual channel gain controls with meters and center detents. The heart of the unit includes the Spatial Imaging controls (which take the place of the SoundField controls on the stereo processor) and features Front Width, Rear Width, and Rear Focus controls. There are also three switches labeled Aux, Mode 1, and Mode 2 that allow for different control cards that electronically set the pickup pattern of the Mark 5.

261

The 451 processor can now be duplicated in your DAW by the Surround Zone software plug-in.

SPL/Brauner Atmos 5.1 Surround Microphone System

The Atmos 5.1 is really a system consisting of two pieces: the SPL Atmos 5.1 console and the Brauner ASM (Adjustable Surround Microphone) 5. The Atmos 5.1 console actually is two units—one main unit occupying a 5U rack space and a 1U power supply. The unit features all the things you'd expect on a small console and more. It starts with five high-quality mic amps, each with an illuminated VU meter, each containing illuminated switches for input pad, phase reverse, phantom power, low-cut filters, aux send, and insert. Each mic amp also employs the unique feature of having the gain trim pots motorized, so all five can be linked to a master control if desired. (See Figure 11.5.)

Figure 11.5
SPL/Brauner Atmos. Courtesy of SPL.

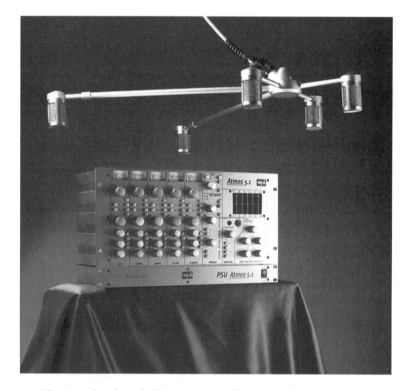

The signal is then fed into a rotary fader that feeds an output assignment and panning matrix. This panning matrix has controls for LCR panning, front-to-surround panning, and divergence. This allows you to place the signal from any mic capsule in almost any soundfield position you'd like.

The output matrix of the unit is also unique. First there is the Sub section, which allows you to derive an LFE channel from L/R, Center, LS/RS, or any combination. There's also a switchable 130-Hz filter and an output gain control. From there, there's a stereo aux input with a gain control that allows a stereo signal, such as a reverb or an additional room mic, to be routed to either L/R, Center, LS/RS, or any combination. Then there are two similar but unique matrix sections that determine the spatial width of the Front and Surround channels. On each of these sections, there's a mono switch, a stereo expander, a rotary pot that determines the stereo width, and a stereo phase meter.

The unit also features a section that allows continuous adjustment of the polar pattern characteristic of each microphone, from omnidirectional up to figure-8. These adjustments can be made remotely from the Atmos 5.1 console and can be monitored while recording.

The Brauner ASM 5 microphone unit consists of five matched Brauner VM1 capsules that are mounted on a machined aluminum spider. The capsules are able to be manually rotated 90 degrees, and the patterns can be remotely controlled from the Atmos unit. The design of the ASM 5 is based on a setup called INA 5 (Ideale Nierenanordnung 5, which, translated, means ideal cardioid setup) that is a result of a master's thesis of Volker Henkels and Ulf Herrmann, although the ASM 5 is said to offer more flexibility and variability than the original INA 5 setup. The L/C/R microphone heads of the ASM 5 are factory-positioned in a triangle, with each microphone being positioned 17.5 cm (about 6.9 inches) away from the center, although they can be moved to form a straight line if that miking position is preferred. The two rear microphone capsules are placed 59.6 cm (about 24 1/2 inches) to the back with a 60-degree offset.

CHAPTER 12

Final Recording Checklist

Here's a list of things to check if something just doesn't sound right. Remember that each situation is different, and ultimately the sound depends upon the player, the instrument, the recording environment, the song, the arrangement, and even the other players involved. Of course, sometimes things are just out of your control. Also, these are not hard-and-fast rules, just a starting place. If you try something that's different from what you read in this chapter and it sounds good, it is good! Remember, take risks, experiment, take notes on what works for you and what doesn't, be creative, and most of all, have fun!

General Checklist

1. Does the instrument sound great acoustically? Make sure you start with a great acoustic sound, with the instrument well tuned and a minimum of sympathetic vibrations and extraneous noises.

2. Are the mics acoustically in phase? Observe the 3-to-1 rule and make sure that any underneath mics are at a 90-degree angle to the top mics.

3. Are the mics electronically in phase? Make sure that all the mic cables are wired the same by doing a phase check.

4. Are the mics at the correct distance from the instrument? If they're too far away, they'll pick up too much of the room or other instruments. If they're too close, the sound will be unbalanced, with either too much attack or too much ring and not enough of the body of the instrument. Walk around the player, put your finger in your ear, and find the spot that sounds the best. Remember, most instruments need some space for the sound to develop. The ambience from the surrounding area is a bigger part of the sound than most instruments.

5. Does it sound the same in the control room as when you're standing in front of the instrument? This is your reference point and what you should be trying to match. You can embellish the sound after you've achieved this.

6. Is there another problem besides the mic placement? A great sound is dependent upon the instrument, the player, the amp, and the room. The player has to be able to achieve the tone you're trying to record with his hands first and foremost. The mic itself usually has less to do with the ultimate sound than the placement, room, and the player and ultimately, the project itself.

   You should always trust your ears and begin by listening to the musician in your studio, find a sweet spot and then begin your microphone placement there. If you don't like the resultant sound, then move the mic or swap it with another. EQ is the last thing you should touch.

7. Is the problem in your signal chain? Don't neglect your microphone preamp. The better your preamp, the less trouble you'll have getting the sound, but sometimes a certain mic/preamp combination will give you the sound you need. Experiment.

8. Is the problem the player's signal chain? A guitarist's signal chain can be a huge help or a big hindrance. You'll get a warmer yet aggressive guitar sound by decreasing the amount of distortion from pedals, but turning up the amp's volume instead to obtain the sustain/distortion from the amp and speaker. Also, smaller amps and speakers tend to sound bigger than large amps/speakers when recording.

> **Remember:** Mics cannot effectively be placed by sight, which is a mistake that is all too easy to make (especially after reading a book like this). The best mic position cannot be predicted, it must be found.

Checklist for Drums (in Addition to the Above)

1. Are all mics as parallel as possible to keep the acoustic phase shift to a minimum?

2. Are any mics underneath the drums at a 90 degree angle to keep the acoustic phase shift to a minimum?

3. Since most mics placed underneath the drums will be out of phase with the tops mics, did you switch the polarity on your preamp, console, or DAW and choose the position that has the most bottom end?

4. Are the microphones aimed at the center of the drum to provide the most attack? Start there first, but for more body or ring, aim it more toward the rim.

5. During your mic check, is the drummer hitting about once per second or slower so there's enough time between hits to hear how long the ring is?

Microphone Selection Checklist

1. Did you select a microphone that compliments the instrument that you'll be recording? For instance, if you have an instrument that has a very edgy top end, choose a mic with the opposite quality so those frequencies won't be emphasized. In the case of an instrument with a lot of transients (like a triangle or tambourine), dynamic mics often work better than condensers.

2. Is the mic designed to be used in the "free-field" or in the "diffuse-field"? Free field means that the sound source dominates what the mic hears. Diffuse field means that the reflections play a large role in what the mic hears. Mics designed for free field use have a very flat frequency response in the high frequencies, and as a result can sound dull when placed further away. Diffuse field mics have a boost in the upper frequencies that make them sound flat when placed further away.

3. Did you select a mic that won't be overloaded by the source? You wouldn't want to put a ribbon mic or many condensers on a snare drum with a heavy hitting drummer, for instance.

4. Did you choose the right polar pattern for the job? If leakage is a consideration, then choose a mic with the proper directional capabilities for the job. If a mic is flat on-axis, it will roll off the highs when it's 90 degrees off-axis. If it's flat 90 degrees off-axis, it will have a rising high end when it's on-axis. You might also consider a figure-8 pattern for its high rejection to sound on its sides.

5. Is proximity effect an issue? If close-miking, will the bass buildup from proximity be too much? If so, consider an omni.

If the Sound Is Distorted Checklist

1. Is the cable working correctly? Try a different cable.

2. Is the mic working correctly? Try a different mic.

3. Is the mic being overloaded? Try a different mic to see if the signal level from the source is too loud.

4. Is the microphone preamp working correctly? Try a different preamp or channel.

5. Is the microphone preamp being overloaded? Check to see if any overload indicators are lit. Try a different preamp, console, or interface channel to see if the problem is resolved.

6. Is the signal chain after the mic preamp being overloaded? Check to see if any overload indicators are lit on your interface and DAW. Bypass any compressors in the signal chain. Play back signal from the DAW to make sure it's clean.

7. Is the monitoring chain working correctly? Is the stereo or control room buss being overloaded? Try a different set of amplifiers and speakers.

Checklist for Overdubs

1. Did you move the vocal or instrument into the big part of the studio? All instruments sound best when there's some space for the sound to develop. You can cut down on any unwanted reflections from the room by placing baffles around the mic and player.

2. When doubling, are you trying to do something a little different on each track? A different mic, mic preamp, room, singer, or distance from the mic will all help to make the sound bigger.

3. When doubling or adding more guitars, do you have a variety of instruments and amplifiers available? Two guitars (a Les Paul and a Strat, for instance) and two amplifiers (a Fender and a Marshall is the classic combination) combined with different pickup settings will allow a multitude of guitar tracks to more effectively live in the mix together.

Vocal Recording Checklist

1. Did you select the correct mic for the singer's voice? Choose a mic with a lot of body for a thin voice and one with enhanced high end for a dark voice.

2. Did you select the correct microphone preamp? Certain mics come alive when they're paired with the right preamp. Also, a certain mic/preamp combination can be just the right color for a vocal. Experiment.

3. Did you select the correct microphone pickup pattern? Not every vocal needs to be recorded with a cardioid pattern. An omni pattern will cut down on proximity effect, and a figure-8 can help with isolation from speakers or other instruments.

4. Is proximity effect wanted or needed? Remember that the closer you get to a cardioid mic, the more the low end will become exaggerated. This could make the vocal too big for the track. Try the mic on omni if you really need to get a close and intimate sound.

5. Is the singer the correct distance away? Too far away, and you'll hear more room, which could change the vocal sound or take away the intimacy. Too close, and the vocal might sound too big or too close due to the proximity effect of a cardioid mic. If the singer is singing softly and breathily, keep the singer close to the mic. If the singer is shouting, screaming, or singing just plain loudly, back the singer off the mic two to three feet.

6. Is the singer drifting off-axis? Some vocalists drift around the room and off-axis of the mic if they feel it's too far away. Put up a dummy mic that they can get close to so they can feel anchored. This also helps when putting up different mics to determine which one works best for the vocalist.

7. Is the singer popping the mic? Place the mic at eye level and point it down at the singer's mouth, turn the mic slightly off-axis, switch the pattern to omni, back the singer off the mic until the pops disappear, or use a pop screen.

8. Would a handheld mic work better? Some singers aren't comfortable unless they feel like they're on stage. Give them a 58 and don't worry about the sound. A great performance beats a great sound any day (and a 58 isn't all that bad combined with the right preamp).

9. Are you limiting the signal? Just a few dB of limiting can help keep the vocal under control and stop overloading the signal chain. Don't use software compressor/limiters because of the latency.

10. Is the headphone mix at the correct level? The phone mix is crucial to a good performance. If the track is too loud, the vocalist may sing too hard, which might not be the sound you want. He may also sing sharply as a result. If the track is too soft, the singer may not sing aggressively enough.

11. Is the ambience conducive to a good vocal? Most singers like the light down low when they sing.

If All Else Fails

1. Change the source (the instrument you are miking), if possible.

2. Change the mic placement.

3. Change the placement in the room.

4. Change the mic.

5. Change the mic preamplifier.

6. Change the amount of compression and/or limiting (from none to a lot).

7. Change the actual room in which you are recording.

8. Change the player.

9. Come back and try it another day.

CHAPTER 13

Chuck Ainlay

Chuck Ainlay is one of the new breed of Nashville engineers who brings a rock-and-roll approach to country-music sensibility. With credits such as George Strait, Dixie Chicks, Vince Gill, Patty Loveless, Wynonna, and even such rock icons as Dire Straits and Mark Knopfler, Chuck's work is heard worldwide.

Do you have a standard setup that you use when you track?

To some degree. I have favorites that I start with, and if that doesn't work, then I try other things. But it depends a lot on the type of music that I'm trying to do. If it's a country thing or if the song is kind of a '70s thing or an '80s thing or a '90s thing, I might try different miking techniques to capture that type of sound.

For example, for Mark Knopfler's album we miked the drums differently for just about every song. We took what the song said to the drummer and Mark and myself, and we just applied different techniques to try to capture that.

But from a Nashville perspective, and maybe where I should start, most things are pretty typical. Somewhat of a departure is that I use two mics on the bass drum and the snare drum. I don't think that's radically different from what other people do, but it's not typically what everybody here does. Usually I'll put an AKG D 112 inside the bass drum slightly off center from the beater head and back about 6 to 8 inches, generally pointing toward where the beater strikes the head. It's not straight in the middle; it's usually off center a little bit. Outside of the bass drum I'll place an FET 47. Usually drummers have a hole cut in their front head, and I prefer that rather than no front head at all. It gives you a bit of that almost double-headed bass drum sound. I'll put the outside mic off center once again, away from where the hole would be cut. Then it's just a matter of time spent dampening the drum with some soft materials to try to get however much deadness you want out of the drum.

Usually then I'll put either some mic stands or chairs or something that I can drape some double-thick packing blankets on so that it makes sort of a tunnel around the bass drum and helps seal off some of the leakage into that outside microphone.

How far away is the 47 FET?

That varies a lot, but usually about 8 inches. Both of those mics go through Neve 1081 modules. I have a rack of those and a fair number of other preamps that travel with me when I'm tracking because I typically avoid using the console preamps for many of the important things and just go straight to tape or hard disc from the outboard modules. The console is used just for monitoring.

I don't usually use any kind of compression on the bass drum, or any of the drums actually, with the exception of the ambient mics. I don't use gates on anything except for the toms.

What do you do for the snare?

The snare drum usually gets a 57 on the top with usually a 452 with a 20-dB pad on the bottom, although that mic varies to some degree because there might not be a 452 with a 20-dB pad in the studio where I'm tracking. The top mic will usually go through a 1081 again, but the bottom mic I'll bring up on a console mic pre. It's always flipped out of phase and combined with the top mic so that I just have one snare-drum track. I like to commit to that because the two mics together really make the snare drum sound, and I don't like to leave that open for judgment later.

Do you do the same thing with the kick?

No, the kick I'll usually leave on separate tracks because that, to me, is one of those things that I can refine later. If I have a lot of leakage on the outside bass drum mic, I can spend a bit of time gating that out or cleaning it up with a hard disc system if need be. That's one of those things that when you start getting into the nuts and bolts of your bottom end with the bass, having those two mics separate will allow you to change how much attack you have in the bass drum or how much "oomp" there is.

The bass drum is actually one of those instruments that requires a lot of EQ. I try to do minimal EQ on most things, but bass drum has always been one of those things that usually ends up taking a lot of EQ. And depending on how you EQ each mic, the results vary a lot.

Are you EQing while you're tracking?

Yeah, I do EQ the bass drum and snare. Actually, drums I EQ a lot while I'm tracking, but I do avoid compression.

So then on the snare drum I like to put it to where the rear of the mic is rejecting the hi-hat as much as possible, but it isn't in the way of the drummer. The main thing with miking drums is for the drummer to never think about hitting a mic while he's playing. The mic usually comes in somewhere between the hi-tom and the hi-hat, but I like to somehow get the rear of the mic toward the hat for the most rejection. It usually is pointing down at sort of a 45-degree angle. I find that the more I angle it across the drum the better side-stick sound I'm going to get. If it's pointed down too straight at the drum, then the side stick becomes too much of a high-frequency click rather than a nice woody sound. So if there's a lot of side stick, then I might have to position the microphone more for that instead of rejection of the hi-hat. Once again, all this stuff varies from session to session.

Hi-hat I vary between a 452 and a KM 184. It depends on what kind of sound I want. If I want a chunky-sounding hat, the mic will usually be over the hat, pointing out across the hat somewhat away from the snare drum, so if you're the drummer it would be on the other side from where you're hitting it. But if I want an airier sound, I'll move the mic more and more off to the side of the hat, to where it's not even over the hat, to get that paper-thin sort of sound. The only thing that you have to be aware of is the wind blast that might happen when he pumps it.

For toms, the microphone choice there varies the most of anything. It will vary from a 57 or a 421, although I've been using these Audio-Technica ATM25s a lot lately. Sometimes if I want a beefier, warm sound, I'll go to a condenser microphone, which can go from a 414 to an 87 if I want a sort of fat '70s sound, to Sony C-37s if they're available and working [laughs]. Once again, Audio-Technica makes a clip-on condenser, the 8532, that I've had a lot of success with. It has a lot of isolation and doesn't have that huge proximity effect that you get from a lot of other condenser mics. It also works great on acoustic guitars. Between that and an AT4033, I get an amazing acoustic sound.

Also on toms, I always put gates on the inserts of the tom channels. What I do is use these little contact mics that were intended to be trigger microphones for triggering sound modules for drums and plug them into the key side of the gates for the toms. Whether or not I turn on the insert depends on whether I want the leakage on the toms. Toms add so much to the warmness of your snare drum and bass drum, but this way I have a really solid trigger on the gates and I don't miss the nuance-type fills. I don't necessarily always use it, but it works so well when I need it. Usually when I do gate toms, it will only be 6 to 10 dB of reduction. I don't gate them to nothing. I usually use the console mic amps so I can do this.

I normally place the mic between lugs of the tom. If you get over one of the tuning lugs, you get too much of the flap from the drums. Drummers usually don't tune their toms perfectly so they don't ring on forever. They'll intentionally detune them slightly so they sort of bend away and stop ringing quicker, so if you split the lugs it sounds better.

Also, I try not to get too close to the head. You're compromising between leakage and tone, but if you get too close you're just going to get attack and no warmth out of the tom. It's usually somewhere between 2 1/2 to 4 inches, probably closer to 3 inches. If I take my three fingers and put them between the mic and the head, that's usually a good starting place. Sometimes I'll mic underneath as well, but that's rare.

Do you flip the phase on the bottom mic when you do that?

Yeah. If we're really going for something like disco drums, then we'll take the bottom heads off and mic it, but that's a pretty old sound.

What do you use for overheads?

That varies a lot, but it's either 414s, or what I've been using most recently is the stereo Royer microphone, the SF-12. Ever since I started using that thing, my drums have sounded so much more real. I can sort of rely on that for the drum sound and then fill it in with the close mics rather than the other way around.

I was just going to ask how you approached setting up the kit balance.

Well, it depends on whether I'm using a stereo mic overhead like that, which then you can use for the main kit sound. If you're using spaced pairs where you're just miking cymbals, then it doesn't work at all. It depends on the intent and if you want this really in-your-face closed mic thing or if you want the drums to be more set back and more real-sounding. If you're going for that '70s/'80s tighter sound, then you'd put the mics over the cymbal. If you want them more real-sounding, then you'd go for the stereo mic.

How do you determine what sound you're going for? Is it the song or the artist or…?

It's the song, really. It depends what kind of vibe I get off the song. The artist influences the decision as well, obviously. Does it strike up a more ambient-sounding thing or does it strike up a more intimate, in-your-face thing?

How about room mics?

I usually put them about 4 feet out in front of the snare drum. Not the kick drum, but the snare drum. I'm sort of splitting the positioning between the hat and the bass drum with what I call a mid-field mic. I'll put up one of the mono Royer mics [R-121] usually and use some severe limiting on it with an 1176, and that becomes my "meat" microphone. It just sort of brings in the drums as an overall picture, and it really adds a lot of meat to them.

Then about 12 feet away—sometimes less—in front of the drums, I'll put up a pair of 149s or a pair of these Joe Meek microphones, the JM47s. They sound amazing on toms, too. Sometimes I'll do like a Led Zeppelin thing with one mic picking up the hi-tom, snare, and hat and the other one picking up the floor tom and ride cymbal, and the JM47s sound great for that.

I'm not hip to that mic.

I'm not sure if they're sold in the States or not. I'm close friends with Ted Fletcher, the designer of the Joe Meek stuff, because his son Guy Fletcher is the keyboard player for Knopfler and has been in Dire Straits all these years. He hipped me to these mics. If you can find them, they're amazing on background vocals, toms, and a whole drum kit. Just put an FET 47 on the bass drum and those two mics, and there you go. But it takes a little bit of time, and you have to have a drummer who has a little bit of patience.

How much time do you usually take on getting sounds?

I'm pretty fast. Maybe an hour at most, and that's for getting things situated in the room. But after that we might change the drums before each song and it'll be 15 minutes. They might change out entire kits, but usually the EQ just works, and I might tweak things a bit as they're running the song down. It's more about changing stuff out rather than tweaking things on my side. I certainly don't take two days like they did on the old Fleetwood Mac albums.

How about bass? Are you taking it direct with an amplifier as well?

In Nashville, most of the guys have their own rigs because it's so session-oriented. They'll come in with these amazing racks full of great gear. They'll have a Telefunken mic pre and an LA-2A or Tube-Tech, which is sort of typical. So usually all I have to do is take a direct line from them to the tape machine, and I don't mess with it in between. I let them dictate by what they're hearing in the headphones because they're used to this stuff since they do it every day.

Sometimes if it's just not happening for me, I'll say, "Hey, I have this really great direct box," and I'll run it out to him. It's an Aguilar, and I love it on bass. It just sounds so big and real, and it really, really works. I don't carry a bass amp, but I really like the old Ampeg B-15s because you can distort those things if you want. Big rigs don't work for me, but the little guys do. Usually I'll just put an FET 47 or the new Neumann 147 in front of it.

If at all possible, I really like the sound of the bleed in the room. If I have a great bass player so I know I'm not going to move a lot of notes—which is most of the guys in town—I'll let them have the amp right next to them. The room mics for the drums pick it up, and you get this big bass sound that fills up the whole stereo image instead of something that's just right in the middle.

I was just going to ask you about leakage.

I like it. Once again, though, if you're dealing with a band where you know you're going to be moving notes, then you have to isolate it. Some places have rooms where you can open it up enough to where you can put room miking on it, and it's really nice to get that spread on the bass.

Do you record everything on Nuendo?

It gets to Nuendo eventually. I prefer to go to tape first if I can, but at 96k I really don't mind tracking directly to it. It sounds really great. Many times I'll find myself sitting there and saying, "Is this really digital?"

How big is your system?

I've got 48 channels of converters—24 channels of Mytek and 24 channels of RME converters. I think the RME converters sound really great, especially for the money. The Myteks are like going the extra mile. I really like them. I've been mixing back to Nuendo and have no problem using these converters.

Did you have mentor or did you learn mic technique by yourself?

It was mostly by trial and error. I wish I had a mentor. The way I came up was to do a lot of demos and freebies. We had a lot of what we called "custom" work in Nashville when I started, which was people coming to the studio on their own dollar, and I did a lot of that. Every now and then I would hear about something that someone had tried that worked pretty well, so I would try it. Like that mid-room thing on the drums with the 1176 squeeze. I'm sure that was somebody else's idea and I tried it. But nobody said, "Put the microphone here." I just put the mic where it sounded good to me and tried compressing it real hard.

When I started, Belmont College had just begun their recording program. Rather than go to school, I stayed in the studio all the time and tried stuff and engineered for all the music classes. So I dropped out of school and did all of this custom, demo, freebie stuff until people started talking about me.

So you didn't work as an assistant first?

Not really. I worked at this studio called Sound Labs, where I got my start. Jim Cotton was the chief engineer there, and he would do all the big projects like Dr. Hook and Helen Reddy and Eddie Rabbitt. He was really cool because he'd let us set up everything. We actually got a lot of the sounds and then he would sit down and interface with the producer and the artist and musicians, and we'd assist him. This was back before there was automation, so there were like five guys on the console during mixing, so being an assistant was always an interactive relationship. You got a lot of hands-on, not like these days, where you're just a note taker a lot of the time.

In those days you got the chief engineer, who would do the gig if someone was paying full rate for the studio, and if they weren't paying full rate, then they got the second engineers, which was us. So I got a lot of trial-and-error experience and made a lot of really crappy records [laughs], but it was fun, and I never regretted it. I never thought about someone judging me on how this record sounds; I just wanted get behind the console and hear sound coming out of the big speakers.

Do you have an assistant who you work with most of the time or do you do it mostly yourself?

For many years I traveled with a guy. In fact, I've had a couple of guys over the years who have stuck with me. But then I became part owner of one of the rooms at Soundstage [Backstage Studios], and now I do most of my work here, so I do it mostly myself. If I travel I use whoever's at the studio. It means there's a lot more work for me because I have to do a lot more of my setting up, and there's not someone who knows how I like to do things and just automatically does it for me.

What do you want the assistant to do for you? Do you set up your own headphone mixes, for example, or do you let the assistant do it for you?

I wish I could say that I was that generous and would let someone else do it for me, but I'm just one of those kind of guys who's got to do it all himself. Kind of the theory of, "If you want a job done right, you do it yourself."

But things like getting the mics and cords and stands out, checking the headphone systems to make sure they work, making sure that the tape machine or hard disc system is set up and happy, all that is what the assistant has to do, and that's a huge job. Then, during tracking, keeping track of location points of the song. We use number charts instead of chord charts in Nashville, so the assistant has to keep track of each take and write it on the chart so after each take he has a chart. There's all this sort of note taking that really needs to be looked after, like who is on each instrument and what microphones are used on each instrument. I make sure that's all documented. I want to know each bit of gear that was used on each track in case we have to come back and set up the same session at a later date.

Is the approach to recording different in Nashville than in other recording centers, such as New York or LA?

I don't think they differ that much except for the fact that we do so much session-musician stuff. Typically, we play back a song demo at the beginning of the session, and it dictates a whole lot about how the recording is going to go down. When the demo is played, the musicians are running down a number chart. They may play it down and change the form of the song afterward, but in a lot of ways the demos are somewhat copied for the master. Many times the musicians will play it down the first time, and that will be the take.

We're not just talking about a small section. We're talking about bass, drums, two guitars [one may be acoustic], fiddle, steel, two keyboards [piano and organ], and vocal. This all goes down live.

Is this typical?

Yeah. So you have to be ready to get the first take, because they'll have it ready by at least the third take. So when you ask how long it takes to get drum sounds, it's got to be fast. It's a blast to cut tracks in Nashville because you're so on fire. You can't make a lot of changes as things are going down. You've just got to make a mental note in between takes. If you've got to move a mic, you've got to do it as the musicians are listening back to a take. You're really flying around. It's a blast.

That's so different compared to the normal rock-and-roll way.

Where they take all day to get a track and it's just bass and drums and guitar and then you strip it down to the drums and replace the bass and guitar? That's drudgery. In Nashville, tracking is one of the most enjoyable things you can possibly ever do. Not only do you have a bunch of really great people that you're hanging out with, but some of the most talented musicians in the world, too.

A typical studio will have at minimum a piano room, a room to isolate an acoustic guitar [sometimes you might jam two acoustic guitars and a fiddle in that same room], and a room for the vocalist. Some rooms, like the Masterfonics tracking studio, have five iso rooms and a couple of guitar lockers. A lot of the tracking rooms here are built that way. You have to have some degree of isolation because often the guys go for their solos as the track's going down. They need some degree of isolation if they want to fix a bar or two of their solo later.

That must mean that you don't spend much time doing overdubs.

Heck no. Most of the track is done when you finish tracking. The singer might sing the song three or four times more at the end of tracking and go home. Then we just comp vocals, do some background vocals, and maybe there might be another guitar added and maybe strings, maybe horns. But usually we just go straight to mix. Nowadays we spend more time tuning the vocals than doing overdubs [laughs]. If we only had singers.... [Laughs some more]

I thought you had some pretty good ones down there.

I don't know. It's just like having these eight-channel mixers for everyone's headphones has hurt everybody playing together as one group. I think that vocalists realize that they're going to get comped and tuned, so it takes away from that studio moment we used to get. And the labels seem to sign artists more on looks than on singing ability these days, too.

What's different today than when you started, besides the things you just stated?

Well, automation changed things a lot from when I started because one guy can sit at the console and do it all. And hard disc is changing the way we work so much now. And having more tracks. When I started, 24-track had just started happening, but we were still using a lot of 16-track gear. We didn't have synchronizers at the time, so if you had 24 tracks, then that's all you had to work with because you couldn't lock up machines. If you needed more tracks you just bounced things down. And we're just not recording live instruments much anymore, with synthesizers, samplers, and loops playing such a big part of a song. The only thing that's recorded for sure anymore is the vocal.

How do you approach recording vocals?

I still base everything around the vocal. To me, you have to find the microphone that fits the vocalist the best because if you get a great vocal sound, you're going to bring up everything to match that. If the vocal is so much bigger than everything else, then you are going to work on every-thing else until it's as good as the vocal. If the vocal sound sucks, then nothing is going to sound good because you don't want to overpower your vocal with the band.

If it's someone who I've never worked with before, I will hopefully get an opportunity to work with the vocalist before the tracking date to find a mic that works. Or I may use what has been previously used if I thought that sounded good. If not, I have to go with what I think is going to work, but usually it's a large-diaphragm tube microphone. I won't stop there, though. I might try other things.

My favorite vocal microphone is a 251, although I have to say that the new Soundelux 251 sounds damn near as good as a Telefunken. I haven't tried their 47 imitation, but I'm betting that it's the same thing. I am so knocked out with this 251. A real U 47 [not a Nuvistor version] works. Sometimes an FET 47 works, too. A U 67 is always a favorite. A C 12 works about as well as a 251, although I like the 251 better.

Do you try to get the best vocal sound and fit the track around it, or do you try to fit the vocal into the track?

It's all the same thing. I think the vocal has to be able to command the track. Maybe in metal or alternative things where the vocal doesn't play a very big role it might not matter, but in most music that is lyrically oriented, the vocal is going to play a very big role. You have to be able to understand what the vocal is saying. I know there are people who hate their voice and want you to disguise it as much as possible, but that's going to be an effect and still has to be a predominant thing if the lyrics are of any importance at all.

The track still has to envelop the vocal, though. The vocal can't sit out there all by itself. There's a pocket where the vocal is going to sit.

Do you approach steel any different than electric guitar?

Once again, I'm fortunate to have the best steel players in the world available. There are no others that even come close. With Paul Franklin, who's probably the most in-demand steel player, a 421 works perfectly, but I'll always off-center it from the voice coil. He and I have just figured that out over the years. He has a whole rig of stuff that he tweaks until he gets what he wants, and it just works wonderfully.

For electric guitar it's usually a 57 off-axis pointed in [toward the voice coil] and a 67 out from the speaker about 6 to 12 inches. A lot of the guys have big rigs, and usually just a couple of 57s off-axis will cover it because they use so many effects to get a stereo spread that an ambient mic isn't worthwhile.

So you usually get a stereo guitar source?

Yeah.

What's your approach to acoustic guitar?

In Nashville, we tend make pretty-sounding acoustic recordings. I guess it's an AT4033 if I want that bright Nashville sound. That mic works nicely. Or a 452. If I want more of a richer sound, I'll use either a KM 84 or KM 56 or one of the new 184s. In all instances the mic is pointed at where the neck joins the body and then out about 5 or so inches. I usually use a second microphone that moves around a lot. It's usually a large-diaphragm mic that's placed away from the guitar. That varies so much. A 67 is probably my preferred mic for that, but an Audio-Technica 4033 or 4050 works well, too.

I'll start out straight in front of the sound hole. If that's too boomy, I'll either move toward the bridge or lower or sometimes above the sound hole, above the cutout. Sometimes off the shoulder near the right ear of the player works. I might just put on a pair of headphones and move the mic until it sounds great. That's about the only way that you can mike an acoustic guitar. You just have to listen.

I'm always trying new things. This stuff will be valid today, but I may be doing something different tomorrow.

CHAPTER 14

Steve Albini

One of the most respected of the new breed of engineers, Steve Albini gained his considerable experience and reputation working primarily with underground and alternative bands. While his most famous credit remains Nirvana's *In Utero*, Steve has worked with a diverse lineup of artists such as PJ Harvey, the Pixies, the Breeders, Silkworm, Jesus Lizard, Nina Nastasia, and even the mainstream Page/Plant *Walking into Clarksdale*.

Do you have a standard setup when you track?

No. I get asked to do a lot of different kinds of sessions—everything from three-piece rock bands, to acoustic soloists, to big sprawling acoustic ensembles, to large electric groups where you have the equivalent of a couple of rock bands playing simultaneously. So I try to have an open mind about what is expected of me because I've been in bands myself, and I know within our band our methodology was different from other bands. I want to give other bands that same freedom to develop their own vocabulary and methodology. What I do is subordinate to what they do, so there isn't really a standard setup.

Given a three-piece rock band, for example, I would prefer to have them try to play live, although not necessarily all in the same room, so that they're interacting with each other and can accommodate each other's little changes in emphasis and timing.

Given a larger ensemble, I've always found that you get better results if it's possible to set everybody up to play live. I've done sessions with as many as 12 or 14 band members playing simultaneously. If it's possible to have everybody play at once, that's the best way to do it.

Do you have standard mics that you use?

Depending upon what the music requires, there is a range of choices to start with. For example, in a drum kit, if the drummer is going for an open, ambient, boomy sound, then the ambient character of the room is really important. But I'll still have close mics on the drums because that's a good way to get a general balance within the drum kit. On bass drum it would depend on whether there was a hole in the front head, or no front head at all, or a closed front head. I normally mic both sides of the bass drum. I'll use either a small lavaliere or a clip-on condenser to mike the beater side of the bass drum. I've used a Crown GLM-100, Shure SM98, or a small dynamic microphone like a Beyer 201 on a little stand by the beater side of the drum. Then if it's a closed front head, I'll use either a large-diaphragm condenser mic like a 414 or an FET 47. Normally I'd use a dynamic mic like a Beyer M88, an AKG D 112, or a really bassy microphone like a Beyer 380 for a really murky, deep, rumbly sound.

If there's a hole in the front head and there's a lot of air coming out of that hole, you have to be careful about where the mic is positioned. I don't have great results with the mic sticking inside the bass drum, but sometimes it sounds quite good with the microphone positioned slightly off center in front of that hole. There I might use an RE20 or a D 112 or a Beyer M88 or occasionally a 421. If there's no front head at all, and it's a very short, dead, thumping kind of sound, then I would put the mic inside the mouth of the bass drum but very close to the beater, and I would probably use either an RE20 or a D 112. I have used other mics, like a Shure SM7, for example.

The idea is that you want to record the bass drum so when you hear it on the speakers in the control room, it sounds like a bass drum. There are quite a few people who opt for a more stylized bass drum sound, where the bass drum doesn't sound like a bass drum but instead sounds like some archetype of a recorded bass drum. I've never had much luck with that. Trying to make it sound like something else always sounds funny to me. I want it to sound pretty much as it does in the room.

The nice thing about having a mic on the beater side as well as the front side is that you can get more attack out of the beater if you need it by balancing that mic against the front mic without having to screw up the sound with EQ. In order to get it to bite more, you don't have to add more high-frequency energy, which can also really exaggerate the spillage from the cymbals and stuff.

What determines what mics you use on the drum kit?

What it should sound like is determined by a conversation with the drummer. Different mics have different character to them. The RE20 has a quite midrange-y sort of popping sound if you're going for a percussive bass drum sound. The D 112 has sort of a hollowed-out sound and doesn't have as much midrange. It has more attack and deep bass. The M88 doesn't have quite as much low energy as a D 112, but it doesn't have as much midrange energy as the RE20, so it's sort of a middle ground between those two. The 421 is much harder-sounding and more pointed. It has reasonable bass response, but it's a more aggressive sound. The condenser mics tend to get used when the bass drum is being played quite softly because you want to pick up the character of the resonance and the character of the front skin.

There's a lot of variation in sound in what you would call the bass drum, so it's important to have a conversation with the drummer and to listen quite closely to what the bass drum actually sounds like.

Do you try to make the sound fit into the rest of the band or just within the kit?

The presumption that I start with is that the drummer already has the sound worked out within the band. I don't work with a lot of bands that are assembled session players. Virtually all the bands that I record are self-contained entities that communicate within themselves in their own way and work out their own problems internally. So if the drummer has got a particular sound to his kit that he likes, I take that to be a part of the innate sound of the band. If somebody doesn't like something at any point, that's your first clue that you have to stop and address something, but I'm not of the opinion that I can discern what the best sound is for the drum kit within a band. I always like to leave those kinds of aesthetic decisions up to the band.

Another thing that I've noticed is that when the drummer has a drum kit that has toms in it, the sort of singing resonance of the toms that goes along with the bass drum can be a big part of the bass drum. Trying to get rid of those rings and resonances is sort of a standard practice, but I've never followed that advice. I like to be able to hear the drum kit as a single instrument rather than as a collection of discrete sounds. For example, when the drummer hits the bass drum, the floor tom goes "Hmmmm." I tend to like that and believe that it's part of the character of the drum kit.

Do you use drum tuners or change heads?

I like to talk to the band before they come in so that they're ready. In the same way that I think it's a good idea for the guitarist to have new strings when he goes in to record, I think it's a good idea for the drums to have new heads. We have drum heads here at the studio so we can swap them out if need be. I tend to think that Remo Ambassador heads record better than other drum heads. Whether clear or coated is sort of a performance choice, but I tend to think that they sound better, or at least are more predictable in their behavior. So I always recommend that the drummer get new heads, and if he doesn't have a preference, I would suggest Ambassadors.

If the drummer needs help tuning his drums I'm happy to help, but generally speaking, a drummer who knows his drum kit and plays regularly will have a preferred sound for his drums, and I don't want to interfere with that.

Do you ever use only two or three mics to capture the sound of the kit?

Yes I do, although it's not a standard thing for me. I've done it when someone is trying to record in an idiomatic way. Some people like the sound of the drums in old Western swing records, where there's a barely discernable drum kit in the background. Some people like the sound of the early Tamala/Motown records, where there's an overhead microphone and maybe a bass drum microphone, and that's the majority of the drum sound. When someone comes into the studio to make something that's making reference to an archetype like that, I like to try to accommodate them rather than recording in a modern fashion and pretending that it's archaic.

I have done some sessions on 8- and 16-track in which it was an aesthetic choice to have a really simplistic sound to the drums where you'll end up using only a couple of mics. I've found that a bass drum mic and a mic on either side of the drum kit, like one by the rack tom and one by the floor tom, is a pretty good way to get a nice, even sound on the drums. Occasionally, just an overhead microphone right over the drummer's head and a bass drum microphone will work. For some reason I've found that ribbon mics work better in that capacity because they have a figure-8 pattern, they tend to attenuate the spillage from the sides of the room, and they keep the hi-hat in particular from becoming overwhelming.

If I'm recording with microphones on either side of the drum kit, then I'll probably use condenser mics, either Schoeps 221s, C 12s, or Sony C-37s.

I recorded an album in northern Ontario in a cabin where we used just a bass drum microphone and two Audio-Technica 4051s as area mics on either side of the drum kit [near the rack tom and another near the floor tom], and that sounded quite good. I'm a big fan of those microphones, especially given how little they cost. I think the 4051s are the bargain of the century.

Do you mike the hi-hat?

No. I will on rare occasion if the drummer is playing really lightly or doing a bunch of tricky stuff that he's really proud of. But generally speaking, there's more hi-hat than you can use. If they came up with a negative microphone that you could suck it out of the record, I would put one up on the hat most of the time.

Do you use the overheads to mike the kit or just as cymbal microphones?

If the drums are being recorded in a live room with a lot of ambient sound, I tend to think that the cymbals sound better that way than with mics right up close to them. I do have overheads up over the drum kit, generally just to correct balance problems with the cymbals. Like if the crash cymbal isn't loud enough, it's nice if there's an overhead mic to bring it up, but I generally prefer the sound of the cymbals at a distance. Of course, it depends what the band is after. There's sort of a '70s characteristic sound where the cymbals are thin and sustaining but there's no real ambience to the sound. It's a dry recording, but there's a lot of sustain on the cymbals. If we're shooting for that sound, it does require you to use close mics rather than ambient mics, and in some cases even use a peak limiter on the overheads so that the snare and toms don't overwhelm the cymbals.

What do you usually use for overheads?

I've had really good luck with Coles and STC 4038 ribbon microphones. I've had good luck using an M-S stereo pair in front of the drum kit, sort of chest high as a cymbal mic. I've used an AKG C 24, the Royer stereo ribbon mic, a Neumann SM 2, a pair of 414s. I've used any number of things for that M-S pair.

For overheads as individual mics on booms over the drum kit, I've had really good luck with Schoeps 221s, an AKG C 60 using omnidirectional capsules, or CK-1 cardioid capsules. I've used 414s. Boy, it's hard to think of something that I haven't used.

Do you tailor your mic selection to the instrument?

To an extent. You can get into a mode where everything is an experiment, and you never make any decisions, and that tends to slow things down. I tend to make a guess as to what should work, and if it doesn't sound like it's doing the job, I like to capitulate immediately and put something else up rather than screwing around forcing it to work. So it's not a long, experimental process, but more like a couple of rapid decisions.

How do you determine where to place the instruments in a room?

If I'm familiar with the studio, like the ones we have here at Electrical Audio, I can tell if a given location is good or bad. The most important things are the band's comfort and their sightlines. There's no point in having one tiny little corner of the room where the drums sound good if the bass player can't see that far. So I tend to avoid the bad spots rather than finding the good spots.

One really revealing thing is to walk around a room and sort of stomp and clap and holler and hear where you're getting reinforcement from the room and hear where it sounds interesting. Wherever you find the place that you like the reflected sound is a good place to start. A lot of studios are designed to have very little reflected energy and support from the room, and those can be frustrating environments to record in. Professionally designed Nashville-style studios can be a real chore to make records in because the rooms don't have any personality. I've found a lot of non-professionally designed studios to be more flattering acoustically.

How do you deal with leakage?

If there are a lot of instruments in the same room, you have to be careful about physically how close they are to one another, what their orientation is, and how close the mics are. If there are many sources in a room, chances are that they're an acoustic ensemble and you're not dealing with high volumes. If there's bleed from one instrument to the other, it normally sounds sympathetic and nice.

So you usually use the iso rooms instead?

Yeah, normally if it's a three-piece rock band there will probably be one room that's an isolation room that will probably have the amplifiers in it. The hardest thing to manage in terms of bleed is if you have really quiet instruments and really loud ones playing in the ensemble, like if you have a violinist playing with a rock band. Then you have to find a location for the violinist where there's enough air around the violin to make it sound normal with a reasonable sightline so he can see what he's doing. But you have to make sure the violin isn't so close to the drums or amplifiers that the violin mic is overwhelmed.

Surprisingly enough, instruments like accordion, frame drum, or things like that are easy to deal with because you can take a small lavaliere and physically mount it to the instrument so it's right by the sound source. You don't need very much gain on that microphone at all, and it's not going to pick up very much bleed. It's much harder to do with instruments like piano or acoustic guitar or mandolin because if you have the mic close to the strings on those instruments, it sounds funny.

Generally speaking, if you have a large ensemble, you try to put physical space between them, and then you try to put the loud instruments in one room and the quiet ones in another one if possible.

What do you use for microphone preamps?

I've used them all, and there are very few that I've not been able to find a use for. We have about 10 Ampex 351 modules that we've modified into mic preamps, and I really love the way they sound, especially if you're using a ribbon or dynamic microphone. It seems like the way they interface with those dynamic systems is just a natural match. They were similar eras of technology designed to work together.

I really love the GML mic preamps. They're dead clean and have a lot of gain and great bass response. I also really like the John Hardy mic preamps. They're clean, really great-sounding, really reliable, and have great metering. We've got a lot of these Sytek mic preamps, which are rather inexpensive but are on par with the others that I just mentioned. They sound different, a little crispier-sounding with a little more extreme high end, but they have loads of gain and are quiet and totally reliable.

The console preamps in our Neotek consoles are also really nice. I use them far more than I use the console preamps when in other studios. The older one that we have, the Series II, has a slightly thicker sound that's really good for rock music and bass and drums. The newer Elite, I don't hesitate to use the preamps on anything.

How do you determine what preamps to use? Is it a preferred combination with a mic?

Generally speaking, it's more of a logistical factor. Like if I have four mics up on the guitars, I'll want to use a four-channel preamp so that they're all in the same place. If I have three vocal mics up that we're experimenting with, then I'd like to have them all in the same place. Again, there's no real exhaustive search done to try to find the perfect preamp. It's more a matter of making sure that whatever choice you make doesn't cause problems.

How did you learn your mic technique? Did you learn from someone?

I did learn some stuff from people who I worked with a long time ago: Ian Burgess, who's an engineer from Chicago, and an English engineer, John Loder, who I worked with a long time ago and who I learned some stuff from. Most of what I've learned about microphones, though, has come from reading and experimenting, in that order. I'd read something that would tweak my interest, so I would try it. I also made a point of making notes of anything I did that sounded good rather than thinking it was a lucky accident. So I did develop my own vocabulary and my own range of experience that way.

What do you use on snare?

I had the hardest time with snare drum when I first started making records. When you listen to a snare when you're sitting at the drums, it can have this really explosive sound, and it can have a really subtle sound. I was never happy with the sound of snare drum on other people's records. It didn't sound like a snare drum to me and usually sounded like some stylized version of a snare drum. So I experimented for a long time before I found something that I was happy with.

The first thing I found that I was happy with was using a Beyer 201 dynamic mic with a small condenser microphone, like a Shure SM98 or AKG 451, strapped to the side of it, with their diaphragms aligned. I used that combination quite a bit because every time I tried something else, it wouldn't sound right. The stock solutions, like an SM57 or a 421, just never did it for me. Every time I would open the fader on one of those, it would just sound wrong. So I like that combination on the top of the snare. It seems like I can vary the balance between those two and get a crisp sound or a thick sound or a popping midrange sound. With a flexible combination of those two, I could either satisfy myself or satisfy the drummer.

Then I went off on another experimenting tangent maybe five years ago. I kept putting other microphones up against this pair that I was used to using, just to see if I could find another option in case I didn't have that pair to fall back on.

I did happen to find a couple of mics that I like on snare drum. For rock drumming, there's this small tube Altec model 75 that sounds quite good. It doesn't clip. There might be some mild distortion, but it sounds good. I've also used a Sony C-37, which was a real shocker. I didn't expect that one to work out, but that mic sounds great on snare drum, especially on a bright but bassy, flat, funky snare drum. And those are the only mics that I've had good results on.

I've occasionally used a bottom mic, but it doesn't get used a lot.

How do you place it?

Someplace where it won't get hit. [Laughs] But that's not even the biggest problem. You want it somewhere where it's out of the drummer's way. You don't want it to interfere with what he's doing, and you don't want the drummer to be preoccupied about not hitting the microphone. Every drummer's set is slightly different, so you try to find a place where it's not going to pick up too much of the hi-hat and it's not going to be in the way of the drummer.

It's nice if you can get a few inches of distance between the snare drum mic and the snare drum, but you have to put it where it will go rather than making the drummer work around it.

How about toms?

For years I used AKG 451s on small toms and AKG 414s on big ones. Occasionally I would use 414s on everything, but 451s had a really great, focused attack and nice, clear, resonant bass. But because the matching on those mics is a little sketchy to start with and because they'd get banged up all the time, I started looking for something to replace them with. The real inspiration for this was that AKG discontinued the 451, and almost instantly those mics were being sold by equipment brokers as "vintage." These used to be a commodity item that you could pick up for $100, and suddenly they were $500. The new reissue of the 451 is completely different and nothing like an original 451, so I had to look for something else.

I talked to a number of microphone manufacturers about commissioning them to make a microphone for me, but no one was interested. What I needed was a high-quality condenser microphone with a small diaphragm that was either side-firing, so I could place it over a tom without it sticking out in the drummer's way, or with a rotating capsule, like the old 451s. Nobody had a product that was equivalent until I talked to David Josephson. I had used some of his microphones in a studio in Japan and found them to be really good general-purpose condenser microphones. He thought it would be an interesting project, so over the course of about two years we went back and forth, and he ended up designing a capsule that would fit on his standard head amplifier that was a side-firing single-membrane cardioid microphone. I think it's called the CK 46. I bought a half dozen from him, and he entered it into his product line.

That mic solved so many problems for me. The housing is rugged, it's a heavy-duty brass housing; and it's a side-firing microphone so it doesn't get in the drummer's way. It's great-sounding, and I use it every day. It's also a good general-purpose condenser microphone. It does a good job on mandolin or banjo, which tend to get thin and stringy-sounding, but it sounds good on those instruments and keeps them from getting too brittle. I've also used it on electric guitar cabinets. But for recording drums, it's the bee's knees. I don't think I have a suitable replacement.

Electric bass: Do you mike or take it direct?

It's rare that I take a direct signal on a bass guitar. Again, I think that the bass player's choice of amplifiers defines the character of his playing and the band, so I tend to try to record the bass amplifier so it sounds the same as when you listen to it in the room. I generally use a couple of microphones, one which is brighter than the other, because depending on the balance of the song, you might have to increase the edginess of the bass to make it poke through more.

One mic that I use all the time is a Beyer 380, which is a very wooly and deep microphone that has a lot of super low end. It's a figure-8 mic so it has a huge proximity effect. If you move it in close on the speaker cabinet, you get all the low end you would ever want. Then I'll generally have a condenser mic as well, like a 451 or a 414, or an Audio-Technica 4033, or an FET 47, or any number of things to complement it.

I will occasionally take a direct signal off the bass if I'm asked to. I'm not crazy about the sound of it. It sounds kind of phony to me, but there's a way that you can incorporate it into the miked sound. The miked and direct signals are never quite in phase with each other, so I've taken to using an analog delay line and sweeping it right around a half a millisecond to bring it back in phase.

I place the mics generally fairly close and in the center of the loudspeaker, but far enough away that none of the excursion of the speaker will run into the microphone.

Guitars: Where do you place the mics?

Electric guitar mics tend to be farther away from the cabinet because if you're really close to the speaker, then the acoustic interactions with the cabinet are more localized. If you pull the mic farther away, then you get a more coherent sound from the cabinet as a whole. I have used all sorts of mics on electric guitars, but I really like ribbon mics on them. I think the 4038 sounds great and the Royer 121 sounds great. Old RCA BK-5s and 44s sound good on small cabinets if you have to beef it up.

One mic or multiple mics?

Normally I'll have a bright mic and a dark mic on the cabinet, like a condenser and a ribbon mic. Since all the speakers in a cabinet sound different, I try to find one that's appropriate for the ribbon mic and another one that's appropriate for the condenser.

I don't have a lot of luck on guitar cabinets, I have to admit. The traditional SM57 or Sennheiser 421 or 409 I haven't had a lot of luck with.

I actually never even owned a 57 until recently. I had to buy one because somebody wanted it, but I had gone nearly 20 years without one.

What do you use on vocals?

That's a real can of worms. There are as many vocal microphones and vocal styles as people singing. I know a lot of people just throw up a U 47 and call it quits. I have used a U 47 with good results, but I can't say that it's my #1 favorite vocal mic.

If I have a #1 favorite vocal mic, it's probably the Josephson microphone called the 700. I've used that quite a bit. But even as great a microphone as it is and as much use as I get out of it, it's not appropriate for fully 75 percent of the people I work with. I end up using everything from RE20s to old tube mics to ribbon mics. It totally depends upon the singer and the delivery. This is one area that you really can go around in circles looking for something that sounds good.

So your mic selection is based on how it makes the vocal sit in the track?

If someone's voice is the center of attention in the music, I like to be able to just listen to that and have it be satisfying. If you're listening to the voice by itself, it should make you think, "That sounds really great." If that's the center of attention, then you want to make sure that it's a rewarding listen.

How about piano?

I've had really good luck with the Neumann SM 2 stereo mic over the piano. AKG C 12s and C 24s sound great, too. Those Audio-Technica 4051s are great piano mics. I'll usually place them perpendicular to the harp, one on the long strings and one on the short strings. You have to shuffle them in and out until the stereo image sounds normal. The SM 2 I'll put in front of the piano with the lid open, sort of looking in on the strings. Same with the C 24.

How do you approach acoustic guitars?

With acoustic guitars it depends on whether there's going to be singing simultaneously with the acoustics. If there is, then you have to try to make the mics not favor the vocal. If there's no singing, then you can record the instrument at a distance and pick up some room sound, and that's nice. Normally I try to have a stereo image either from the audience's perspective or the player's perspective. The Neumann SM 2 is a great acoustic mic. Schoeps 221s are great. I've used the ATM4051 at a distance. They get a bit brittle if you get too close.

If you have an instrument that's really stringy and thin-sounding, a ribbon mic up close tends to make it sound a bit heftier. The same basic thing holds true for things like mandolin and banjo. With banjo you have to be careful because it's a brittle instrument, and you have to use a darker microphone.

Just out of curiosity, do you record to tape? You sound like an analog guy.

Oh, yeah. There's still way too many problems with digital recording. I don't like what it's done to music. It's completely changed the way music sounds. I think it'll be one of those signifying trends that when we listen to music from this period, people will be able to pick those records out and laugh at them because they followed all the conventions of the day. The way digital recording has changed the way records are made has created this whole new vocabulary of clichés that is scarring music really badly. But I think it's a fad. People will go back to making records in studios when people get tired of making records in their practice rooms. There's a big inflation in the number of people making records and a big dilution in the quality of the recording. That will play itself out, and it will stabilize again. It's exactly the same way as in the '80s, when everyone was using drum machines and drummers were looking for work. It looked like it was the beginning of the end, but that played itself out and things got back to normal. It's the same thing with this.

CHAPTER 15

Michael Beinhorn

With credits including Aerosmith, Soundgarden, Soul Asylum, Red Hot Chili Peppers, Ozzy Osbourne, Fuel, Korn, and Marilyn Manson, producer Michael Beinhorn is no stranger to music that rocks. But unlike many others who work in that genre, Michael approaches the music with a care and concern usually associated with more traditional styles of acoustic music. And as you'll read, he's elegantly outspoken on the current state of modern recording.

How much do you engineer?

I try to avoid it entirely. [Laughs]

But you still have your fingers in it because you obviously know what you're doing and you know the tools.

That's hopefully what I bring to the work that I do. To me it's fun, but there's also an amount of responsibility. I think if I'm going to have some sort of say in how a recording is done, then I should know a little something about what the tools can do. I should know what kind of SPL a certain mic can stand, or what the mic can actually do, or what types of things it doesn't marry best to.

I understand that you have a tremendous vintage microphone collection.

I've got a couple. Actually, more like 17.

What got you on the quest for vintage mics?

To me, if you are able to have access to them, you can't really have enough of them. [Laughs] Especially pertaining to vocalists, because a different microphone will marry better to a different person's voice. There's no one microphone that does every single thing. You're not going to take a U 47 and use it on every single vocalist just because it's your favorite mic and it works great. That being said, it's a great workhorse mic, and as tube mics go, it's one of the best for multiple varieties of tasks. But they all serve a different function.

For me these things are like the tools that an artist uses. It's like the palette, the paint, and the colors. But there are things that are being made today that are every bit as essential as those old microphones are. I've been using a lot of Audio-Technica stuff, and I've found that for the functions they serve, there really isn't anything I've heard that is comparable. There's a certain amount of speed in regard to transient response that you can't get with the older stuff. [In the old days] they weren't thinking about how fast you could reproduce a sound; they were just concerned about capturing it, although after a while with a greater degree of accuracy.

How much pre-production do you usually do?

Whatever it takes. It's a broad answer, but it's a broad question. Some bands are rehearsed and prepared and have their songs written, and maybe all they need is to have a couple of arrangement alterations, but other bands may require months. I worked with a band where their pre-production took about seven months. They also didn't have any of their songs written, so that was somewhat of an issue too. [Laughs]

When you're doing pre-production with someone you've worked with before, does it go faster or slower?

It's not something that I have a whole lot of experience with, to be perfectly honest with you. That's really only happened one time, and there wasn't any difference. Really, it has more to do with what the circumstances dictate. Sometimes, if the band has achieved a certain amount of notoriety, they're more likely to have more of a lackadaisical attitude about things, and that just equals more time spent.

When you're tracking, what's the most important thing for you in terms of setting the vibe?

Making sure that the band is well rehearsed and they know their music. You can coddle people all you want and act like a cheerleader, but at the end of the day if they don't have their songs rehearsed, there's no amount of glad-handing that's going to be more effective than if they know every single thing that they're supposed to play. If you want to make variations on that, and if everyone's okay with it, then it's cool, but if people don't feel good about what they're doing and have some sort of confidence, then there's no amount of cheerleading that you can do to help them. That's like the greatest vibe killer in the world as far as I'm concerned.

Once a song is played and done really well, there's such a sense of relief and at the same time happiness about hearing something sound so good. That's the thing that really makes it all move.

Do you feel that you contribute to their confidence level?

I can't say for sure, not being able to get inside someone else's head, but I can assure you that once someone has done something well, they have to beat me down with a stick because I'm usually incredibly enthusiastic about it.

Do you usually try to track with a full band and try to keep everything?

I usually try to keep everything, but the reality is that stuff, in my experience, tends to get a little more forensic and clinical. So no matter how much we keep in the end from the actual tracking, what's used is pretty minimal.

I don't like to dictate to people how their records should go, but I think it should be illustrated to the individuals I'm working with that we find a method that works. Sometimes it involves the whole band playing, but I haven't found that to be the case unless the band has developed some kind of ideology that really involves them playing constantly together. Generally speaking, if you don't have that, I haven't found that people are going to give the type of performance that I want to put on a record. But I'll try everything to achieve that goal. Lately, what I've done a lot is to just start out by recording the drummer.

What does the drummer play to? The rest of the band or just a guitar or something?

It's really at his discretion initially. I find that a lot of times, in the bands I seem to work with, the drummer is a fantastically good musician. The only problem is that when you hear him on a record, he's playing like shit, and the main reason is that he's not listening to himself. He's listening to somebody else perform. What that means is he's not listening to his own internal sense of time; he's listening to somebody else's. Usually it's one of the guitarists, because they can't hear the bass in a live situation, so they gravitate to the guitar. It's like a natural kind of impulse. There are very few drummers who listen to what they're doing exclusively and use everyone else as sort of a reference.

It's hard to explain, but I sort of go for a sense of interdependence rather than people performing independently. The drummer, who's the backbone of just about whatever musical endeavor you're in, is pretty much existing in his own framework, and his dominance of the band from a rhythmic perspective is unsurpassed when cutting his track.

Do you have him play to a click?

Only if he wants to. I personally would rather hear the drummer's natural time. Unless the drummer insists on using a click, I'm not going to make a fuss about it. The only time I feel a click is necessary is when the drummer might be playing along with loops, and even then it's something that needs to be addressed, because there's also something nice about a drummer playing out of time a little bit with a loop.

My feeling is that if you have a drummer play to click and then edit him and line him up in Pro Tools or something like that, you might as well have gotten a drum machine to do the same thing. So why are we spending all this money tracking these drums? You could program the whole thing and pretty much get the same exact effect.

So you don't mind things breathing and pushing and pulling?

No, as a matter of fact, I think it's essential. You don't want a sloppy drum track, but at the same time, if you don't get a sense of a person's natural groove or rhythm, you might as well get a drum machine. For some types of records I think it's ideal, but for the type of records I've made, it's kind of pointless.

Is your approach in the studio the same for each artist?

I think it's good to go in with a plan but at the same time it's also good to expect the unexpected. You never know when something is going to change. You never know when someone is going to flip out and go crazy. On this last project that I was working on, they asked to do the guitars first and the bass afterwards. I've never done a record like that before, but what are you going to say to them: "No, I don't work like that. No, it messes up my flow?" [Laughs] They wanted to work like that, so I said, "Fine, okay."

What's the hardest thing for you to do in the studio?

Mix. I'm a shitty mixer. In all honesty, I haven't devoted myself to it, so I can't say that with absolute certainty. But I don't fancy myself to be that guy.

There's so many "specialists" these days anyway.

I'd like to eliminate the specialism of recording. The concept of a mixer has always been "bring in a guy at the end who has a fresh perspective" or "more objective" or whatever you want to call it. I began to realize that it's kind of a con that the record companies do. It's something they've come to rely upon as sort of a security blanket, and it also stems from the fact that in the old days mix engineers were generally the people who recorded it.

They were referred to as "balance engineers" because everything had been recorded to taste just the way they wanted it. At that point it was just a question of balancing everything properly. Nowadays we can't make a record without a "mix engineer" attached to it. I don't think that model will continue. It can continue, but it's going to become irrelevant pretty soon, especially if people ever learn how to record properly.

And this is a tremendous issue, as I'm sure you're aware, and one of the reasons why you seem to have gotten in touch with me. There are a lot of people now who have a tremendous problem with way records are made regarding the lack of quality and so on.

The reality of the situation is that traditionally when people had less to work with, they were more creative. You're throwing a whole bunch of recording techniques at people that look easier, but deceptively so, as they really aren't. Digital recording is way more complicated than analog ever was. So you have this problem right now where you have this tremendous "de-evolution" of the technique of recording where there's not enough consideration about what goes into making a good-sounding record. On the one hand, there are people who say, "What difference does it make? No one really cares anyway." But I think the only people who don't really care are the people at record companies who want the record done for X amount of dollars, who say, "Just get the thing done. Just do it fast and do it cheap." That sends a very negative message to people and takes quality control out of the picture. Fast, cheap, and good—you can only have two! [Laughs]

If you really know what you are doing, you can make a good-sounding recording with Pro Tools, but it only happens like two times out of a hundred. Most guys who are recording at home don't realize that the internal clocking on Pro Tools sucks. Nowadays with the HD system, you can't even clock it to anything else or even use outboard converters if you want to. I want a modular recording system. I want to be able to pick my clock and converters. I like the Euphonix R-1, but I prefer the dB Technologies Blue converters. I want to clock it with a Lucid rather than the internal clock. I want those choices, but Digi isn't giving me those choices.

The problem is that the world wants convenience. We've been turned into a culture of convenience addicts, all of which is fine and good because we can expedite whatever functions we happen to be performing in our daily lives. What it does for the quality of that function is a completely separate issue. So the question becomes, "Is faster really better or more efficient?" Is quality such a necessary aspect in recording anymore? The answer isn't necessarily no, it's more like maybe.

Some of the acts you produce have a lot of distorted layered guitars and distorted things that some say don't necessarily need to be recorded pristinely.

That's the whole point of why it makes sense to do that there. The reality of the situation is that harmonically, there are immense similarities between a symphony orchestra and a band that uses multi-tracked, multi-layered distorted guitars. Really, from a harmonic standpoint, there's no difference at all between the functions that these types of things serve. They're essentially operating in the same general frequency range. Guitars and string sections; it's all the same. I believe you get the same psychological effect that you get from a group of violins that have been miked closely to pick up the grit as you do on the electric guitar. The electric guitar is a very complex sound. How the distortion works and what you do with it are key to being able to understand it. Distortion is a very important thing in modern recording. Things like how it's dealt with, what function it serves, where it sits in the mix, and how you get separation are all important.

If you're dealing with a band that has two guitarists, both of whom use extremely distorted sounds, like in a situation such as Korn, what distinguishes a record that you would make from any other record? Being able to perceive what's going on [between the parts on the record]. Tape compression is not your friend at this point. It's only going to obscure these issues. In the meantime, those issues, to me, are paramount. I would like to make a record, and I try to with those guys, where you can hear aspects to the sound that you wouldn't otherwise. Unfortunately, this is not a popular viewpoint, owing to the fact that bands of this genre are seen as a bastard form—something like an aberration that may someday go away if we close our eyes long enough so we don't have to deal with it anymore. Most label people are highly dismissive. They don't treat it with the care that any form of art deserves. They're willing to shine it on as a bunch of distorted guitars by a "kid who can't play anyhow." That's the reason why I try to do it as best as I can. To try to stand away from the pack and fight mediocrity. That's what I care about.

Do you go for perfection or vibe?

What is perfection, first of all? To me, perfection is the vibe. To me, perfection is the feeling you get when someone is giving a great performance. The reality of the situation is this: Listen to a Led Zeppelin record. Those drum tracks are pristine. Now listen closely to how Bonham is playing; the guy is all over the place. He's slowing down and speeding up. There's no consistency at all. But you get the vibe that this is not someone to be trifled with, and he's holding the whole band together.

If you want to listen to perfection and something that's lined up to the nearest sixteenth note, get a dance record. By the way, I happen to love electronic music, and it's one of my first loves, but it's a different type of music. It's a different aesthetic, so don't make the comparison. Don't hold them up to the same reference.

In the '80s people started doing everything with clicks and chopping tape like maniacs and making everything as tight as they possibly could. While production went to a new level as far as how anal people could get about things, it also took a lot of the life out of music.

Beat Detective and Auto-Tune do the same thing.

Again, these are tools that, in the right hands, can make creative music. But in the wrong hands of people who are just trying to work as quickly as they can and have no interest in things having some sort of feeling or atmosphere to them, then they're more like a gun that's used to kill people rather than to protect them.

What advice would you give to someone starting out about how to make his or her recordings better?

I don't think there's any one piece of advice that you can give somebody. Most people don't know how to record, so learn how to engineer the right way—and I don't mean by going to a recording school. From a technical side, make sure that your source is the best that it can possibly be and make sure that whatever you're picking it up with is the best transducer you can possibly afford.

The reality is that there's a chance that in spite of all this, you could make one of these crappy recordings that everyone else is making these days and wind up with a record that sells 3 or 4 million records and be riding around in a Lamborghini. But all that sort of stuff is short-lived if you still don't know how to set a microphone up.

The bottom line is this: If you're not willing to devote yourself heart and soul to recording, you may as well not get into it. The key to me is devotion and respect for the people who are listening to what you do, so you have to try to make something of lasting value.

CHAPTER 16

Michael Bishop

There are few more versatile engineers today than Michael Bishop, who easily switches between the classical, jazz, and pop worlds. Shunning the current recording method requiring massive overdubbing, Michael instead mostly utilizes the old-school method of mixing live on the fly, with spectacular results. Working exclusively for the audiophile Telarc label, Michael's highly regarded recordings have become reference points for the well done.

Do you have a particular recording philosophy?

Yes. I like to get out of the way of the musician's intentions and be as transparent as possible to the end listener.

For acoustic music I'm hopefully not reinterpreting the musicians' intent. I want them to interpret what they're doing and keep the recording path as clear as possible, which will allow that. That includes everything from what type of microphones I choose, to what position they'll be in, to the cable and preamp and master recording system used.

That's for acoustic music, of course. Once you get into regular studio pop or jazz or blues, then it's a completely different animal in that now it's completely open to interpretation.

Let's go there for a second. I know you do a lot of sessions where the mix is done on the fly, either direct to two-track or multitrack with no overdubs. How do you handle leakage?

I let leakage be my friend. Leakage is inevitable for the kind of recording I'm doing because I like to keep the musicians together as a group in the studio, rather than spreading them all out with isolation for everybody. I keep them together in as live a setting as is possible. That means there's plenty of leakage, and I just deal with it. I don't have to have the isolation because typically I'm not doing overdubs and replacement of tracks. We fix things by doing new takes to cover the spots we need to cover. They'll take a running start at it to cover the measures that they need, and we'll edit it later, which is very much a classical orchestra style of recording.

By keeping people close together, the leakage generally becomes less of a problem. The farther apart you get the musicians and the more things you put in between causes delays and coloration, particularly on the off-axis side of a microphone, which is already colored. This only exaggerates the effect of the leakage. That's something I learned from John Eargle's very first microphone handbook.

How did you learn your microphone technique? Did you learn it empirically or did you have a mentor?

I had a mentor who hired me for my very first studio job; his name is Ken Hamann. Ken did a lot of classical and jazz recordings in the '50s and went on to do some rock stuff at Cleveland Studios, like Grand Funk Railroad, James Gang, Bloodrock, Outsiders, and things like that. I could only follow his example because he never really answered questions. I could see what he was doing and make notes, but he never gave me any formal instruction. So most of my early microphone technique education was empirical, by watching his example and testing it on my own, but I didn't really know why something worked well until I picked up that first edition of the *Microphone Handbook* [by John Eargle]. I studied that thing from one end to the other, as there weren't any other publications like it at that time [the early '70s]. So that book really told me why I should be using a particular microphone in a particular situation, or why I wanted to use it, or why I liked a particular microphone in a particular situation. It taught me the characteristics of the different types of microphones and how to know your tools thoroughly.

So that changed everything, as it taught me that everything I knew was wrong! [Laughs] After that, I started using omnis [microphones with an omnidirectional polar pattern] a whole lot more in the studio, where I was doing primarily rock recordings and jingles at the time. Using omnis, I started to learn how to work with the leakage in the room and make it a pleasant experience instead of something to be avoided. Luckily, that carried on through my work here at Telarc, where we're recording everything direct to two- and six-channel.

Are you still using primarily omnis?

I like to start with an omni before anything. Now there are particular instances where I'll immediately go to something like a figure-8, but I'll use figure-8s and omnis more than anything.

I do, too. I learned early on that they sound better than anything more directional in most cases.

I wish I would've learned that earlier.

Does the type of music you're recording determine your microphone selection?

Of course, because there are certain things that the musicians or the producer or even the end listener expects to hear on a particular style. Like if it's a straight-ahead blues recording, then there's a sort of sound that's typical of a drum kit on that kind of recording. So you use something fairly raunchy, like a 414, in places, where on a jazz date I might use a 4006 or a Sennheiser condenser. Or there's the plain old thing of putting a 57 on a guitar amp where it just works, so why reinvent the wheel?

What's the hardest thing for you to record?

A very small acoustic ensemble or a solo acoustic instrument, but particularly small acoustic ensembles, like a string quartet. They have less to hide behind, and I have less to hide behind. [Laughs] Actually, I think recording a symphony orchestra is fairly easy in comparison to a string quartet. It's pretty easy to present this huge instrument, which is an orchestra, because just the size and numbers can give a good impression almost no matter what you might do. You have to really screw it up to do badly there. But a string quartet is really difficult because you can hear every little detail, and the imaging is critical, particularly if you're working in stereo. It's really hard to convey a quartet across two channels and get proper placement and imaging of that group. That's one of most difficult tasks right there. It becomes easier in surround.

Is your approach different if you know that the end product will be in surround instead of stereo?

Absolutely, because a stereo recording has to present width, depth, and all of the correct proportions of direct to ambient sound, and in surround you have more channels to present those aspects.

Is your approach similar to the norm when recording an orchestra, with a Decca Tree and house mics?

My approach on an orchestra has never been with a Decca Tree. It started out very much following along in the steps of Jack Renner, who originally hired me here at Telarc and who developed the well-established Telarc sound on an orchestra that this label is known for. So I needed to be able to continue that tradition of the so-called "Telarc Sound." At that time, when I first started here, Jack was typically recording with three omnis across the front of an orchestra and perhaps two omnis out in the hall, and that was it. So I followed along in that tradition until I came up with something of my own to contribute.

I changed it from the three omnis across the front to four omnis across the front with the two center mics being 24 inches apart, so it was a little like a half of a Decca Tree in the middle, but the positioning was very different. A Decca Tree typically has that center front M50 [or whatever microphone] well up above the conductor and into the orchestra somewhat. That, to me, presents a sort of a smear when the mics are combined because of the time-delay differences between the front microphone that's ahead of the other two mics. These delays destroy some of the imaging and produce a bit of comb filtering to my ears, which is why I never liked the Decca Tree. If you were taking those microphones and just feeding three separate channels it would be okay, but that's not how it's used.

So having the microphones in a straight line across the front gave a clearer sound, and I could get perfectly good focusing with careful placement of those two center microphones to get good imaging through the middle of the orchestra. That's one thing that I always look for—the imaging across the orchestra that lets me feel where each musician is on stage. Use of spot mics pretty much destroys that, so I tend to shy away from using them.

Anyway, I quickly moved from that to using a Neumann KU 100 dummy head in the middle as part of the quest for better imaging across the middle. It got in there by accident. I was really just trying it as sort of a surround pickup and experimenting with binaural, and one time I got brave and threw it up there in front over the conductor, and that became the main stereo pickup on the orchestra with omni outriggers out on the flanks.

What do you do for the hall?

For stereo I continue to use a couple of omnis out in the middle point of the hall, but when I started actively doing surround some years ago, that wasn't satisfactory anymore for the rear channels. They were too far removed in that they got the reverb, but the sound was always somewhat disconnected from the front channels.

So early on I brought my surround mics fairly close up to the stage and started to experiment with a number of different setups, which I'm still fine-tuning, and I probably forever will be because it's such a difficult thing to capture properly. Often those surround mics are anywhere from 15 to 20 feet out from the edge of the stage, depending upon the house. They're not out very far at all. The most common surround pickup that

306

I've been using is two M-S pairs out there, looking forward and back on each side. They would be assigned to Left Front/Left Rear and Right Front/Right Rear as far as the decoding output of the double M-S pair. So I'll be using a figure-8 and a supercardioid, usually the Sennheiser MKH 30 and MKH 50, which are the easiest ones to use in this case. I like the sound of those microphones. Often I'll be using the Sennheiser omnis as the flanks to the KU 100. Sometimes they'll be Schoeps, depending upon the music and the hall.

How much time do you have to experiment on sounds in a new hall?

Luckily, I'm pretty good at enrolling people to go along with my crazy ideas. I'll get the orchestra management to allow me to hang microphones during the orchestra rehearsals in the days leading up to the session. I'd like to have a good day during their rehearsal time to experiment with placement. I'll always get up on a ladder and get up in the air to listen for where the sweet spots are. There's that magic blend up there that just doesn't seem to happen out in the house. So I'll find the right height and distance for my mics relative to the orchestra and try them there during the rehearsal if at all possible. This is probably against all AF of M [American Federation of Musicians] rules, but I don't ever roll tape when doing that sort of thing, so there's no danger of using material that isn't paid for. But this is all due to the good graces of the management of the orchestra that I can even attempt this.

In cases where we can't do this, all I have is what the AF of M allows, which is technically five minutes at the top of the session. That's one of the drawbacks of recording in the States, which is where I work most of the time. Jack Renner is doing most of Telarc's overseas recording, and there you have the luxury of being able to have mics up and do extensive sound checks during rehearsal. Of course, the time there is not as tight either, because you're not restricted to the three- and four-hour typical orchestral session.

Have you done any experimenting with the surround mics that are presently available, like the SoundField or Atmos?

I've used the SoundField on a number of sound effects recordings. I tried it briefly on a couple of sessions and came to the conclusion that I really didn't like that much of a point source for picking up either stereo or surround. While it was technically correct and it's a wonderful way of manipulating the sound later, there's something about the musicality of it that I didn't like. It doesn't have the width that I look for either, which is something that I'm accustomed to getting with spaced omnis and the various combinations that I use.

The other thing that I've tried is the Schoeps Sphere, which is an excellent means of recording surround, particularly in the Jerry Bruck combination of figure-8s combined with the brightening center in the sphere. But it's somewhat limited for the type of recording that I typically do with an orchestra.

I haven't tried the Holophone or the Atmos. Most of these are interesting concepts, but they don't give me the leeway that I like to have with separate microphones, where you can fit the microphone to the situation. It's too much like doing broadcast recording, and people who do broadcast recording have their hands tied severely.

The thing I like about the Holophone is the height element.

Yeah, that's a nice element to have built into a system. I have to do that separately because I have recorded the height channel for a couple of years. It doesn't often make it out onto a release, but I record it.

Do you fold it back into the other channels?

I haven't had very good luck with that without having it smear things up. I treat it as a separate element now that we can put out six-channel releases. I wasn't using it on our first DTS-encoded releases because typically that channel wouldn't be coming out as a full-range channel anyway, but I started recording it back then. Now that we have a way to put it out, I am including it in the mix. We don't say anything about it in the notes on the SACD because it seems to confuse the consumer. They'll say, "I don't have a height channel, so will I be able to play your recording?" So we don't want to put that doubt in people's mind while surround music is just getting started. We're trying to clear the doubts and make it more user friendly, I hope.

What I'm doing is recording the height channel on a typical orchestral recording and then making a combination LFE and height channel that are band-split, since the height channel doesn't need any low end and even any extreme high end.

What I like about the height channel on the Holophone is that it gives you the ability to add a little of it back into the other five channels. But as you say, if you add too much it's just like reverb in that it washes out really quickly. Seven or eight percent really brings the recording to life, though.

Yeah, it doesn't take much. The height channel's very minimally used even when I'm using it as a separate component in a playback system. The level is perhaps 12 dB down from the main channels, but if you remove it you notice that, "Gee, this isn't as nice." But the one place that I have folded it in is sometimes in the rear channels, in an effort for the rear channels to better connect to the front channels. The biggest stumbling block on any surround recording is to get that connection between rear and front, since we can't hear the phantom imaging to the sides. Our hearing mechanism isn't much help to connect those front and rear channels to get a really convincing reproduction of the space you were in. So we're playing with smoke and mirrors to get that illusion, and playing with pan pots or miking to get the orchestra to somewhat wrap around the listener a little bit. That's where a height channel—and it only needs to be a very small speaker somewhere over and behind the listener's head—can bridge that gap. Tom Jung has been doing the very same work and using the height in the very same way, but I have to imagine that the two people out in the world who can play it are enjoying it. [Laughs]

Do you start with the same setup every time?

Every session is unique, but there are places that I visit regularly [in an orchestral setting], so I know where to start on those. But there are still a lot of things that need to be different given the piece of music that we're recording.

How about the electronics?

The electronics are steady. I use a standard setup of Millennia Media pre-amps all around.

What's your approach to doing an ensemble in the studio?

There the performer is taken out of the natural setting of a performance space, which you are trying to re-create because you don't usually want to represent a studio sound. Since people are goboed off and set up more for sightlines than for anything else, you're not necessarily presented with a nice acoustic blend out in the studio, so there isn't a whole lot to record ambience on. But if I'm in a situation where I'm in a tracking and overdub situation, I will often record, if the tracks allow, at least a three-track pickup. Like for a sax overdub, there'll be a single pickup for the sax with at least a stereo ambient pickup, which will give me something to work with later on.

How far away is the ambient mic?

Oh, not very far away at all—maybe 6 feet. If that doesn't get enough ambience, I might change the mics to cardioid and flip them around to face away from the instrument. One thing that I've been working with a lot has been double dummy heads (Neumann KU 100s)—one facing the instrument or ensemble and the other with its back to the ensemble and pointed upward and away from the group, up into the room.

I tried this a couple of years ago with a small acoustic ensemble in a little performance space outside of Baltimore. I had a second borrowed head that I just put out there to try. It didn't sound right facing the group, but as soon as I turned it around facing the room—and this is with a spacing of only 3 to 5 feet between the two heads—it became a 3D sort of experience with four channels only. I did add a center mic [an MKH 50] to solidify some stuff that was further in to the stage, and that helped.

Were the mics back to back?

They were back to back with hardly any spacing. If you listen to the rear channels only, it sounds like almost the same recording as the front channels except that the timbre has changed because it's coming in at the back of the head. So now the high frequencies are somewhat muted, and of course the delays are somewhat different. The combination with the front head was just about ghostly.

CHAPTER 17

Bruce Botnick

Few engineers have the perspective on recording that Bruce Botnick has. After starting his career in the thick of the L.A. rock scene recording hits for the Doors, the Beach Boys, Buffalo Springfield, the Turtles, and Marvin Gaye, Bruce became one of the most in-demand movie soundtrack recordists and mixers, with blockbuster credits such as *Star Trek*, *Poltergeist*, *Air Force One*, *Aladdin*, *Mulan*, *ET*, and *The Sum of All Fears*, *Scooby Doo*, and *Star Trek: Nemesis*. Always on the cutting edge of technology, Bruce has elevated the art of orchestral recording to new heights.

How do you approach an orchestral session? How is it different from a rock-and-roll session?

They're mutually exclusive. On a rock-and-roll date, there's more close-miking than in orchestral recording, which uses mostly distance microphones. Back when I started in the early '60s, I learned from Ted Keep, Val Valentine, John Paladino, and Armin Steiner where to put the microphones. I learned by watching and listening. They placed a microphone somewhere, and I thought, "I'll try that." Also, on the back of almost every record album in those days was a list of microphones used and all that sort of technical stuff. If you heard something you liked, you'd go, "I'm going to use a U 47 on the trumpets." So placement experience came from that. I started trying things to see what would work for me.

At Sunset Sound, where I started, you really had to get in close in order to get separation because the room was so small. It was common to put mics up close to the drums and guitar amplifiers, but at the same time you had to back away when doing strings. So a lot of the same things work for me in the studio today. For instance, I went from distance-miking over the vibes and timpani, to going in close to get separation, to back out again for orchestral recording. So it's like I made a full circle.

So separation is something that you're not concerned with?

No, I'm really not. I like leakage. If it's a good-sounding room, leakage is your friend. It's what makes it sound bigger. Let's say I've got 12 woodwinds, and I'm using 4 microphones. In other words, one for the flutes, one for oboes, one for the bassoons, and one for the clarinets. They're going to be pretty tight, meaning about 5 or 6 feet over them. That's not rock-and-roll tight; that's orchestral tight. But if you open that microphone, you're going to pretty much hear what that mic is pointing at, and the leakage from the other microphones on the woodwinds makes the size bigger on the instrument. Same thing with the overall microphones. If you listen to your overalls and then open up your sweeteners into it, you can control the amount of presence that you want from that distant pickup.

Are you concerned about cancellation from all the open mics?

If they're pointed in slightly the wrong direction from one another, you will get cancellation. It's like when you multi-mike drums. You get lots of phase shift between toms. I remember there was an English engineer who had just done the Bee Gees' first album, and he showed me what they were doing over there, which was what a lot of people do today. Overheads on the cymbals, individual mics on the toms, and getting really tight in and building a drum sound from scratch, rather than being a little distant and getting an overall picture of the drums and then adding things into it. At that time I noticed major phase shift, where by moving the microphones even an inch from the two center toms, I could change the total character of what was happening. I was always amazed how much things would change, especially if you changed microphones or patterns. I used to try a figure-8 next to a cardioid to try to avoid the phase shift.

How did you transition from doing mostly music to doing film work?

There was a point in time when I just stopped being a mixer and focused on producing. That was in my Columbia Records days. I was hiring Andy Johns to do a bunch of my recording because he was doing things that I didn't know how to do. The great thing about growing up in the business in some bigger studios, and I'm not sure if it's the same today, is that the second engineers that have eyes to be mixers get a chance to sit behind the greats and watch and learn. That's the best schooling there is.

I never stopped recording, but I basically let Andy and some other people do the basics and then I would do the overdubs and mix. It allowed me the freedom to produce because it's hard to sit in both chairs. A point came when I started doing motion pictures where I could do both at the same time, and I got back into it with a fervor.

Doing movie dates was just something that happened. I did a lot of movies for Disney when I was working at Sunset because Tutti Camarata [who owned Sunset Sound] was running Disney Records too, so he used to do some pictures there as well. I did all the beach party movies and some movies with Jack Nitzsche, but they were all basically rock-and-roll songs for films.

Later on, when I went to Columbia Records as a producer, one of the gigs that they gave me was to be executive producer for the soundtrack of *Star Trek: The Motion Picture*. So I was on the stage every day and somehow or other developed a relationship with Jerry Goldsmith and then later John Williams, and it just started to expand. I also got tired of being a psychiatrist for my artists, and albums that should have taken six weeks to make were taking over a year, and we were forgetting about why we were there. It became drudgery, and I got burned out. Then the movie thing happened, and I found it very enjoyable—not to say that it isn't complicated, though.

Yeah, but you must get the satisfaction that it's relatively quick.

Yes, it goes back to my days of doing things live. That's the way I learned. We always did things live to mono and live to stereo and ran a three-track as a backup. Today it's not very different. We go for live mixes on the sessions, so it's basically what I did when I started.

When you're doing live mixes, are you running a multitrack backup as well?

Yes. One of the things that I think is interesting for me is that I get to use the cutting edge of what's happening. I use pretty much every hard-disc system that is out there, as well as the best converters. It's a lot of information coming down the pike, but it's really interesting. Like on this new *Star Trek* film that I have coming up, we're going to run a multichannel Pro Tools|HD at 96k with some external converters at 192k for the M 50 overalls, for the multitrack with on-board Avid video. So that's very cool if you think about where we were even five years ago. Five years ago, we were still running mag and film, and now it's totally off of a workstation. Now we can do the edits on the spot as well as any update mixes if we need to.

Do you use a Decca Tree?

Sometimes I use it and sometimes I don't. Sometimes I just use three Matthews stands, and sometimes I use outriggers. It depends on the score—that determines what I need. I don't do everything the same way twice because I find that rooms will change acoustically depending upon the temperature and humidity, and all of a sudden you have to change the mics in order to compensate for wherever the room's going. It can be a big change.

Is this during the course of a session?

Yes. I've had it where the first two days sounded amazing, and all of a sudden the third day is as dry as can be, and you have to either raise the mics or go in closer or change them. It's not uncommon, but it can be shocking when the orchestra hits that first note and things are suddenly different. You have to move really fast.

So your approach is different every time.

Yes, I basically have a standard way that I work, but sometimes I will change the microphones that I have on my strings or woodwinds. Basically, my percussion mics and overall mics stay the same from show to show.

I use M 50s as my overalls. Years ago, I went through 26 of them to get 6 good ones when they were readily available. In my library I have three omnidirectional Beyer 48k/24-bit digital mics that are extraordinary. The sonic landscape and imaging is spectacular. It's sort of like watching a Cinerama movie with one camera with a very wide lens instead of three cameras. They don't have the same kind of reach that the M 50s have, though.

I run my Decca Tree in the 2-meter-by-1-1/2-meter configuration, although I've been subsequently told by various engineers that those aren't necessarily the correct dimensions.

What do you use for spot mics, and how do you determine which ones you should use?

The determination is based on the score. If I'm looking for a more aggressive sound because I need to compete against sound effects, I will use different microphones on my strings, like my AKG C 12s. Normally I would use Sony C-37s, which are the same things I use on the violas. But on the celli I generally always use the C 12s. I try to look at my sweetener microphones as something complementary to my overalls so that when you open them up, everything stays within the same color. That way, if you equalize in one area, it doesn't start to make other things sound weird.

Over the years I've tried to find microphones that were compatible color-wise. As a result, a majority of the microphones that I use are tubes.

Do you EQ much?

Not too much. I use some EQ, but it depends on the score and how the stage is responding. I don't use the same microphones in all the rooms either, because they react differently as well. So not only do we have the microphone choices on our palettes, we have the rooms as well.

How do you choose where to record then?

I'll talk to the composer to see what he has in mind, and that will determine where we go to record. We want the sound of the room to enhance the score.

Some stages are deader than others. Like if I go to Paramount, it's a very sweet-sounding room, but it's a little on the dead side so I have a tendency to use more reverbs and room-sampling reverberation to make things sound good. It's almost like rock-and-roll recording because since you're in a deader environment, you have to create a more live environment. If I go to Todd-AO I use less of it because the room's so live already. Sony has a great deal of clarity so you can add a lot of reverb to it. It's not as reverberant as Todd-AO, but it's not dead either. Warner is a deader room so you can get away with more effects. I like that.

Taking a room that has a lot of room sound, like Todd-AO, and adding another room to it, you're putting a room within a room, and it doesn't always work. So you have to find different kinds of reverbs that work in the room you're in that don't clash.

So you don't use the same reverbs all the time?

No, it all depends. I use TC 6000s as my constant and Sony 777s, Lexicon 480s, and EMT plates to help fill in the color.

Do you worry about surround, or do you just try to get a good stereo image first?

I don't deal with stereo at all until we make an album. Surround I'm always concerned with, but when I'm recording I set up my surround mics so that they all have the same amount of reverb on them and then I turn them off. They make everything sound bigger than it is, and you can fool yourself, so most of the time I turn them off. I turn them back on for playbacks.

How do you determine where to place those mics?

Again, it depends on the score. Sometimes I go the old-fashioned way of just sticking two way up in the air really far in back of the room.

Do you have them looking back at the orchestra?

That's what's normally done, but now I don't do that all the time. If the room is reverberant, I'll face them toward the rear of the stage to get the reflected sound.

Do you do anything special for the LFE?

I use Tom Holman's Bass Manager for my system. I don't generally provide a separate LFE track because I've found that it sometimes creates a huge collision at the dubbing stage. I generally only provide that track if there's something effect-wise that we're doing or if I need to get more bottom end out of the basses that I can't get otherwise. Sometimes I might use a Harmonizer and drop it down an octave and kick a little bit in there. It depends on the situation and what you're trying to achieve. If you've got full-range speakers, which they are in the theater, the majority of the time a separate sub-track is meaningless, especially if you've got a bass management system that's doing all the work.

When I've done my Doors remixes in 5.1, I've used the sub a lot. I've put bass drum, bass, and effects down there. There's a DVD-A out of the *L.A. Woman* album.

Do you bring your own monitors?

Yes, I use Questeds. I just bring the LCR and a sub. I don't bring any surrounds because all the stages have them built in, and they're the same ones that are on the dubbing stages. I also bring some McIntosh tube amps to drive the main speakers and a Yamaha to drive the sub.

Do you bring your own mic preamps?

The majority of it is tube-based, along with some Martechs and Avalons. I've got eight Martechs, and I'd like to get four more. I go for the noise with tube mics and tube pres. [Laughs]

What determines what format you record to, because I know that has evolved for you over the years?

Sound quality and convenience, because we're moving so fast today. I can barely wait for a Sony 3348HR to rewind anymore. We used to use a 3348 for backup, but we don't use it anymore. We go right to hard drives and then back them up to optical.

On most film mixes I'm recording with a DSD Genex [8500] and a Pro Tools rig for them to take to the stage. The last couple of films I've used Radars, which sounded quite good. I generally use a lot of outboard dB Technology converters.

What's your approach to building a mix with an orchestra?

I don't know how I do this, but it's developed over the years that I balance all of the microphones out and preset my EQ before I hear a note of music. Generally, when the first note of music is played, I'm 95 percent of the way there. After a while you start to know your gain structure and where things should be and how a particular room responds. I make notes about EQ for a starting place, but I can just go.

I would say the same thing about a rock session. If I was doing rock and roll, I'd put it all up at the same time and balance it quickly. I know what I want to do on the drums from years of experience. Generally, I'll just ask everyone to play at once and listen to the whole thing. Then I'll go in and tighten up anything afterward. I might ask them to play a little by themselves and refine it. But there's something good about getting your sounds all together and defining what's happening as it's going down, rather than making everything an individual sound and then putting it together and wondering why it doesn't work.

What's the hardest thing for you to record?

When I'm in a room where the room itself starts to get loud the louder an orchestra plays. Then the brass and percussion can completely wipe out the strings, and you have no control over it. That's the hardest thing. You have to manage the levels through the conductor to have them play lower, but then your balance becomes unnatural because if you go out and listen in the room everything sounds right, but microphones don't hear it that way. A lot of the time I'll have to have the brass play really quietly but with attitude in order for it to sound right and not overpower everything else.

What are you using on the brass?

I only use one microphone. Sometimes I'll put a sweetener on the tuba. Generally, I have a special M 49 that I'll put on omni. I use a U 47 occasionally, but I find that 99 percent of the time the brass pickup comes from the overalls and leakage into the viola and woodwind mics, which are sitting right there. So that's where leakage comes into play.

It sounds like you use omni patterns a lot.

A great deal. Bones Howe talked in an article years ago about how omnidirectional microphones were the best, even on vocals. I tried it, and he was right. They just sound more open. Bones was actually one of the main guys who I learned from. Not from sitting behind him, but from listening to his records and then later getting to know him when he worked at United Recorders as an engineer.

I'm very fortunate to have been around some of the really great guys. Even Wally Heider was tremendous. Bones loved Wally because Wally was one of the few guys who could put just a few microphones in front of an 18-piece big band and have it sound like an 18-wheeler, it was so big-sounding.

Do you have any advice for someone just getting into orchestral recording?

One thing we didn't talk about—and it's one of the biggest things, oddly enough—is balancing a microphone boom so that it doesn't fall over and kill your microphone. I find that amazing because I see studio setup guys set up a stage where they have microphones unbalanced on a stand—one slight push, and over it goes. It's such a simple thing, but it's so important.

Did you give away any of your secrets in this interview?

Have I given away any secrets? Actually, there are no secrets. I could tell you every microphone that I use, and it wouldn't matter because the difference is in I how hear it, or how Bobby Fernandez or Dennis Sands or Shawn Murphy hears it. We all hear differently. A lot of us have the same microphones and preamps and do things similarly, but it's a combination of how you put it together and how you hear it. That's why in the end there are no secrets.

CHAPTER 18

Ed Cherney

One of the most versatile and talented engineers of our time, Ed Cherney has recorded and mixed projects for the Rolling Stones, Iggy Pop, Bob Dylan, Was (Not Was), Elton John, Bob Seger, Roy Orbison, and the B-52s, as well as many others. Ed also recorded and mixed the multiple Grammy–winning *Nick of Time* and *Luck of the Draw* CDs for Bonnie Raitt, as well as engineered the Grammy-winning "Tears in Heaven" track for the Eric Clapton–scored film, *Rush*.

Do you use the same setup every time when you track?

Yes and no. It's evolved over the years. You have favorites for the moment and for the style of music that you're doing. For standard rock stuff, lately I'm doing it the same way, at least for a starting point.

What is that starting point?

For overheads left and right, I'll start with a couple of Coles. Then for toms, I've been using the Audio-Technica ATM25s. They're good for speed. You just set them up and go; you don't usually even have to EQ them. On the kick I've been using a 421 inside fairly close for snap and an FET 47 about 2 or 3 feet out. On the snare bottom I've been using a 441, and for the top an ATM23HE.

Are you miking the hat?

Yeah, with a B&K 4011. Then typically I'll put up an 87 in omni about 10 feet in front of the drums and maybe about 6 feet high as a room mic, just to have a listen to things to get it going. That's to start. It doesn't mean it will end up anything like that, but it will enable me to get things going as quickly as I can.

How long does it take you to tweak things?

About 10 minutes. I find that when I do it faster, it works better. I get the drummer to play a little time but don't wear him out, and if it's not right you know it right away. And sometimes if it's not right, you go ahead and cut the song anyway. When you have a listen, good musicians will go, "Oh yeah, my snare's too dark" or something like that.

When you're placing the overheads, are you using them more like cymbal mics or are you trying to capture the whole kit?

It depends. If it's a gentle song and the drums are being atmospheric, I'm going to spot-mike cymbals and rides and swells. But with a rock kit I'll try to get a pretty good balance with the overheads, yet still get the cymbals without them ripping your head off.

Did you have a mentor when you first started?

I sat behind some really great engineers. I assisted Bruce Swedien on 10 or 20 records at Westlake when I moved to Los Angeles. He was very generous with information. Mick Guzauski is another guy who I assisted who really gave up a lot of information.

Is anything different from the way you started to the way it is now?

In a lot of ways it's exactly the same, and in a lot of ways it couldn't be more different. For example, when you would cut a drum kit 10 years ago, you would have to get the sounds down when you tracked. For certain kinds of music it was really difficult to replace snare drums and kick drums. You could do it, but it wasn't easy. So you were going for overall sound and feel. Now, a lot of times when you record drums, you're just printing triggers. I still try to get the best sound that I can on tape, then if something isn't right you can certainly add to it.

When you're tracking, do you just go for a good drum track or do you try to get as much as you can?

I try to get as much as I can. I think it's musically a lot better that way. Also, with a lot of instruments, I don't isolate that much anymore. When I did the Rolling Stones, and the amps were in the room with just a little bit of baffling, but basically open so that they could hear them. Everything was leaking into everything, but that just gave it that glue, especially when it was played well.

So leakage doesn't bother you?

It depends on the band and what you're trying to do. If you know that everything is going to be swinging with the drums, then you're going to try to get it. Otherwise, you're just laying down a template so you have to isolate things as well as you can if you know you're going to be layering guitars and that kind of stuff.

What are you using on guitar amps?

Like pretty much everybody else, I've used 57s forever, but lately I've been using Royer R-121s. I've been liking those, and the musicians I've been working with have been liking them, too. It's pretty much just put the fader up, and they capture what's going on with the amp. They've got a very sweet character.

Do you only use one mic on the cabinet?

Usually, unless it's in stereo. Sometimes I'll use a 414 or a large-diaphragm condenser back off the cabinet if we want the room sound, but typically I've been putting up a 121 in front of the cabinet.

What are you using for mic amps? How much does it matter to you?

It matters a lot. I'm still using as much Class A as I can. I've got a bunch of 1073s that I use in critical situations.

Do you take bass direct or do you use an amp as well?

I try to do both. Again, it depends. If you don't have a lot of space and you don't have any isolation, I'll go with a direct depending on the player. But usually I'll go with both with an FET 47 or something like that on the cabinet and a DI. I like using the Groove Tubes DI, but then again it depends. If it's an active bass, then you might want to use a DI with transformer in front of it.

Do you EQ when you record?

Heck yeah! But dipping more than anything. If something is a little dark, then it might be because 2 or 300 is building up, so you dip a little of that out and maybe add a little top. If you're going to tape, then you might want to add a little top anyway. If you're going to Pro Tools, then you might want to dip a little 2, 3, 4K to take the edge off it.

Are you compressing going to tape?

Not too much. Vocal, obviously. I'll do a little peak limiting on the direct of the bass to protect the input, but not with the mic on the cabinet because usually that will relate pretty well. So I'm really not compressing a lot. I'm trying to get it as fat and clear on tape as I can.

Do you always record to tape first?

Not always. When I say "tape," I mean hard disc or whatever the storage medium happens to be. I just really try to fill the meters and get it on there fat and good.

What's the hardest thing for you to record?

The human voice, because every one is different. You know what to expect from a drum kit or a guitar amp or piano, but the human voice is so personal. Even if you have a microphone that works 90 percent of the time, you're always looking, and you're always guessing. And it's the most dynamic instrument, too. So it's the most difficult instrument because it has the most variables.

Do you have a signal chain that you start with for the vocal?

It depends, because a lot of times I'll be tracking bands where the vocalist will be out in the room with the drums. Then I'll get stuck with that performance with a few fixes, but that means I'll end up with an SM7 or an RE20 for the project.

For rock vocals I'll use dynamic mics a lot of times, like an RE20 or SM7. I did Hootie and the Blowfish, and he [Darius Rucker] sounded great on an SM7. A lot of times a C 12 sounds good for a female voice. Jagger loves it too, but he sounds about the same on any mic he uses. [Neumann] 47s usually sound good. I've used the Audio-Technica 4050, and I kinda like that. That's a pretty good place to start.

You need to start somewhere just to get something going instead of scratching your head. Get something up and get people playing music. Then you hear it back, see what it sounds like, and adjust from there.

Are you trying to make it fit in the track or are you trying to make it sound as good as possible by itself?

Pretty much fit in the track.

How concerned are you with the headphone mix? Do you do it yourself or relegate it to the assistant?

It's critical. I'm really concerned with it, so I do it myself. What I typically do is feed what I'm hearing [the stereo buss] to the headphones, and if I'm lucky enough to have a headphone mixer I'll add some kick, snare, bass, and vocal, and whoever else needs more "me." A lot of times I'll even add the stereo buss to the stereo cue mix so I can be additive. So I'll have the stereo buss coming up, and on the console I'll also add some kick and snare, because you have to get it up over the sound that's in the room. So I'll sweeten the drums, and that's where I'll usually start.

The idea is to be making music quickly with everybody hearing themselves. If I'm hearing them, then they're hearing it. I just don't want to spend any more time getting sounds than I have to before people are playing together with the red lights on.

Do you send a lot of effects to the phones?

I start simple. Maybe I'll have a couple of reverbs—something short and bright and something a little longer. I might have a delay sitting there ready to go. But typically, I'll start it out pretty dry since most rock tracks are like that now anyway. And if I add something, the stereo buss is feeding the headphones, so they'll get what I'm hearing. Sometimes that can be inspiring, and musicians will react to it.

Was recording the Stones any different than recording anyone else?

It's a rock gig, but there are five guys there who have been around and know what they want to hear. You're really not allowed to screw up. Some younger guys might let you get away with something, but you've got to be on top of your game more so than with anyone else.

How did you approach Charlie's drums?

It's just a straight-ahead rock kit. The less you do, the better off you are. You put some mics up and try to capture the drum kit like it's one instrument rather than separate drums. You just get out in the room, have a listen, and try to re-create that. But there's not a lot of work involved. The work is in the perception and not in the knob-twisting.

How did you determine where to place everyone in the room?

I think I sat there for a day and half before I did it. I'd go out and sing a song, clap my hands, and stomp around and try to create a space where everyone could see each other. I tried to get some things off-axis yet keep the room kind of open and live so people weren't just relying on their headphones and could hear their amps and have that interplay. I tried to make sure that the line of sight was intimate yet keep some separation. Also, I'll ask the assistant where they usually set everything up. [Laughs]

What are you looking for in an assistant?

Somebody who's eager, sharp, and enthusiastic. Somebody who knows their room. And they better have some interpersonal skills. And somebody who can look 30 seconds into the future and anticipate what's going on.

How much do you rely on the assistant? Do you do everything yourself and let the assistant take care of the client?

It depends on the client, and it depends on the assistant. You don't want to get burned. Sometimes someone who thinks they know more than they really do will get you into trouble. You have to make sure that information isn't lost, or a track in analog gets wiped. I do a lot of it myself, though.

Are you doing much to tape anymore, or is it mostly to hard disc?

It's mostly to hard disc. We did the Stones to tape and Pro Tools. We ended up using the tape after doing an A/B. There was absolutely no comparison. We would get a take, then put it into Pro Tools, then manipulate it there.

Do you have a philosophy of recording?

I want to get the sounds to tape as quickly as possible, then play it back so you can talk about it. It's real at that point. "That's too bright. That's too dull. That should be louder. That should be a different part. That should be a different snare drum." It's easy to modify once you can hear it. I've been in places where you mess around a lot before you play any music, and the session doesn't move forward. You just can't make music that way.

CHAPTER 19

Wyn Davis

Best known for his work with the hard rock bands Dio, Dokken, and Great White, "Wyn Davis style" in that genre is as unmistakable as it is masterful. From his Total Access studios in Redondo Beach, California, Wyn's work typifies old-school engineering coupled with the best of modern techniques.

Do you use the same setup every time you track?

I'll generally choose the same mics all the time and then modify those selections as seems necessary.

Basic tracks these days are pretty much just drums and bass. Rarely do I work in situations where people are going for keeper guitars on the rhythm track date. Occasionally that happens, so I try to isolate the rhythm section as much as possible so there are options at the end of the session to go punch something in without having to worry about leakage.

What's your drum setup?

I'll tell you what my overall approach to drums is. I feel that the drums are sort of like an orchestra in the sense that there are a lot of instruments, so I don't make any attempt to isolate drums from one another or to do anything that would take away from the overall sound. For instance, if you hit the snare, the whole drum kit rings and vibrates. In my opinion, that's a part of the sound of the set that you want to keep. So I don't make any attempt to narrowly focus mics or baffle things off or anything like that. I just use the mics that I like and don't do any gating or a lot of compression while track-ing. I just try to capture the sound of the drums as closely as possible to what they are in the room.

I use 87s on the toms and generally a dynamic mic on the snare. Over the years I've taken to using a couple of C 12s as overheads. Depending on the kick drum I sometimes will use two mics—a D 12 and either an RE20 or a 421. The D 12 has a scooped-out response, and the RE20 or 421 will sort of fill that in a little bit.

Do you put them both in the same place?

I usually have the mics about midway into the kick. Generally, I don't say anything to the drummer about making the bass drum sound good. If the drummer comes in and he has a front head with no hole in it, I have a cable that I've made that I can slip in through one of the ports. I have a sort of shock mount that I'll mount inside and then we'll put the head back on. The most important thing is for the guy to feel comfortable and have the response from the drums that he's used to getting. If you change that, then his performance suffers, and you don't get what you're after to begin with.

Do you use something like a 47 FET or something outside the drum?

Well, I have used a 47 FET before, but because the characteristics of every kick drum are different, it really depends on how much fundamental is in it and how empty the shell is. Some people fill their shells up with pillows, and some keep their front head on. Some people have a giant hole cut in the head, while some people have one just big enough to put your fist through. It really depends on the drum. In my opinion, there are few magic-sounding kick drums out there that have everything you want, so you basically have to tailor the mic to the kick drum and figure out which mic is going to represent the best part of the kick drum for what you're after. I'm usually after something that will be at the bottom of the track fundamentally.

Do you use the overheads as cymbal mics or to capture the kit?

I use the overheads to capture the whole kit, but with an emphasis on the top end of the set, meaning all the cymbals, hi-hat, and accent cymbals. I basically use C 12s almost over the toms and not directly facing the cymbals. I put them off-axis from each other a bit so that the two C 12s are looking in the opposite directions a little bit. They're sort of close together, maybe a foot or 18 inches apart, looking in two different directions back toward the mic stands.

If the intention is for the drum sound to be real ambient, which is the case in a lot of rock situations, I usually put the overheads about 2 feet above the cymbals so they're capturing a fairly wide angle.

Do you mike the hat?

Yeah, usually with some kind of small-diaphragm condenser microphone, like a 451 or a KM 84. It depends on the sound of the hat and what the guy is going to be playing. If it's going to be bashing on a hat with a really loose pedal, it'll be different than if Vinnie Colaiuta is playing and doing a lot of intricate hi-hat work.

Do you use a bottom mic on the snare?

I've taken to doing that about 6 or 7 years ago. I rarely use very much of it, but sometimes it really comes in handy. It really doesn't matter much to me what that mic is. It can be just about anything. It usually comes down to whatever's left. If I have a 451 with two 10-dB pads available, I'll put it under there.

What are you using on the top of the snare?

I pretty much use a 57 all the time. Occasionally I'll put a 451 on the snare, but it has to be the right kind of snare and the right kind of player.

How about the bass? Do you usually just go direct or do you use an amp as well?

Always both direct and with an amp if the bass player has an amp that he wants to use. I put a 67 about a foot away from the cabinet.

Where did you learn your techniques?

The person who I learned a lot from early on was Ken Scott [engineer for the Beatles, Pink Floyd, and David Bowie, among others]. I watched a lot of what he did when I worked with him, so he was the guy who I learned the most from. I had a lot of respect for him because he went through that traditional British engineer training and had a lot of experience with different types of music, having worked back in the heyday of all the stuff that people revere nowadays. I figured out a lot of things on my own later, but I learned the initial stuff from him.

For instance, Ken always used a KM 84 on the snare, but it just never worked for me. In most of the music that I do, people are hitting the drums so hard that I really don't want to risk damaging the mic. I have a couple of 87s that are of the early '70s vintage that I still use on the toms, but they've really taken some whacks over the years. Because of that I never replaced the baskets on them, but they still work great.

How do you handle leakage?

For a modern multitracked recording session where people are planning on going back and having another look at what they've done on the tracking date, it's important not to have a lot of leakage so that anything can be replaced without interfering with something that's on the track.

When I'm at my studio, I've set it up so that there's virtually no leakage. I have sliding glass doors that adjoin the dead room to our live drum room, so the drums are isolated. Then we have a couple of iso booths, so the leakage really isn't a factor.

In situations where the band wants to play and capture the rhythm section as a unit on the spot, I don't worry about leakage. I actually treat it as part of the overall sound and try not to have any glaring phase anomalies.

How do you get your guitar sounds?

It's just a process of guitars, amps, and the players. It's trite to say, but so much of it is really in the fingers of the player, so I really work with them and try to find out what it is that they're doing and what it is that they want to capture. On hard-rock guitar with screaming Marshalls, the one thing I try to avoid is placing the mic straight on to the speaker. I usually try to be off-axis a little bit so that I can avoid the buildup of that 1 to 2k screaming, tear-your-face-off sound.

I have the mic back about 2 or 3 inches depending upon how loud it is. Lately I've been favoring this Royer mic [the R-121] for guitar. That mic takes EQ so well after the fact. It automatically shaves off some of that 1 to 2k brittle Marshall thing that really builds up after four or five tracks of guitar.

Are you using just the one mic on the cabinet?

Yeah, I usually use just one mic close up. I haven't had a lot of luck introducing much ambience into multitracked, layered guitars. It just creates a mess. With more minimalist stuff it's really cool, though. I usually end up asking the guitar players to turn whatever treble control they have on their guitars back a hair. It takes just little bit of the edge off. At first they're a little bit hesitant, but there's usually plenty there to go around. It really warms things up a lot if you just crack that tone control back a couple of numbers. It makes it sound a little bigger, especially if you're layering three or four guitars on top of one another.

When you're layering guitars, are you changing the mic or the mic placement at all?

No, just pretty much changing the guitar. I generally try to use different guitars and different pickups, but I use the same input path for multiple guitar passes.

Do you have any mic preamps that you like in combination with specific microphones?

Yeah I do. Back when Dean Jensen was alive, I bought 12 of those Boulder mic pres that he made. They never really caught on, but I really like them. The only problem is that some consoles can't handle their output on a loud source even when they're turned all the way down, so I've made some passive inline pads that I can put on those guys. I use Dean's stuff on things with a lot of low-end content, like bass, toms, and kick, because of the linear nature of the low end coming out of those things.

I like the old Neve stuff on guitars. The overheads and guitars I'll usually put through a pair of 1073s.

Are you compressing while you're recording?

I usually don't add any compression on the tracking end of things. I try to maintain all the dynamic range that's there because I find that later it leaves me a lot more options about how I want things to sound.

What's the hardest thing for you to record?

Somebody who can't play very well. [Laughs] Truthfully, that's a lot of people nowadays. The art of being prepared for the studio, along with a lot of the engineering arts, is being lost in all the cutting and pasting. I've found that the preparation that people have before coming into the studio has diminished over the last few years by an astounding amount. People will come in and work hard to get something on the first chorus and then say, "Okay, can't you just paste that everywhere now?"

When people used to play these performances from top to bottom, there was a synergy with the track that happened. Something would evolve as the track went on. You definitely lose that if you're just using a hard disc recorder as a glorified musical word processor.

How do you approach vocals?

Vocals, on the other hand, I do compress going to tape all the time. It depends on the vocalist, but I'll use any number of mics. It's almost always some kind of condenser mic and some kind of tube mic. There are a lot of really great vocal mics out there that do a great job; it just depends on who's singing. It can be any number of microphone preamps, depending upon who's singing and what kind of sound you're looking for. For tracking I use an LA-3A with a quick attack and a slow release, letting that lightly catch anything jumping through.

Are you looking for something that sounds good by itself or something that fits in the track?

Usually something that works in the track. If it's a ballad where the vocal is going to be way out in front and has to stand on its own, I'll just be looking for a good vocal sound. But usually I'll make adjustments to make it work with what's being played back.

Do you send the same FX to the headphones as what you think will be used on the final mix?

I do it as requested, but I generally try to keep the headphone mixes pretty dry. I want them to be punchy and fat and basically in their face because I think it keeps everyone really honest. If somebody wants some verb or delays it's not a problem, but I try to keep it down to the very least that they'll accept. I'll slide it in there and keep on asking if it's enough and explain to them that I prefer they just go ahead and sing it sort of *au naturel*.

Do you use room mics on drums?

Depending on where I am, I really love M 50s. I don't own them, but I'll rent them. In my drum room, I'll Velcro a couple of PZMs to the wall that the drums face and use those as room mics sometimes. I'll also use a couple of 87s sometimes. If I use 451s on the overheads or an old set of 414s, then I'll use my C 12s as room mics.

What do you look for in an assistant?

I'm looking for somebody who does not have a problem with his or her role as a service provider. I don't need somebody to look after me all the time, although I do like having someone watch my back to make sure that a mic or a track is not too hot or something. But I need somebody who doesn't have a problem doing whatever's necessary to make the client happy. Whether it's getting them a Coke, making coffee, or replacing a guitar cord, I like somebody who feels pride in the ability to facilitate a session. Not somebody who feels like, "I'm just doing this until I can get my own gig."

I don't have a problem with doing anything on a session. I don't feel that I'm above any aspect of any part of it, whether it is scrounging around on the floor trying to find the right mic placement or getting somebody a bottle of water. So I want an assistant who feels the same way. That's the most important thing that I need in an assistant for me.

How much responsibility do you give to them?

As much as they can handle, but I'm such an odd case because I really don't require much of a second. I do it all pretty much myself. It's not a matter of wanting to do it all, but by the time I tell someone what I want, I could've done it. I'm really more interested in the assistant looking after the clients and making sure that they have all they need.

Are you EQing when you record?

I do whatever it takes to make it sound the way I want it to sound. Generally I'll start with the microphones, but then I'll do whatever I have to. With a really good studio drummer, there's very little that has to be done because the kit will sound great right off, but that doesn't happen too often. For the last half-dozen years or so, I get the guys from Drum Paradise to bring some drums or tune the ones that are there if there's a budget that can accommodate it.

When you're doing basics, are you comping drum tracks or going for one good take all the way through?

We always go for the best take possible, but I'll edit when necessary if there are sections that are outstanding. With all the recording for the last year and a half being dominated by Pro Tools, editing drums on 2-inch is not a necessary thing anymore. We simply make multiple passes to Pro Tools inside a playlist and comp them in there.

Do you move beats around?

I like to treat drums as one instrument, and moving beats around flies in the face of that. Sometimes I do, but I'll tell you, as soon as you start moving things around and taking things out of their phase relationship to each other, it's over.

Do you have a philosophy about how you record?

The overall philosophy is to make everybody as comfortable as possible. In a tracking situation, aside from your responsibility of getting something decently recorded, the most important thing is to get good headphone mixes for these guys. In fact, to get the best one possible. Amazingly bad things happen to even the best players when the headphone mix is all screwed up. I don't relegate the headphone mix to anyone else. I make sure that I have a set of headphones in that I can switch across all the cues that are being fed to the guys playing in the studio. Beyond that, after almost every take I will have an assistant make a sweep of every headphone position and listen to a playback to make sure that none of them have gone south or an amp is starting to distort or something like that. I don't think you can pay enough attention to that part of it because if the guys are hearing something that feels good, it moves the session from sort of a technical exercise for the musicians to a really inspiring and fun thing. When you can create that atmosphere in the studio for them, that's when you're going to get the best work out of the players. And when you get the best work out of them, it's going to sound better. It's really amazing how no matter what tools you're using, if people aren't having a good time, it's just not going to work.

CHAPTER 20

Frank Filipetti

From Celine Dion, Carly Simon, James Taylor, Tony Bennett, and Elton John to Kiss, Korn, Fuel, Foreigner, and Hole, Frank Filipetti's credits run the entire musical spectrum. Known for his fearless ability to either extensively experiment or get instant sounds as the session dictates, Frank's old-school wisdom combined with his adventuresome and modern approach continues to push the cutting edge.

Do you use the same setup every time you track?

There are certain microphones that I'll start with based on experience and the nature of the session. For example, on a Broadway show date where we've got to record a whole show pretty much in a day, I will go to a predetermined setup regardless of who the drummer is, only because we don't have time to play around. On the other hand, on a session like Korn or Fuel, where I know we have a lot more time, we'll work with four or five different mics on every drum or instrument and try to zero in on the best one. So in that particular instance, it's less about starting with a prearranged setup than ascertaining where the drummer's going and how he plays. With the guitar it would depend on how much he plays, if he plays softly, or things like that. But if I'm going into the session and it's essential that it runs fast, I'll go with what I consider the safest and not necessarily what I consider the best.

So what's your setup when you have to be safe?

Basically, I'll be looking for microphones that may not always give me the best sound but will keep me from having to worry about overloads and spillage. So I'll go for something that I know is reliable, that I know from experience will give me a good enough place to get started.

In those particular instances, if we start with the drum kit, I'll stay away from condensers on anything but overheads because my experience is that they break up with a hard hitter. If I'm in a session that has to move quickly, I don't have the time to break down those mics and set something else up, so with the drum kit I'll go with a lot of dynamics. On the snare would be a 57. Under snare would be a 57 or a 441. Toms would be either a 421 or a 57. A lot of this is amended now because in the last year or two, Audio-Technica has come out with a new line of condensers that actually do take the sound pressure, so recently I've been using the AT3000 on the snare, the 5100 on the under-snare, and the ATM35 on the toms. The only problem that I have with those is that they're high output, so on some of the older consoles, like a Neve 8068, they come in a little too hot. But for the most part I'm starting to use more condenser mics on the kit now because the new mics that they have are pretty good for handling high SPL.

Then there's the AT4047, which is just a great general-purpose mic that takes high SPL. Recently, I've been using those on guitars. On the Korn session we used them on guitars because they were very loud—so much so that your standard condensers, like 67s, just can't take the level, especially if you're miking close to the speaker.

Do you experiment with overheads? Do you use the overheads as cymbal mics or as the basic sound of the kit?

I experiment a lot with the overheads, and I've gone through a lot of permutations with them. I started out as a drummer, and one of the things that I dislike about a lot of recordings is that the sound of the snare is coming mostly from the snare mic. As a drummer I know that the sound at the snare is not exactly what I want to hear on the track. There's a lot of bloom around the snare and around the bass drum as well that I feel is essential to capturing the reality and the dynamics of the snare and bass drum in particular. So my overhead technique is to capture the overall sound of the kit and not just the cymbals. I tend to want to mike the kit so that I do get leakage of the snare, bass drum, and everything into the overall sound. I want to be able to put up the overheads along with the bass drum mic and get a pretty nice sound on the kit. So my tendency is to mic a little farther away from direct impact of the cymbals.

I've experimented with a lot of different positions, and I've come up with a placement that works best for me. Most engineers seem to come in with the mics coming from the front of the kit, looking back toward the drummer. I put my overheads in the back near the drummer, looking ahead toward the kit. I just found after years of experimentation that's where the best sound for me is. Just above the snare looking out toward the cymbals gives me the depth and the impact that I'm looking for.

The microphones are probably a foot or so above the drummer's head. I don't want him banging his head or hitting them with his sticks. They're far enough back that if he raises his sticks to hit a cymbal, his sticks might hit a mic in front of him but not one slightly behind him. Not only is it great for the snare and the cymbals, but it's great for the toms as well. What I end up generally having to do because of that is to also mike the ride cymbal separately because the ride sometimes needs that little extra "ping" that you can't get from farther away.

Are you using an X/Y or a spaced pair?

You know, it depends on the amount of time that I have to experiment. If I have to set it up really fast just to get going, I'll go with something resembling an ORTF for starters. I may move it up or down or in or out a bit from there, but the mic positions themselves are along the lines of ORTF. I find that gives me more spread and depth than X/Y and less stuff to fool around with than M-S, although I do like M-S miking occasionally. If I do use M-S, I usually supplement it with a wider array as well.

Do you use multiple mics on the kick?

Yes. Not only multiple mics but multiple distances, which is something similar to what I do with guitars. I know that the object is to get all of your mics in phase, but I find that with guitars and the kick drum there are varying distances from the drum or the speaker that actually work in a way that's complementary. They can create certain combs [filtering] that work to your advantage and sometimes work better than doing it with an equalizer. I'll play around with various distances on a kick drum and guitar amp because on those two instruments in particular, we're not always looking for the most natural sound. We're looking for impact. It's a visceral thing that may not happen live, but something that you're trying to capture onto tape or disc. So I'll work with multiple mikings for those instruments.

On the bass drum I generally start with a D 12—the D 36 is my favorite mic, but you can't always find one—for the dynamic part and then I'll put a condenser on it as well, with the capsules as closely aligned as possible. The condenser mic will usually be a 4047 or a 47 FET or something like that. I'll make sure that both capsules are as phase-aligned as I can make them. They're generally placed just at the outside of the drum, looking at the beater head. Then I'll play around with an array of two or three other mics at varying distances. Sometimes we'll use a sympathetic beater kind of thing, where you'll have just a shell in front of the drum, which vibrates to get a little more depth and bottom. Sometimes I'll build a little tunnel out of packing blankets and mic stands and put another mic or two at the end. So there are a lot of different things that I try, but the basic setup starts with the two mics just off the front head looking at the beater.

Do you mike the hat?

I always mike the hat. I've tried various things on it, but it's the one area that I've never been totally happy. I've tried such an array of mics—AKGs, Neumanns, all kinds of things. Most recently what I've settled on is a 451 with a 10-dB pad or a KM 84 with a pad or a Schoeps CMC 5 with a pad. But to be perfectly honest, the hi-hat is the one instrument that you can't really get too close to because of the low-frequency information. If you get too close, it tends to color the sound somewhat, yet you can't get too far away either because you lose the impact.

So if you have the time to experiment, you're going to put a lot of different mics up on the drums and see what sounds best?

Basically. On the snare I have a bunch of mics that I've used over the years that go from a 441 to a 57 to a B&K 4012 or an AKG 451 with a pad on it. And then there's the newer range of mics from Audio-Technica, like the AE5100 and AE3000, that work well. But most of the condensers, except for the ATs, I would only use on a jazz date or where I know the drummer isn't a hard hitter. If I didn't know the drummer or the material, I would start off with a 57 just to be safe. I now use the ATs a lot, although with certain heavy hitters, the 5100 gets overloaded, but the 3000 will give the speed of a condenser but also hang in there with SPL like a 57. What's interested me is that the 3000 is a very small side-address mic that makes it easy to place within the kit.

How many do you usually use on kick?

On a date where I have a lot of time to play around, I'll use four or five mics. Like I said, I generally use both a dynamic and a condenser to get the sound of both, but Audio-Technica has just come out with a mic that is a dual-capsule mic, where one capsule is dynamic while the other is condenser. What's interesting about that is that you get both in one head.

On the setup that I just finished, we had the 47 FET along with the D 36 and the dual condenser AT all on the head. Then I had a 47 and a couple of CMV 3s and a CM 51 farther back off the bass drum. But again, that's because I had a session where I had a lot of time to play.

How are you balancing all of those?

The main sound is the overheads, the bass drum mic, and the snare mic. That's my basic drum sound. Then I'll fill it in with tom mics and these other mics around the kit. Many of them are faced at the bass drum but also pick up ambience from other drums. The most important thing is to be careful about the phase relationships because you don't want to smear anything. My general rule of thumb is this: I'll listen to a drum with and without the additional mic. A lot of people will just add a mic or take it away to see if it's adding something, but the bottom line is when you add a mic, you're adding 3 dB to the signal so almost always it will sound a little better with it in. What I do is make sure that when I take the mic away, my level is still the same. That gives me a much truer taste of whether that mic is adding something.

I'll just have the two mics on the snare—top and bottom with the phase swapped on the bottom, adding just enough of the bottom to add a little of the snare rattle. I don't like the sound of just the top head by itself. I find it to be very unnatural. So then I mix just a touch of that in with the overheads. For the overheads I've been using Schoeps CMC 5s either in cardioid or in omni, depending upon the drummer on the date. I've just recently purchased an interesting pair of Sanken CU-44X mics. These are new microphones in the same sense as the AT in that they have a dual capsule with two condenser capsules in the same housing. One is a large-diaphragm and one is a small-diaphragm, with each capsule designed to pick up a different frequency range. I love it for overheads because you get all the power and depth of the larger capsule combined with the speed and transient response of the small one, so you get the best of both worlds. It's also a great vocal mic for the same reasons. It gives you a lot of air without sacrificing that low end. Also, its off-axis response is very, very linear.

Considering that you're getting most of your drum sound from the overheads and kick drum mic, how does that influence the placement of the rest of your drum mics?

It influences it a lot. I pretty much try to keep with an audience perspective on the drums and place the mics as if you were facing the drum kit. I tend to shy away from a full pan of the overheads across the stereo soundfield because that sounds a bit unnatural to me, unless I'm using it for an effect. One of the things that I do, because I know that my overheads are going to be so important in the overall sound, is to make sure that the distance from the snare to each overhead capsule is identical. I want to hear the snare in the center when you just listen to the overheads. When you just mike the cymbals and you solo those mics, the snare tends to shift depending upon your perspective. So I make those mics identical in distance from the snare as well as identical in distance from the cymbals that they're miking so no mic gets a signal prior to the other one. With just the overheads up, I want you to get a good idea of the kit but with the snare in the center, which is not really how the kit is since the snare is always placed slightly on one side. The bass drum is in the center, so in the best of all possible worlds, I try to make the snare right above the bass drum, and I mike it accordingly.

Do you use room mics at all?

Yeah. On the Korn dates, for example, if I'm ever thinking about 5.1, which I am more and more these days, I set up a set of rear overheads and front and rear room mics. Sometimes my room mics will be high over the kit, and just as often they'll be low to the floor.

How do you determine that?

The sound of the room and how much metal the guy plays determines the position. Some guys are splashy cymbal players and other guys aren't. If there's a lot of cymbal activity and a lot of splashy metal work going on, my tendency is to go lower to the floor to get things warmer. It's one of those things determined by the amount of time there is to play around. Otherwise, I'll just set them as best as I can.

Another thing on the drums that I tend to do if there's a lot of cross-sticking is to slip a mic in close to the cross-stick, because I generally find that a mic coming in across the cymbals doesn't always give me enough of the meat of the cross-stick sound.

When you're putting four or five mics on a kick, do all of these go on separate tracks or do you combine them?

It depends on the session. On a Broadway date or a quick pop date, I'll generally stick with two mics on the bass drum and maybe just put a room mic close to the floor, a couple of feet out from the drums. But if I have the time to play around with it, then I'll use the multiple mics. Generally speaking it's a production call. If I'm producing, then what I'll do is meld as many as I can ahead of time and just go with it.

But since we've gone to hard disc–based recording medium, it's given me a flexibility that I didn't have before. What I tend to do now is keep these mics on separate tracks because I tend to play around with the timing after the date is over. Visually, I try to place the capsules as close together as I can, but no matter how close it looks to be, you usually don't get it down to the sample. One sample is on the order of microns, so I'll play around with moving the later one to see what happens when I move it in time. Sometimes you'd be amazed at how much of a difference that makes in the quality of the sound.

The same thing with guitar amps. I'll have three or four mics on one guitar amp, like a Marshall cabinet with the slanted front, and three or four mics on a Marshall cabinet with a straight front. If you go in after they're recorded and you move those things so they're aligned to the sample, you'd be surprised how much better they sound when they're collapsed into mono and totally phase aligned. So if I'm on a hard disc recorder like an [Euphonix] R-1 and I have the ability to keep them on separate tracks, then I do so until I can phase align them and combine them later.

You own an R-1, don't you?

Yes I do. It's just an amazing machine. It's the only tape machine that I've ever bought, and it's one of the few purchases that I haven't actually regretted years later. It just keeps getting better and better. The reason why I bought it was that when I started using it, I loved it so much and realized that I never wanted to go back to a 3348 or a Pro Tools system. But it's not that easy to rent, and when you *can* rent it, it's expensive. So I said, "I'm doing this for me because it's the machine that I really want to work on."

I have a system that's 48-track at 48k. On both the Korn and Fuel dates, we used it as a 96k 48-track, which means that I had to add another two audio decks to my system. In this instance, Michael Beinhorn [the producer] also owns a system, so we just put our systems together. I've used them all, and to me there's nothing better. I have never used a workstation or any computer device that was so stable.

Do you usually mike an amp when recording electric bass guitar?

Whenever possible, I take both an amp and direct. I used to align the signals with a good digital delay, but now you can phase align in the workstation. I always take a direct because you never know. There may be a spillage issue or crackling mics or something, so I always take a direct if they've got one, even if it's an acoustic upright.

On an electric bass I will take the direct and put at least a couple of mics on the amp and pick and choose among those as I would with a guitar amp. I generally end up with one, but I'll start out with a couple to see what I like, again depending upon the time. If I have to get it done quickly, I'll put up a 4047 or a 47 FET and mike one of the speakers on the bass cab and just go with that. On the other hand, if I have the time to play around, then I'll go with a variety of things, like a tube 47, an AT4062, the 4047, and a variety of dynamics and condensers, just to see what works. Then I'll either choose one or blend a couple together to get the sound that I'm looking for.

On Korn, for example, we needed to get a really good range that encompasses the deep lows with that really crispy, crunchy top end, so I would mike for both of those. The 4060 was catching the really crispy top end, while the 4047 and the 47 were catching the meat of the bottom.

On guitar amps, do you put the mics close together or do you mike for distance?

Again, it depends how much time we have. The first thing I'll do is try to choose the best speaker on the amp. Usually we're using a four-speaker cabinet like a Marshall, and generally the speakers don't all sound the same. I try not to mike from too far away because you start to introduce phase anomalies from the different speakers coming from the cab. I tend to get as close as I can with whatever my miking scheme is. For instance, if I'm using a 4047 or something like that, they have shock mounts that keep you from getting too close, so the mic that's farthest away from the cabinet will determine my distance. But I'll try to get them as close as I can to the grille cloth.

I don't have any hard-and-fast rules about miking the center of the speaker or the side or going in directly or off the side because I've found over the years that every amp and every guitar player sounds different. So I'll try them all. I'll put a mic right up on the cone looking right down the center, then I'll put one looking at the center but placed where the voice coil meets the cone itself, and then I'll just put one on the edge of the cone and then just see which one sounds the best. But I do try to cluster a few mics so their capsules are as close to identical in distance from the sound source as I can get them. Then I'll put another mic about 6 to 10 inches away and play with it in phase and out of phase to see if it's adding anything or taking it away. Generally, the 4047 is my main mic because it takes the high SPL really well, but in addition it gives me both the lows and a good balance of highs. But then I'll add a little bit of something like a 57 or a ribbon mic, like an RCA BK-5 or something like that. If the 4047 is at 0 on the console, these will be at −10 or −15 to add a little bit of crunch to it. Then I might add the mic that's off 6 or 8 inches to either scoop out a little midrange or to add something because of its phase characteristics. But I might not even use it all. It depends.

That sounds like a big setup.

That's the thing. There are two ways that I approach these things. On a setup that I have time to play, then all of the techniques that you and I have learned over the years and all of the stuff that we've read about all come into play, so we get to try some things and experiment. That's why I really love those sessions.

On the other hand, if you do a date where the tape has to be rolling in 15 minutes, and you have 40 musicians sitting out there in the studio, you stick a mic in the most logical place and go. I'm grateful to have the opportunity to do both. Every year I used to do "Pavarotti and Friends," which was Pavarotti with guests like Elton John, Stevie Wonder, Mariah Carey, BB King, and Celine Dion, with a 70-piece orchestra and a rock-and-roll house band. There were jazz, classical, opera, and rock all intermixed. You'd have anywhere from a minute to a minute and a half to set up for the next type of music. Under those circumstances you just rely on all of your experience and just stick a mic in front of the instrument and pray. I love doing the gamut of all that stuff.

How long did it take with Korn or Fuel to get to the point of actually recording?

It's hard to say, but generally within the first two or three days. With Korn it was a little longer because we spent the first day and a half deciding what recording format we were going to use. What we did was set up some instruments and record them into an R-1, Pro Tools, Nuendo, analog 24-track, and an 8-track 2-inch. We went to every format we could think of. What we ended up with was the R-1 with dB converters on the front and back. So that was a day and a half. The next thing we did was have the drummer set up and play in different parts of the room to determine the best-sounding placement, which took about a day. Then we spent about a half day trying out bass drums, different snares, different heads, and things like that. So now you're three days into it and really now only just starting to mike up the kit. David, the drummer from Korn, has a huge kit, so after trying a bunch of different mics, we only started to get things together by the end of the fourth day. On the fifth day we started tracking.

Fuel was much faster. We did one day of setups, the second day of moving the drums around in the room, and on the third day we started cutting drums.

How do you handle leakage?

Generally I view leakage as a positive as opposed to a negative. My view is that leakage is your friend and what makes the sound real and live and wonderful. I like the way it makes things blend with each other and fills in a little as it would in a live situation. It's just like on the drums. I don't mike the overheads for the cymbals, but for the overall sound that comes from around the kit.

On the other hand, one of the first questions I ask is, "How much flexibility are you going to need for overdubs?" For example, on most Broadway shows that I do, having the chorus in the room with the orchestra sonically is by far the best thing to do because it sounds amazing with the leakage. You might have 30 people in the chorus, but it sounds like 100 because of all the leakage. It's big and warm and wonderful. On the other hand, if it turns out that the show will be sent to Europe and done in another language [as is the case in most shows these days], you have no choice but to isolate the chorus so they can use your basic track and add a foreign-language chorus later. So I try to find out up front how much flexibility we'll need in the overdubs.

For example, when I was doing the Rod Stewart album [*It Had to Be You…The Great American Songbook*], we had everyone in the room. We then came to realize that some of the piano might be changed later, so we had to isolate it, because even though it sounded great, it was going to be too obvious if you punched in a new part.

Is there a standard set of mic preamps that you use?

Again, it really comes down to a matter of time. On the Fuel session that I just left, we had seven or eight different kinds. Michael Beinhorn, who was producing the session, has a bunch of old 1057s, 1073s, 1081s, and even some old 1058s. I got in some of the new Neve 88R remote mic pres. SSL was kind enough to let me use a prototype of their new super mic pre, which is also a remote pre. I also have some of my own Tube-Techs. I'll usually go in with some preconceived notions, but I'll also play with stuff if there's time. Many times you're surprised how good a particular pre can sound with a certain mic on a particular instrument. On the other hand, I'll go with whatever I have to go with. Generally speaking, I'm not a real snob about these kinds of things. I have pres that sound better than others, but the mic pres on the new Neves and SSLs all are good enough if I have to get a session up and running that I'm not going to complain. If it doesn't sound good, it isn't because I'm using the console mic pres, it's because I'm not doing my job.

What's your philosophy about tracking?

My only philosophy is that I want to get the best sound under the circumstances and make it sound great. If there's any philosophy at all, it's that I will only go to the equalizer as a last resort. I've been doing this long enough to know that a change in microphones or position is worth a lot more than tweaking EQs. I have a tendency to think that if you start tweaking EQs too soon, then you going to miss some obvious things, so the first thing I do is get the session sounding great flat. Then I'll make a few adjustments with an EQ. I'm not a purist in the sense that I will record with an equalizer and processing, but my first instinct is to get out of my chair and go listen in the room to make sure of what I'm hearing. So I spend a lot of time listening to the actual sound of the instrument and then go into the control room and try to pick that up on the microphone.

Do you compress when you're recording?

Not a lot. The only time I do some EQing or compressing while recording is when I know it's going to be mixed to tape and I won't have a chance to do it later. So, for example, if I'm mixing all the toms and overheads together onto a stereo kit track, I'll do the processing then. I will use compression occasionally. I did so more when we were in 16-bit than now with 24-bit because in the 16-bit world it was more important that you stayed close to the zero end of the scale. I would compress things just to make sure that I stayed close to that range, but in 24-bit you have a lot more leeway, so I'm less likely to do that now.

Whatever I want to hear I do want to put on tape, though. In other words, if I think that compression is important for the playback, then I will compress to tape. But for the most part, I really want the sound to do what it does naturally.

How did you make the transition from drummer to engineer?

Actually, I had a couple of deals as a singer/songwriter. By 1979 I was a staff writer for Screen Gems, where I was getting a weekly salary. I had just finished an album for Life Song records when they lost their distribution deal with Epic. At about the same time, Screen Gems decided not to pick up my publishing option. I had been kicking around New York for seven or eight years trying to make it as a musician, and it looked like everything was caving in. So I went to the studio owner of Right Track, which was just a demo studio at the time and the place where I used to do my Screen Gems songwriter demos. I said, "I'm 30 years old now and too old to be an assistant, but I know I can do this." I always had good ears, and people always had commented on how good my demos sounded, so he gave me a shot. Inside of six months I was the chief engineer. A year later Peter Asher came in to do a movie, *Pirates of Penzance*, and he wanted the chief engineer, which was me. From there he took me to England with him, and from that point on I just started doing it. So it was a very easy transition in that once I got going, things happened almost so quickly that I never looked back. I really never had a chance to miss being a musician and songwriter.

For years I was trying to get songs to Peter Asher, and just three years after I started engineering I was in Montserrat with him, co-producing James Taylor. There was nothing in that scenario that made me regret my decision.

How have things changed technically in the way you do your gig between then and now? Has your approach changed?

My approach has changed in that I used to try to make up for what I thought were the inadequacies of analog. I used to come into every session an hour early and go through the tones and alignment, and then there was the hell of listening off the sync head. I didn't get into digital initially because I liked that even less.

There are a lot of people who like to wax on about the wonders of analog recording, but I'm not one of them because I used to hate the compression that analog would put on things. As a drummer, I used to hear this amazing sound coming through the monitors in the room with a real crack on the snare and a real punch in the bass drum, and then I'd put it on analog tape and I'd hear all this squashing and extra harmonics going on. I never liked the sound of analog. I thought it took away so much of what we were going for.

I think now the challenges are remarkably different. There are two things going on. One is our ability to stay ahead of the curve in that it's getting harder and harder to know all your equipment. Back 15 years ago, I dare say there wasn't a studio that you could walk into where you didn't know the gear. As long as you knew the SSL and Studer or MCI and Harrison console, there really wasn't anything you couldn't do. Nowadays you walk in, and you're going to have to pretty much know how to record on Pro Tools and Nuendo, too.

I've had to take on a lot of things myself because I'm amazed at how many studios don't know how to deal with digital. They don't understand it and are very lax on things like clocking and cabling and related issues. So there are a whole lot of things right now that an engineer has to be on top of because there's so much gear and so much misinformation out there. On one hand the technology is remarkable, but if you don't stay on top of it all the time, it's very ripe for very bad mistakes.

What's the hardest thing for you to record?

At the end of the day, the voice. I could put any mic in front of a voice and record it and it's done, so in a certain sense it's easy. However, to catch the dynamic range and nuances and personality of a really great singer like a Barbra Streisand or a Carly Simon or a James Taylor really does require a focus and an interest that I see missing in a lot of recordists these days. Voice is a fascinating instrument. I never stop learning. Every time I think that I have it together, I get surprised. There are so many things about the voice that you can miss unless you're really tuned into it, so in the end it's the easiest and the hardest to record.

Do you have an approach to recording the voice?

If I know the singer, then I have an idea ahead of time which mics I'm going to use. If I have the time, my approach is to put four or five mics in front of them and have them sing a line. It's similar to when you have a speaker that sounds great with a certain amp and not as good with another amp. There's a certain coupling, a synergy that happens between various stages of audio equipment that can be really special.

It's the same thing with a voice. There's a synergy that happens between a mic and a voice, so the first thing I do is try a variety of mics running the gamut from a U 47, to an M 49, to a 251, to a C 12, to one of the newer mics like a 4060. Usually you'll eliminate all but two or three right away because there's a connection between the harmonic content of the voice and the mic that just tends to work. Then when I'm set with the mic, I'll start to play with preamps.

But if someone said, "You have a vocalist coming in and we have to record right now," then I'd probably just go with my standard setup, which is my 269 or one of my 47s into a Tube-Tech mic pre with more than likely just a touch of 1176.

Do you have your own assistant?

I should, but I don't because my setup is so complicated. I do most of my work here at Right Track, and each time they hire a new assistant, they get to spend a "hell week" with me to break them in.

To me the assistant has two main jobs. One is he's your liaison with the studio, obviously, and the second is documentation. One of the things that is sorely missing is the need for proper documentation from studios. I'm amazed that studios don't require every assistant to write up a proper track sheet on a session. I don't care if it's recorded to Pro Tools or a DAW; I want to see a track sheet at the end of the day.

CHAPTER 21

Jerry Hey

There may be no other trumpet player as respected and widely recorded as Jerry Hey. The first call for a Hollywood recording date for more than 25 years, Jerry has not only played on thousands of recordings by almost every major artist and movie soundtracks too numerous to mention, but he is a widely sought-after arranger as well. So when it comes to what it takes to make a trumpet sound great in the studio, it's best to get the facts straight from the master.

I understand that you have strong feelings about how people mike your horn.

I guess I have strong feelings because over the course of my experience, being in great situations and then being in awful situations, I've learned a lot.

You carry your own mics, don't you?

I have for about 10 or 12 years. When you go into studios like Capitol or Ocean Way, they have a good microphone collection so you don't have to worry. But with home studios being such a big part of recording now, a lot of times they don't have any good mics. It forced me to take one part of the equation and make it the same every time so I always know it's not the microphone's fault if something doesn't sound right.

I carry three Royers with me now. Before that I had a KM 54 for a while.

Why three Royers?

Usually in my horn section there are two trumpets, one trombone, and one sax. The trumpets play on one mic, and trombone and sax play on a mic each.

The Royer has become sort of a standard now. They're almost like the new RCA 77 and much more reliable, in my opinion. If you had a great 77 that was well taken care of, it was a good microphone, but nine times out of ten it's been dropped or mistreated over the years, so they don't sound that good. Plus they can't handle the level like the Royers do. Most of the studios now have bought Royers, so I don't have to even take them to a lot of places.

So do you just have someone use your mics right away, or do you wait to see what it sounds like?

It depends on the engineer. For instance, Bruce Swedien has a great mic collection that he bought new that no one else has ever touched, and he's put a whole host of microphones in front of us. We did a very high-intensity tune for Michael Jackson once where he put his RCA 44 on the trumpets, and I told him, "Bruce, you're the only guy I'd ever let put that microphone in front of us." He said, "Wait until you hear it." It just sounded amazing because it was in such pristine condition. In a situation like that, where a guy has world-class microphones, there's usually not a problem.

But in situations where I'm in somebody's home and they have little or no microphone selection and they put up something that I know doesn't sound good, I'll tell them I have the Royers available. Nine times out of ten now they'll say, "You've got those Royers? Great."

Do you have a favorite placement?

Because the Royers have a figure-8 pattern, the room is an issue in the placement. If you're in a smaller room with four horns, you can't have the mics too far away from the trumpets at the level we play because the room becomes a factor on the back side of the mic. So the placement can be anywhere from a foot and a half to 4 feet or so away. We've done some Earth, Wind & Fire stuff where it's been 6 feet away. That was kind of roomy because the room was small, but that was the sound we were going for—kind of a "live" sound. So it does depend on the size of the room, how far away you are from the wall that you're playing toward, and how much slap off the wall you're going to get. But generally I'd say about 2 feet from the end of the trumpet bell takes most of the room away from it.

Is that directly on-axis to the bell?

Yes, directly on-axis. I'm of the feeling that if you play off-axis it sounds off-axis. I know that when you play right at somebody it's much more present than if you turn even a few degrees away, so that same thing translates directly to the microphone.

How do you determine where in the room you're going to play?

That depends on the acoustics of the room. In a moderate-size room like Ocean Way, Conway, or Capitol, when you play softly it sounds like you're playing softly, and when you play loudly it sounds like you're playing loudly, and you can hear yourself all the time. Almost anywhere in those rooms sounds great. If you go into another room that has carpeting on the floor or soft walls or ceilings, the quality of sound doesn't change that much [from soft to loud], and you feel like you have to work harder. In a deader room it helps to be closer to a wall so you can get a little feedback from what you're playing; otherwise, it's easy to overblow and work harder than you need to work.

Do you mean play into the wall?

Not into the wall, but move a step or two closer to get a little bit of feedback. When you're playing trumpet, your effort is a factor in how much you can hear yourself, so in a deader studio it makes it a lot more difficult to play and to hear everybody. So if you move up a little closer to the glass or the wall, it can make you not work so hard.

Does that still matter if you're wearing headphones?

We always use one-sided headphones because it's very difficult to expect the engineer to get your balance good enough with the rhythm section and also balance the horn section the way it should be in order to play in tune with double-sided phones. That puts another cog in the link of recording when you have to make the engineer work that hard. Also, with one headphone we can hear everyone in the room, which helps keep the time and phrasing the same.

Where is the mic placed on the trombone?

Because we generally only have one trombone, placement's not that much of an issue because the mic can handle the level, and he's the only one on that microphone. If the mic is farther back and we're in a live enough room, the trumpets will get on the back side of that mic—and even more so the one on the saxophone—because there are two of us playing loudly and only one of him. So the bone mic is about 18 to 24 inches away from the bell.

What other mics have been used on you that have worked?

Al Schmitt loves 67s, and so do I. I've seen some Coles. Allen Sides always puts KM 54s on the trumpets, and they always sound great.

Do you always play with the same guys?

If I can. The other trumpet player is Gary Grant, and we've played together for over 30 years. I know what he's going to do, and he knows what I'm going to do, so it's just like a clone standing right next to you. The saxophones have changed a bit over the years with Dan Higgins or Larry Williams or a few others that I've used. Bill Reichenbach on trombone has been the guy for a very long time. It's understood that we go in there as a team with everyone going at it at the same level. It makes life easier, and we have a good time.

CHAPTER 22

Eddie Kramer

Unquestionably one of the most renowned and well-respected producer/engineers in all of rock history, Eddie Kramer's credits list is indeed staggering. From rock icons such as Jimi Hendrix, the Beatles, the Rolling Stones, Led Zeppelin, Kiss, Traffic, and the Kinks to pop stars Sammy Davis, Jr. and Petula Clark, as well as the seminal rock movie, *Woodstock*, Eddie is clearly responsible for recording some of the most enjoyable and influential music ever made.

How did you get started in the recording business?

I was a classically trained pianist, but my real interests were in how to improve the sound of what we had. I had a fascination with sound dating back to growing up in South Africa. There was no TV, so I used to fall asleep listening to shortwave radio. Modifying that and trying to make it sound better was a goal of mine, so when I left South Africa and came to England in 1960, I gravitated toward that part of the business. I eventually got a job as a tea boy at Advision Studios in 1962, where I learned by watching. It was all mono in those days. I learned how to record on 35-millimeter mag dubber, how to operate a projector, and how to a cut disc. Prior to my getting a job at Advision, I was experimenting at home with a Brenell tape recorder with a couple of ribbon mics and recording jazz groups in my living room, which was my earliest recording experience.

At Advision we recorded mostly commercials in mono onto a Telefunken tape machine, which was a direct descendant from the Magnetophon that was captured from the Germans during World War II. Whenever you hit the stop button, sparks would fly out and burn your fingers if you were not quick enough. The microphones that we used in those days were Altec small-diaphragm condensers, RCA 44s, and an oddball selection of English ribbon mics.

I guess I really learned by watching what the other engineers did while they were recording, and I sort of adapted their technique in recording my first jazz groups. From there I went to Pye Studios, and that's really where I got my first lesson on how to record pop music. My mentor there was a guy named Bob Auger who was an absolute genius. We used to go out on the road with the Pye Mobile recording 90-piece symphony orchestras on a three-track Ampex machine. We would use three Neumann U 47s placed strategically left, center, right for the balance. The conductor would draw out from orchestra what was necessary, so if you got the mic placement correct and you got the conductor to help you, then you would theoretically get a great recording. I learned a lot from that situation.

Upon our return to Pye Studios, we would record a band like the Kinks, on which I was an assistant, or we would record Petula Clark. So there was a wide range of pop and classical stuff that I got to witness and be a part of. This was all three-track in the beginning and then it evolved into four-track.

From there I started my own studio, KPS Sound Studio, which was a little demo "hole in the wall" where we recorded John Mayall and some of the Kinks. It was a very basic, very primitive two-track studio.

Eventually I landed at Olympic, where I met my next mentor, Keith Grant, who I owe a lot to. Keith was a monster at doing large sessions. He'd do big orchestras with a choir, rhythm section, horns, and lead vocal all at the same time. Olympic was the best independent studio in London, with a capacity of between 80 or 90 musicians, and it's where I ended up doing Hendrix, Traffic, the Stones, you name it.

We'd do a lot of music to picture and just a tremendous variety of stuff. For example, in the morning we'd do a movie soundtrack from about 9 a.m. to 1 p.m., in the afternoon we'd do a jingle, and then break it all down and record the Stones in the evening! Many times the instruments that were left lying around from the orchestral sessions wound up getting used on the rock sessions later at night. The rock guys would come in and say, "That's cool. I'm gonna use that," which is how I recorded Jimi using the glockenspiel on *Little Wing*, because it was just left in the studio.

Having been trained as a classical musician, then getting into jazz, then into rock, I had this very wide range of taste in music that was very eclectic. So when anything weird came into the studio, I was the guy they picked.

That must have influenced your philosophy about recording.

In regards to mic techniques, what I adapted was this classical idea of recording—*i.e.*, the distance of the microphones to the instruments should not be too close if you wanted to get anything with tremendous depth.

Obviously I used close-miking techniques as well, but it started with the concept that "distance makes depth" that Bob Auger taught me. Generally, the basic philosophy of getting the mics up in the air and getting some room sound and some air around the instrument was what we used. Then you'd fill in with the close mics.

Of the microphones that we used, 67s were probably the favorite—and still are today—but we used 47s, 251s, a lot of KM 56s and 54s, ribbon mics, AKG D 12s, D 20s, and D 30s. In fact, on some of the Hendrix stuff I used a D 30 on the bass drum, which I still think is a really great bass-drum mic.

Once I came to the United States in '68, utilizing that philosophy seemed to work, but with some modifications. Obviously, watching how the American engineers did things influenced me to a certain extent.

How was that different?

It was different in that they didn't use as many mics and they would be very tight in, which I though was a cool thing. So I adapted that close-in technique of getting right in on the speaker cab, which seemed to work very well.

Were you using a combination of close and far mics?

Yes, I was. In fact, the Hendrix stuff in '68 at the Record Plant, the *Electric Ladyland* album, if you listen to "Voodoo Chile," you can hear the way the room just resonates. That's because I had mics everywhere, and the fact that he was singing live, too! I wasn't scared of recording an artist in the room live as he was cutting. To me, anything that was in the room was fair game to be recorded. Don't forget that I had an artist who was an absolute genius, so it made life a lot simpler. When you're recording someone of Hendrix's ilk, you're not going to be overdubbing much if it's a live track. You put the mics up, place them correctly, give the artist the room and the facility to work in, and make sure it sounds cool so when they walk into the control room they say, "Oh, that sounds just like I was playing it out there." That's the goal: to capture the essence of what the artist is actually doing in the studio.

Obviously, there are other ways to do it. You can do it in sections and pieces by overdubbing and re-cutting, and that certainly works too, but to me there's nothing more exciting than having the band in the studio cutting live straight to tape, where that's the performance and that's what gets mixed. That's the essence of any great recording. I don't care if it's classical or rock or country, you've got to capture that performance, and the hell with the bloody leakage.

Too bad that DAWs have changed that these days.

It has, and I think to music's detriment. I strongly feel that music should be captured as it's going down. If you make a mistake, too bad. You cut another piece and chop it together, but you still have the essence of that live performance.

So you mostly did multiple takes and then chopped together a good one?

Yeah, absolutely. Chopping multitrack tape was the name of the day. I think that a lot of producers and engineers that grew up in the '60s and '70s hold to that philosophy. I think that even today, with Pro Tools, one can still do that, although it also can be slower in the long run. I urge anyone who's cutting tracks now not to record directly to Pro Tools. Go to analog first. Get a nice 16-track headblock, record at 15 IPS, put Dolby SR on if you desire, then transfer over to Pro Tools. But, I'm very, very careful about that transfer process. The critical trick is to use the best converters that money can buy. Even after that, I love to lock up the original analog drum tracks with Pro Tools for mixing.

When you started you were pretty limited by the number of tracks and channels available.

Definitely. You have to use your imagination and think really hard about how to plan it out. For instance, on Hendrix stuff, which is the classic example, it was done on four-track. On the first record we used mono drums and mono guitars and so forth. So on *Are You Experienced*, we would fill a four-track up and then dump it down to another four-track, leaving two tracks open. Then you may have to do that again. On *Axis: Bold As Love*, I was doing stereo drums, which made a big difference.

Was your approach different when you went to stereo?

Yes. When it was mono I just used a single overhead, a snare mic, and bass-drum mic. There might be one or two tom mics, but that would be it. When I went to stereo my approach changed. I probably used a pair of 251s or 67s, I can't remember which—probably more than likely 67s. I was just trying to get that left-to-right image when the toms would go left to right. I always record from the drummer's perspective and not from the listener's perspective.

Has your approach to tracking changed when you do it today?

Yes, it has been modified in the sense that you don't have to use an enormous room to record the drums anymore. In fact, bands today don't want that huge reverberant drum sound that we used to love, so you can record drums in a smaller, deader space and still get a big, fat sound. Obviously, I'm using more mics, multiple mics on the bass drum, multiple mics [top and bottom] on the snare, which I didn't do before. I use a lot of mics on the guitar and then pick the ones that I like.

Is your setup the same all the time?

Pretty much. I will experiment with different microphones as they come in. I work with Shure and helped develop the KSM44 series of microphones, so I use those a lot because they sound really great. The KSM27 is a great guitar amp mic. I love the new KSM141, which is a cross between a 451 and a KM84, on hat, percussion, acoustic guitar, and underneath the snare. The SM91 and SM52 are my bass drum mics of choice. And I use KSM44 on overheads. But I still use vintage mics, like 47s, and the new Neumann TLM 103s, 147s, and 149s. To me a microphone is like a color that a painter selects from his palette. You pick the colors that you want to use. So the mics are my palette. In the end it doesn't matter to me too much. Whatever is available, I'll just look at it and think, "I wonder what this will sound like on the guitar, or bass, or whatever instrument." I know what my standard stuff is, and if I need to do something really quickly, I'll always go back to it, but I'll often experiment with whatever happens to be in the studio.

Do you tailor the mic preamp to the microphone? Do you have certain combinations that you like?

No, I just blanket it with vintage Neve modules, either 1033s or 1081s. I like the 1081s because of the four-band EQ so I can carve things out, particularly when I'm recording bass drum. Lately I've been using the Vintech X81, which is a copy of the 1081.

So you're EQing to tape?

I always do. I have done it my whole life. If I hear a sound that I like, then it goes to tape. If it's a guitar, then I'll print the reverb as well on a separate track so the sound is there and locked in. I usually have an idea of what it's going to sound like in the final analysis, so the EQ and compression are done right then and there. I think if you bugger around with it afterward, you have too many choices. This isn't rocket science, it's music. Just record the thing the way you hear it! After all, it is the song that we're trying to get and the guy's emotion. We're becoming so anal and self-analytical and protracted with our views on recording, I think it's destructive and anti-creative. It's bad enough that we have to be locked into a bloody room with a sweaty musician. [Laughs]

Recording music should be a fun-filled day. To me, making a record should be about having a ball because it makes the day go quickly, and yet you're still getting what you want on tape. There's a friend of mine who has a bar in his studio, and after the session is finished everybody has a beer and relaxes. What a wonderful thing! I think artists today have a tendency not to do this. You cut to a bloody click track, go to Beat Detective, do a lot of overdubs in Pro Tools, and then spend a lot of time searching for the right plug-ins to make it sound cool. But the track has to move and breathe. Listen to all the great songs and albums that have been recorded the last 30 years. The ones that really stand out are the ones that breathe and move. With human beings, their tempo varies. I do admire what can be done in Pro Tools, but if there's something that wrong, you should have done another take and maybe chopped things together.

What's the hardest thing for you to record?

The toughest thing to record is a full orchestra. Getting the right room and properly placing the microphones is really tough, but it's also so rewarding. The other thing that's tough is the artist who can't get the right feel, so you have to go through a lot, changing microphones and instruments and placement, to make it work. That can be boring.

I like to think that going into the studio is a challenge. What are we going to do next? Can we do it any better? Can we really top the one that went before? What usually happens is that the artist, unbeknownst to him, has done a brilliant job on the first take, and it all goes downhill very rapidly after that. The reverse can also be true in that the first take is weak because the person is just getting used to it, and he builds up gradually to point where it is great.

Didn't you tell me once that "All Along the Watchtower" was Take 27?

That's a great example of an artist of Jimi's stature starting from square one with a very difficult arrangement. He's yelling at Mitch, "C'mon. Here's how you do the rhythm part." Then Mitch eventually gets it. Then he yells at Dave Mason because he can't get the secondary rhythm guitar part. Eventually he gets it, and Jimi keeps going at it and going at it. At one point Brian Jones walks into the studio drunk out of his mind and starts to play piano. Jimi politely lets him play, I think on Take 20 or 21, and then excuses him by saying, "No, I don't think so, Brian." Then by Take 25 it's a four-star, Take 26 is good, but Take 27 is the master, you can just tell. It's got everything right. Everything is perfectly placed and has the intensity that Jimi wanted. So the song evolved because it had to. There was no time for rehearsal. This was something that had to be learned in the studio. It's not the way you want to do it, but because he's a musician of that stature, you don't mind if it takes 30 takes.

So you recorded even what you knew would be a rehearsal?

We recorded everything because you never knew when the magic might happen. It could be Take 14, but it could also be the first or second take, which often happened.

When you're tracking now, do you still have everyone in the studio playing and going for keepers?

As much as I can, I encourage bands to do that. I go into pre-production making the band really understand what the parts are and what the options are. You've got to know what the options are because when you go into the studio and start recording, even though you're well rehearsed something might not work, so you've got to have a backup plan. Sometimes when you hear something in the studio it doesn't sound the same as pre-production, so you've got to be able to change things. You may only end up with a great drum track and a great bass track, and maybe the guitars have to be replaced, which is not a problem, but I at least try to get as much of it on tape to preserve that feel.

So before you weren't worried about leakage. Are you more worried about it now?

It depends on the situation. If the band is of the type that can execute perfectly and doesn't require any replacement, you want to capture it with the leakage. If you know that you'll have to work on the parts and they might require a lot of attention to detail, you have to look at the leakage factor as being important.

How do you determine where to place the instruments in the room?

I go for the best studio that I can find, and they usually have great-sounding rooms with terrific monitors and a great mic selection. You can't really go too far wrong. You have to have a great room first, but if you have, then it's pretty simple.

CHAPTER 23

Mark Linett

Hollywood's Sunset Sound has not only produced a tremendous number of hit records over its 40-plus years in business, but an impressive number of wonderful engineers as well. There's something about the sound that those schooled the Sunset way get. It's big, fat, punchy, and distinct all at once. Mark Linett is a Sunset alumnus who went on to a staff position at the famous Warner Bros.–owned Amigo Studios before subsequently putting a studio in his house. You've heard his work many times, with engineering credits including the Beach Boys, Brian Wilson, America, Rickie Lee Jones, Eric Clapton, Christopher Cross, Buckwheat Zydeco, Randy Newman, Michael McDonald, and many more. Having worked on numerous best-of compilations and remixes of famous '60s recordings (the Beach Boy's *Pet Sounds Sessions* and several Jimi Hendrix reissues, for example), Mark has the unique ability to compare the techniques of the past against those of the present.

Do you ever find that people are hiring you specifically to get that "vintage sound?"

Yeah. What I've discovered is that a lot of records I do are either intentionally or unintentionally trying to sound like the records cut at Western or Sunset or Gold Star from around '66 or '67. Of course, in those days of three- and four-track recording, leakage wasn't something you worried about and was actually something that contributed enormously to the sound. The players were mildly baffled at best, and you had these small rooms with everyone playing at the same time. So the leakage had a tremendous amount to do with what things like the drums sounded like. It wasn't about a mic in front of every instrument and that's all it picked up.

So now you want that kind of sound, but you still want some kind of control, so I try to isolate all the instruments so that in the event that the inevitable happens and somebody wants to replace their part, it can be done. There's a tradeoff for that in terms of playability, but since most players are attuned to playing with headphones and the person that they're playing with can be across the room—or across the world, for that matter—it's really not so much of an issue.

So a lot of what we end up doing with room mics sort of emulates what that sound would have been if all that leakage would have spilled into the other mics. One of the problems with multitrack recording is we get very concerned about being able to isolate every sound but yet have it sound really good when it's all pushed up together, and that gets really tricky. You start to understand where they got the sound on those old records. It might have been only on three-track, but it was pretty well soldered together using leakage to their benefit. Once headphones and multitracks came along, all that sort of went away because people wanted to have options.

On a lot of great records they had the vocal slightly baffled out in the room, but they weren't planning on replacing them anyway.

I've heard all sorts of '60s sessions from Western and Gold Star. I did some things for Nancy Sinatra last year where I got to hear some outtakes from "These Boots Were Made for Walkin'," and that is a 100-percent live track, except for her singing. It's just amazing. You think "How can these guys play that well?" and the answer is that the technology required that they either play that well or get somebody who could. Also, there weren't a lot of guys wearing headphones in those days, either.

They played well because they had to. Imagine most players trying to do that today.

My personal feeling is that all this technology certainly has a place, but it's so affected by the playing. We tend to get caught up in the technology and forget that fact. A few years ago I was hired to take a band into Studio 3 [at Western] because that's where a lot of Beach Boys records were made. The fact is that the band didn't record anything remotely like the way that stuff was done, so it was really kind of irrelevant. Even if you did try to record the way they did, I'm not sure that it would work anyway because nobody can really play that way anymore.

Once, not long after Pro Tools came along, I was doing a kids' record where we did the basic tracks with an acoustic bass and live drums. The bass was in another room, but if you soloed it, you could hear that there was a drummer on the premises, which was no surprise. I didn't have Pro Tools at that point, so they took it somewhere else to mix it. I got a call about a week later from the engineer mixing the project, saying that there was something wrong with the transfers that we did. I asked him what was wrong, and he said, "When I solo the bass I can hear the drums." It never occurred to him that the two guys might have been playing at the same time in the same room. Because it's now technically possible to do just about anything that you can imagine, everybody automatically thinks that's what's going on. It's kind of sad, really.

When you track, do you always start with the same setup?

Pretty much. For the past 9 or 10 years, I've been doing most of my tracking here at my studio with a house drum kit, just like the old days. A lot of places that we admire from the mid-'60s had a very set way of doing things. Not that you wouldn't experiment to a certain extent, but you developed what worked in the room. Traditionally, in the earlier days, people went to a studio as much for the engineer as the sound of the room. It was really about the sound that was coming out of the room that people wanted, so they assumed that the engineer had a lot to do with it. [Laughs]

So at my own place, maybe 60 or 70 percent of the time we end up using my house kit. Whether we do use it or not, I end up miking it the same. That's changed a bit over the years, but not much. It's kind of nice to work in a linear way and to be able to more directly play on what you've done before than when you're under the gun of the clock. Getting it good and fast is probably more important than anything else.

What's your setup for drums then?

At this point I generally will have at least two and sometimes three mics on the kick. Usually a D 112 inside and an FET 47 about 2 feet back, and a big old AKG D 35 for that '60s oomph for the bass drum at about 3 feet back—you have to play with the placement. It definitely picks up a lot more than just the kick, but fed in a little bit you can get more of a '60s sound.

You want to put a windscreen on a condenser on the drums so you don't pick up too much air to keep it from popping the woofers. You want the drum and not the air moving out of it.

What do you use for snare?

I usually use a 57 top and bottom with the bottom out of phase. Usually a 460 on the hat. When I use tom mics, which is most of the time, I'm rather partial to Beyer M500s. The last bunch of years I've been fond of a stereo ribbon mic for overheads. I was using a B&O, but now I use the Royer SF-12, which is kind of a fancy version of it. I like ribbons over a live drum kit because of the silky top for the cymbals. And you can do all sorts of processing to them without it getting too stupid.

Then I always use all sorts of room mics. The last bunch of years I've been favoring a pair of BK-5s—one behind and one in front of the drums. Sometimes I'll use a condenser across the room and usually one or two kind of "crummy" mics, like a Reslo or an EV 635, usually sitting on the floor compressed heavily. It's amazing what you can do with a small room. In some ways if everything is properly miked with compressed room mics, you can actually get a bigger drum sound than in a big room.

How did you determine the positioning of the room mics?

Pretty much just trial and error. The nice thing about having your own room and drum kit is that you can do that, although years ago I discovered just how much the player affects the sound.

I was doing Rickie Lee Jones' third album at Amigo, and Steve Gadd was going to play drums. We set the room up the night before, and they brought his drums in. I figured I'd get a bit of a head start, so I asked the second engineer to hit them. The second sits down and starts to hit them, and it was like, "This sounds terrible." I figured it was a rented kit and he'd come in and tune them up before the session or something. He comes in the next day and doesn't change a thing, and when he hits them, it's maybe the greatest drum sound I ever heard. The simple answer is that I've never heard a good drummer sound bad, and I've never heard a bad drummer sound particularly good. It's one of those instruments where the technique of the player really matters, like most acoustic instruments. When you get electric, it gets less important because the variables are much less.

You seem to do a lot with acoustic bass.

It's very difficult to do right, and if you don't have a good player, then it's especially hard to get what you need to make it sound good. For a rock thing I usually have something pointing at the bridge. I'm fond of an Altec 639 there and then sometimes another mic up on the neck, like a Beyer or an EV 666. It depends on the music. Traditionally in rock sessions, you would place the bass near the drums and fill in the sound from the drum mics.

All of us who aren't old enough to have made records when everything went on one track don't realize that recording back then was more like the way you'd record an orchestra now. On a rock date now, everything gets its own mic, and you try to weld it all together as opposed to capturing a realistic sound.

What are you doing for electric guitars?

I change it around, but a 57 is usually a constant. I usually use some combination of a dynamic and a condenser. I've gotten into using Sennheiser 409s over the years. EV 635s can be really nice on electric guitar. I've got some Gefell Neumann 582s with big lollipop Blue capsules on them.

If it's a fairly straightforward band of two guitars, bass, and drums, I like to cut stereo guitars. I'll pan them left and right so I can bring the other mic in toward the center so you get the sense that it's not just pinpointed in one speaker or the other. Again, this makes it seem as if you were picking up the guitars through some other mics in different parts of the room.

Are the two mics in the same place?

The dynamic is generally crammed right up on the speaker, but the condenser is back a little bit. You don't want the condenser right on it because then all you end up with is a lot of low-frequency stuff.

How about piano?

I have an upright piano that works out pretty well, actually. I've done all kinds of things with it, like a 47 up top and a ribbon on the back. Just yesterday we used a dynamic on the high end and a 47 on the low end.

If I'm in a studio with a grand piano, I tend to prefer to use a C 24 in M-S pretty well off the soundboard and out from under the top. If there are other players in the room, then I'll go with a pair of 251s if I can get them, over the soundboard with the piano bagged for isolation. If I was doing something orchestral, I'd just put a single spot mic on it.

I didn't realize that you do orchestral dates.

Not as many as I'd like. I did a 65-piece orchestra last year at Fox, where I used about 70 percent of the sound from a Decca Tree with M 50s, with the rest of the sound from spot mics. Orchestral recording is so much about the room and players and the arrangement. It's a thrilling thing to have that much music coming at you.

The things I like to do most are tracking and live records because live records are another instance where you have all the players playing together, albeit with PAs and monitors and mics stuffed really close to keep the enormous bleed down. But the mere fact that everyone is playing together makes up for that.

What's your approach to record live? You obviously have to think differently about how you do it in comparison to the studio.

In some ways it's simpler, and in some ways it's not. To start with, if it's a reasonably successful act, they've got their miking together and they just hand you a split. Then I'll just add a couple of things. If they're not doing it already, I'll want a bass amp mic because it makes a big difference. I'll probably want an under-the-snare mic, which they're probably not giving me. I used to use my own overhead mics, but I don't have to do that anymore since what people carry is normally quite good. I usually have to change the kick drum mic. SM91s seem to be the standard for live rock these days because all they want is the click of the drum, although I have used them in the studio just to get a little of that sound in there. I'll usually go with a D 112 and maybe a Beyer M160 as well to get that low-end ribbon sound. If I can afford it, I always try to put up a couple of mics on stage left and right to sort of have the ability to hear what it sounds like standing there. In the ideal situation, where you don't have to replace too much, they can add a really nice sound to the mix.

A lot of what I do, at least here in town [Los Angeles], is with my own rig that I've built and refined over the years. I can now do it with two racks and whatever we're recording to. I have a big rack of API preamps and another rack with these Roland 24-channel mixers. It shocks me sometimes how good the rough mixes sound. First of all, you do have everyone playing together, so it's a little more obvious what it's supposed to sound like. But another thing also happens that I firmly believe: if you force an engineer to make it sound like something on the spot, it's much more likely to come out pretty good than if you sit down with the tape and say, "Okay, let's spend eight hours on the snare drum sound." The toughest thing for me when going back to do the real mix is not getting it to sound better, but getting it to all stick together and get the performance vibe again.

I do my rough mixes with no processing at all. The room mics get a little EQ, and I compress the audience mics so when the band plays they don't overshoot, and when they stop playing the audience is good and loud. But other than that there isn't an EQ or compressor near these rough mixes. And they are shockingly good-sounding most of the time.

Do you ever keep them?

Yeah, I did one record last year where we kept 90 percent of the rough mixes, partly out of economic necessity, but they sounded good, so there was no reason to go back and remix them. Now with a DAW, I can fix some things by editing, without having to do a full remix.

What do you usually use for mic amps?

Here at my studio 90 percent of what I record goes through my old Universal Audio tube console that used to be in Studio 2 at United Western from about '61 to '69. It has 610A modules, and I just like the sound of that thing. I have a big API here, but not very much tends to get miked through it. It's generally just a remix console. If I'm doing a big tracking date, I may use a combination of the Universal console and maybe a few APIs and some other outboard preamps, like Neves, or some tube stuff, like V74s or Langevins. It just depends on the session.

You always seem to have some really nice vintage pieces for sale. How did you get into the vintage audio business?

I'm a collector at heart. At some point very early on, I started buying gear for myself and then built a studio. There's always stuff you buy that you don't want anymore, or you buy a big pile of stuff to get the one or two things that you want. I also collect other things with a passion as well, like jukeboxes and pinball machines. I don't do it so much any more because I've just got too much gear—way more than I can use at any one time, which is good and bad. I'm actually trying to lighten it up a bit because it can sort of take over. I've got a Universal Audio board in a crate that was the original board out of Studio B at Universal in Chicago in the '50s. I bought it from a guy who had it in his garage for 20 years, as much to keep it from being chopped up as anything. I'd love to restore it just to hear what it sounds like if I ever get around to it. At least it didn't go to the metal shop.

I'm down to one [Studer] 820 24-track now, but I really only use it for the archival stuff these days. I'm not sure if the next project we'll go to analog first or directly to Pro Tools.

So you're still in the Pro Tools world?

Yeah, I own Nuendo as well, but I don't really use it that much. I was using it for a couple of 5.1 remixes where I needed 96/24. Now I have a Pro Tools 96/24 system, so I really don't need it.

How about vocals?

I'm pretty much in love with a couple of 47s. I have five or six of them, but there's one in particular that's my vocal favorite. Of course it depends on the artist. I may use a 67 or even an 87. It goes through one of the 610 modules and then maybe into a [Fairchild] 670 or an EAR 660. I used to do a lot with an API preamp into an 1176 set at a 12-to-1 ratio, which is sort of your standard setup.

Do you EQ when you record?

No, I'll use what I get from the mic. If I'm using the UA console, then there are limited choices anyway because there's only low and high at plus 3 or plus 6. Since I'm monitoring back through the API, I might EQ on the monitor side. What I'm always trying to do is make it sound as much like a record as possible, even if it's not complete. When I get it to a point where I like it, I figure it's going to work all the way down the line. I find that one of the toughest things to learn—and I'm still guilty of this—is when you get it to a certain point to just stop.

How about effects when you track?

No, I might have a slap available or maybe a couple of reverbs.

What the hardest thing for you to record?

Probably acoustic bass. It's a very problematic thing to record solo. It doesn't record very well when you isolate it. That plus the fact that most guys don't play that well makes it more often than not a difficult instrument. I'd rather record a standup bass in an orchestra setting because it'll sound better and the player will probably be better, too.

Do you use an assistant?

I don't, but I go back and forth on this. Sometimes it would be great, but I don't have enough to do to keep somebody around. When I worked at Sunset, when you weren't seconding for someone else and you did your own session, they generally didn't give you a second, so you did it all yourself. Then when I worked at Amigo, you always did it yourself if it was an overdub date. So I spent an awful lot of time engineering by myself. I must admit that when I go somewhere else to record, I love to have somebody else there just to run Pro Tools so I can just worry about the sounds. That's kind of nice. On the other hand, it's pretty good to do it all yourself so you're aware of what's going on.

With a DAW, it's important to know how to be creative without it controlling the session. In my mind it's almost like it's tape, except I can see the waveform. If I want another track, I can easily make another track. If I want to move something, then I can move it. It's like everything that you want a tape machine to do, but it can't. If I want this vocal track to be on this track, okay, now it is. If I want to move it two frames, now it is.

CHAPTER 24

Mack

With a Who's Who list of credits such as Queen, Led Zeppelin, Deep Purple, the Rolling Stones, Black Sabbath, Electric Light Orchestra, Rory Gallagher, Sparks, Giorgio Moroder, Donna Summer, Billy Squier, and Extreme, the producer/engineer who goes simply by the name Mack has made his living making superstars sound great. Having recorded so many big hits that have become the fabric of our listening history, Mack's engineering approach is steeped in European Classical technique coupled with just the right amount of rock-and-roll attitude.

Do you have a philosophy about recording?

Yeah, to get the most "meat" or the biggest possible frequency spectrum from each instrument, because you only have that chance once. You can always screw the sound up later, after you've recorded it. [Laughs] Sure, you can say, "Okay, this requires a small-sounding piano," or something like that, but you're confining yourself, and you can't change your mind later.

That goes for multitrack recording, which in the old days, if you had to put a band down on an eight-track machine, then you'd record them on two tracks and have six left for overdubs. So you had to have a precise image of what the balance needed to be when you started recording.

I try to get the biggest, most pristine sound that I can so it can be bent in any direction later. Something tiny is really hard to make bigger.

Do you have a standard setup that you start from every time?

No. It's totally dependant upon the type of music. Different types require different setups. If it's something with a really fast tempo, you would mike things tighter than if it was a slow bluesy thing, which is better with some open space. I would pick the microphones and placement of the mics with that in mind.

How long does it take you to get things where you like them?

Probably anywhere from 20 minutes to an hour or so. I tend to work really fast. I don't want anything technical to get in the way of the music. You usually don't get a lot of time anyway, because people are frequently wandering around and anxious to play. You start a session, and people are sort of playing around. I like to use that time to get the whole setup done when the players are pretty uninhibited. When we start taking, I don't want to interfere with the creative process and go, "Can you give me that left tom again, and again, and again?"

That doesn't give you much time to experiment.

Not all that much, but I get that time back because it's inevitable that the band will go through a song and come to a passage where they want to change something. While they run over things again and again, that's when I use the time to check individual things out and experiment.

Do you use your overheads as the basic sound of the drums or just as cymbal mics?

The basic drum setup would be bass drum and overheads. My favorite would be B&Ks but I like to use Schoeps if it's not a hard drummer. Then I really know what the kit sounds like. Everything else is there to augment that sound.

Do you put the overheads over the drummer's head in an X/Y configuration?

No, as an A/B. I try to make sure that they're an equal distance from the snare. It does depend on the room. In a huge room I might use an X/Y thing, but the rooms for rock stuff are usually on the smaller side, so I use an A/B.

Are they pointing straight down or at the snare drum?

They're pointing directly at the snare drum.

What do you do with the kick?

I use two mics—a close one and one far away. I use something like a D 12 up close but a little off-axis, angled downward, depending upon if you have a front skin or no front skin. I use a U 47 for the far mic, about 3 feet away but very close to the floor.

I really like to use my own microphones because I know what they sound like. Even though a mic might have the same label, it still might sound different. So I like to use my own because I know what they do.

So if your main drum sound is coming from your overheads, what are you looking for from your other mics, because the sound will be different than if you were going for a close sound?

Actually, apart from the close kick mic, which is a dynamic, everything else that I use is a condenser. For example, I use 67s or 87s for the toms and something like a KM 84 or an AKG 224 for the hat. Probably what's really different, because I haven't seen anyone doing it except really old guys, is I put the snare drum mic exactly parallel to the drum.

Pointing at the side of the drum or pointing across the top?

No, pointing directly at the drum. That's a very old-fashioned, classical drum-recording technique.

Are you pointing it at the hole on the drum?

No, because that tends to cause the occasional wind noise.

How far away?

About 10 to 12 inches away. I like an AKG 414 in hypercardioid. Ideally, I would like to use every mic in omni because they sound best that way, but you can't always do that.

You have a very classical approach. Did you have a mentor?

I had a really old guy by the name of Martin Fouquet who ran Teldec in Berlin. He used to record all the symphonies on the label until about 1975 or so. He was the coolest guy ever. He came around when I was doing ELO or any other bigger-name rock group to check things out. He would say, "How did you do that?" and then say "This is the way we used to do it." That's where I got the snare drum thing. He would just throw these things in, and I would pick them up because they were different. At the time I didn't have much of a clue since I was only engineering for a couple of years, so I was happy to try anything. He taught me that there's nothing as dead as the side of a figure-8. The things I learned worked under nearly any circumstances, and you never had any screwy phase things happening.

You've done so many great guitar bands with great guitar players. What is your approach to electric guitar?

Just leave enough distance from the amp so you get a bit of room reflection to it. I used to do the thing where you crank the amp so it's noisy, then put on headphones and move the mic around until you find the sweet spot. I usually use two mics—which is sort of contrary to my beliefs because you get a lot of phase stuff—because you get a natural EQ if you move the second one around. If you can remember what the hiss sounded like when you had a good guitar sound, then half the battle is won.

One of my big things is not to use EQ, or to use as little as possible, and not to add any, but to find what's offensive and get rid of that as opposed to cranking other stuff to compensate.

The simplest thing is what translates. It's kind of like when you're frying eggs; the whole house immediately knows it. But if you have a French chef with a lot of ingredients, you know that somebody's cooking something up, but you don't know what it is.

So what mics do you use on guitar?

I like a KM 84 and an SM58. One is straight on-axis and one is off to the side.

Does it matter where the amp is in the room?

Yes, that matters very much. It's the same philosophy as with a monitor speaker. If you pull it away from the wall by a foot or two, then your whole system sounds different, and the same thing applies to guitar amps. Little things like tilting it a bit or changing it around. For some reason, amps are usually put in place by somebody like a roadie, and nobody ever moves them after that. But moving it around a little and angling it can really make the sound change a lot.

Do you usually have everyone playing together, trying to get keeper tracks?

I try to get everybody at the same time. I recently worked with Elton's band, and everyone was like, "Wow, he's letting us all play together in the same room. This is pretty cool."

You don't care about leakage then?

I do, but there's gobos and blankets to help out. But if it's a good band, then you do notice the difference. Stuff that has been layered in parts is just not the same. The little accelerations and decelerations are so together that it just makes things come to life. I'd rather leave the little flaws in or repair them later. You don't notice a lot of them anyway. It's the performance that counts.

I try to keep everyone pretty close so they can communicate outside the headphones. There's nothing worse than putting someone in a box out of his environment.

What do you do for bass?

My first thing is direct. I do record the amp just to have it, but unless it's really good I don't use it. I prefer small amps to big ones. The big stuff never really does it. For guitar amps, Marshalls are pretty standard, but with everything else, smaller is better.

What do you use for mic amps? Do you have a certain combination that you like for certain instruments?

I'm totally sold on Millennia's because I think that transient response needs to be the best that it can, and I like the cleanest possible sound to get it on tape. I don't want any extra ingredients. I just want it to sound on tape the way it sounds in the room.

Do you use them on everything?

I use as many as I can get my hands on. Neves are good, too. They have a certain sound that I can deal with. Martin Fouquet tried to explain it to me early. I told him that I didn't understand, and he told me to get a signal generator and put it on square wave. I recorded it on a piece of 1/4-inch tape and looked at the input signal as compared to the output signal. The in signal looked like a square wave, and the out signal looked like a sine wave. And he said, "That's your problem." The actual sound of something is mostly determined by the initial instant of the sound. If you cut that off, then it could be any instrument. Just try cutting the attacks off almost any instrument. You can't tell what it is any more. So that made a lot of sense to me, and I got really hooked on preserving the transients after that. With digital, it's actually easier to do that.

What do you usually use for piano?

My favorite mics are the Sennheiser shotgun mics, the MKH425, in X/Y. It's totally inappropriate, and I know that, but it really, really works. I never have to do anything other than put them in the piano.

Where do you place them—where the strings cross over?

A little lower than that. They're about 5 inches off the strings. It depends on how hard the piano player hits the keys and what range he's playing in. I was forced to do this one time because there was a really hot amp right next to the piano, and I had to get in really close. All of a sudden I realized, "Hey, this is better than anything I've ever done." So I stuck with it.

How do you record vocals?

I like 47s. Just for the heck of it, I once had 10 new 414s set up against one another with a willing singer, which is usually a problem because if you have too much of a Christmas tree setup, people get intimidated. It was unbelievable. It sounded like you were putting in various filters from one mic to the next. They were all supposed to be the same. I found that experience shocking, so from that point on I always carried one mic for vocals that was not used for anything else.

Do you use it for every vocalist?

Yes. I just got a new one that's a TLM 147, which was a fluke. I got it really cheap, but when we put it up against the other one, it was actually better.

Are you using the Millennia for vocals as well?

Always. I always use the HD3C Millennia with the built-in Apogee converter. I've had it for about eight years. I come straight out digitally to whatever I'm recording onto. I use a Manley Vari-Mu for a compressor.

Do you ever compress much while recording?

I do compress the bass with like an 1176 or the Manley by about 6 dB or so to keep it tight. The better the bass player, the less you need it. You want something that has a slow release time so it's not pumping.

You do some orchestral recording as well, don't you?

Yeah, that guy from Berlin got me in and told me to try anything I liked.

With a Decca tree?

Yes, that and the EMT hinges, which is such a great thing because it makes microphone placement so easy to adjust. You have one fixed point on the ceiling, and the other two are on these little motorized hinges that allow you to move them across any given space. They have them in Germany in most big studios and recording venues for classical music.

That's yet another eye-opener. After you place the mics where you think they should be and then are able to move them while you listen in the control room, you realize that the energy of an orchestra is entirely different from where you thought it was. The energy is up high and way farther back.

Are you using tape or going directly to the digital domain?

For rock things I use tape because you get much more apparent level by shaving off all the peaks on the tape. The actual noise of the tape is really not that much of a consideration if everything is cut at like +6. A really great thing that I rediscovered is the EMT 218, which is an ultra-fast analog limiter that EMT developed for the post office. If you record a piano digitally, your average level is probably at about –20 with spikes going to 0. If you put the EMT in front of it, you can lift your gain by 10 to 15 dB, and you don't hear it work. You set it and forget it, and you're really safe. It gets rid of all those annoying peaks. It works great for just about any music application, and it's an especially great thing for digital.

Do you use an assistant?

Actually, I don't care at all. I had an assistant for a while, but then I realized that I was doing everything myself anyway. I don't mind getting on my knees and pulling cables. By the time you tell somebody something, you could have done it yourself faster. Besides it gets you off your butt and moving. When you go out into the room, sometimes you go, "This sounds really good. Why does it sound so crappy where I am?" [Laughs] You also know where everything is and why everything is the way it is.

What's the hardest thing for you to record?

I don't like doing vocals with people who can't really sing. That's probably the most tedious thing for me. Also, I'm not that good of a liar. I have a hard time not being honest, especially when you know from the first take that a vocal is going nowhere.

But with people who can really sing, doing vocals is not that big a deal. With Freddie Mercury, you'd know that you'd be done within the hour. He'd do a few tracks that would be great and then just leave you to put it together.

When you were doing all the layered harmonies with Queen, were you doing that all on 24-track? Did you use a slave reel to put them together?

It was all 24-track. The drums had four or five tracks, and there'd be a bass track, a guitar track, and maybe a piano track. There might be a quick guitar overdub if Brian had a sound he liked. That left maybe 10 or 12 tracks available for vocals. So we'd do six vocal tracks and bounce them down until we ended up with a stereo pair, which was really nice because everything was done then.

Were those vocals all the same part, or did they sing in harmony with it doubled or tripled?

They would sing all unison for one part and we'd build up the harmonies and then bounce it. Once we had all the parts together, then we'd make a stereo pair out of that.

Was Freddie doing all the vocals?

No, they all did the vocals. That's what made the sound, because Brian was thin and piercing while Roger was like a raspy soul-type thing and Freddie was the body.

All the ELO stuff was done on 16-track, and there'd be a lot more bouncing going on. I came up with this idea of bouncing while you were recording. That way I'd save a generation. You always had to play it right, but that made them sound better as opposed to double-bouncing them.

The ELO stuff was always so squashed, even back then. But that's Jeff Lynne's sound, isn't it?

Yeah, he always liked any compressor that was used set to "stun," and he still does that today. And he didn't want any reverb or effects. You always had to sneak some stuff in to make it a little more roomy.

Al Schmitt

After 19 Grammys for Best Engineering and work on more than 150 gold and platinum records, Al Schmitt needs no introduction to anyone even remotely familiar with the recording industry. Indeed, his credit list is way too long to print here (but Henry Mancini, Steely Dan, George Benson, Toto, Natalie Cole, Quincy Jones, and Diana Krall are among those on it), but suffice it to say that Al's name is synonymous with the highest art that recording has to offer.

Do you use the same setup every time?

I usually start out with the same microphones. For instance, I know that I'm going to immediately start with a tube U 47 about 18 inches from the F-hole on an upright bass. That's basic for me, and I've been doing that for years. I might move it up a little so it picks up a little of the finger noise. Now if I have a problem with a guy's instrument where it doesn't respond well to that mic, then I'll change it, but that happens so seldom. Every once in a while I'll take another microphone and place it up higher on the fingerboard to pick up a little more of the fingering.

The same with the drums. There are times when I might change a snare mic or a kick mic, but normally I use a D 112 or a 47 FET on the kick and a 451 or 452 on the snare, and they seem to work for me. I'll use a Shure SM57 on the snare underneath, and I'll put that microphone out of phase. I also mike the toms with 414s, usually with the pad in, and the hat with a Schoeps or a B&K or even a 451.

What are you using for overheads?

I do vary that. It depends on the drummer and the sound of the cymbals, but I've been using M149s, Royer 121s, or 451s. I put them a little higher than the drummer's head.

Do you try to capture the whole kit or just the cymbals?

I try to set it up so I'm capturing a lot of the kit in there, which makes it a little bigger-sounding overall because you're getting some ambience.

What determines your mic selection?

It's usually the sound of the kit. I'll start out with the mics that I normally use and just go from there. If it's a jazz date, then I might use the Royers, and if it's more of a rock date, then I'll use something else.

How much experimentation do you do?

Very little now. Usually I have a drum sound in 15 minutes, so I don't have to do a lot. When you're working with the best guys in the world, their drums are usually tuned exactly the way they want and they sound great, so all you have to do is capture that sound. It's really pretty easy. And I work at the best studios where they have the best consoles and great microphones, so that helps.

I don't use any EQ when I record. I use the mics for EQ. I don't even use any compression. The only time I might use a little bit of compression is maybe on the kick, but for most jazz dates I don't.

How about mic preamps? Do you know what you're going to use? Do you experiment at all?

I know pretty much what I'm going to use. I have a rack of Neves that I'll use on the drums.

How do you handle leakage? Do you worry about it?

No, I don't. Actually leakage is one of your best friends because that's what makes things sometimes sound so much bigger. The only time leakage is a problem is if you're using a lot of crap mics. If you get a lot of leakage into them, it's going to sound like crap leakage. But if you're using some really good microphones and you get some leakage, it's usually good because it makes things sound bigger.

I try to set everybody, especially in the rhythm section, as close together as possible. I come from the school when I first started where there were no headphones. Everybody had to hear one another in the room, so I still set up everybody that way. Even though I'll isolate the drums, everybody will be so close that they can almost touch one another.

How did you learn your mic technique? Did you have a mentor?

My uncle had a recording studio in New York City when I grew up, so I've been around it all my life since I was 7. I learned a lot from him. He was a great engineer that did Caruso and the Andrews Sisters and those types of things, and I got to watch it all. And then when I first went to work in the studio, I was fortunate enough to have Tommy Dowd as a mentor, and then a guy by the name of Bob Dougherty, who was a genius at recording large orchestras. I learned so much from him about things like capturing the sound of French horns and woodwinds and so forth.

The major trick in all of this, and I learned it from both Tommy and Bob, was that you go out in the studio, stand next to the conductor, and listen to what's going on. Your job is to go in and capture exactly what he wants to hear out there. So my microphone techniques are still the same as they were 30 years ago.

Let's talk about when you do an orchestra. Are you a minimalist, mic-wise?

I try to use a few as possible. On some of the dates I'll just use the room mics up over the conductor's head. I'll have a couple of M 150s, or M 50s, or even M 149s set to omnidirectional. I'll have some spot mics out there, but lots of times I don't even use those. It works if you have a conductor who knows how to bring something like the celli up when it needs to be louder, so I'll just try to capture what he's hearing out there.

For violins I prefer the old Neumann U 67s. If I'm working on just violin overdubs, I'll use the 67s and keep them in the omni position. I like the way that mic sounds when it's open and not in cardioid. It's much warmer and more open this way, but it's not always possible to do that because if there's brass playing at the same time, then I'll just have to keep them in the cardioid position on the violins.

On violas, I like the Royer ribbon mics, the Neumann M 149s, or the 67s, depending on availability. On celli I usually use the Neumann KM 84s or M 149s if they're available. The mics on the violins are about 8 or 10 feet above them; the same is true for the violas. For the celli, the mics may be 3 or 4 feet above them.

On harp, I like the Schoeps, the Royer, or the Audio-Technica 4060. On the French horns, I use the old M 49s. I use the M 149s on the rest of the woodwinds.

Do you have a philosophy in your approach when you're recording?

I get with the arranger, find out exactly what he's trying to accomplish, make sure that the artist is happy, and get the best sound I can possibly get on everything. Then if there's something that's near and dear to the artist or arranger, I'll work toward pleasing them. Most of the time they're happy with what I get. Most of the guys I work with, like Tommy LiPuma or David Foster, nine times out of ten concentrate on the actual music and leave the sound up to me.

I'm always very early on dates. I want to make absolutely sure that everything is working. I don't click through mics. I talk into them to make sure that they sound right. Then during the session, I'm constantly out in the studio moving mics around until I get the sound that I'm happy with. I'll do this both between songs and every time there is a break.

What's the hardest thing for you to record?

Getting a great piano sound. You know, piano is a difficult instrument, and to get a great sound is probably one of the more difficult things for me. The human voice is another thing that's tough to get. Other than that, things are pretty simple.

The larger the orchestra, the easier it is to record. The more difficult things are the eight- and nine-piece things, but I've been doing it for so long that none of it is difficult any more.

What mics do you use on piano?

I've been using the M 149s along with these old Studer valve preamps on piano, so I'm pretty happy with it lately. I try to keep them up as far away from the hammers as I can inside the piano. Usually one captures the low end and the other the high end, and then I move them so it comes out as even as possible.

How about on vocals?

I try to keep the vocalist about 6 inches from the windscreen with the windscreen an inch or two from the mic, so the vocalist is anywhere from 7 to 10 inches from the microphone. That's usually a good place to start depending on the kind of sound you're looking for. If the vocalist is trying for a breathier quality, I'll move the mic up closer.

Chapter 25   Al Schmitt

The microphone I'll use generally depends on the voice, the song, where it's being recorded, and the acknowledged favorite mic of the vocalist. For example, Barbra Streisand has been using this particular Neumann M 49 since we did "The Way We Were." It matches her voice so well that she will not use anything else. This particular mic is a rental, but she knows the specific serial number, so that better be the right mic sitting up there when she's ready to record. That being said, I've done 12 song albums where I've used three different mics in the recording—one for up-tempo songs, one for medium tempo, and another on the ballads.

On Diana Krall and Natalie Cole I've been using a special 67 treated by Klaus Heine into a Martech preamp, then I go into a Summit compressor, where I pull about a dB or maybe two. I use very little compression, but I use it for the sound a lot. I also do a lot of hand compression as I record. I always have my hand on the vocal fader and ride the level to tape.

It sounds like you're a minimalist. You don't use much EQ or compression.

No, I use very little compression and very little EQ. I let the microphones do that.

What's your setup for horns?

I've been using a lot of 67s. On the trumpets I use a 67 with the pad in, and I keep them in omnidirectional. I get them back about 3 or 4 feet off the brass. On saxophones I've been using M 149s. I put the mic somewhere around the bell so you can pick up some of the fingering. For clarinets, the mic should be somewhere up near the fingerboard and never near the bell.

For flute, I usually use a U 67 positioned about 3 to 4 feet above the middle of the flute, but I may have to move it around a bit to find the sweet spot. If I want a tight sound, I may have the mic about 18 inches away. I may move it closer to the flautist's mouth or further down the fingerboard depending on the sound I'm trying to get. For flutes in a section, I usually have to get in a bit closer and more in front of the instrument.

How do you determine the best place in the studio to place the instruments?

I'm working at Capitol now, and I've worked here so much that I know it like the back of my hand, so I know exactly where to set things up to get the best sound. It's a given for me here. My setups stay pretty much the same. I try to keep the trumpets, the trombones, and the saxes as close as possible to one another so they feel like a big band. I try to use as much of the room as possible.

379

I want to make certain the musicians are as comfortable as they can be with their setup. That means that they have clear sightlines to each other and are able to see, hear, and talk to one another. This means having all the musicians as close together as possible. This facilitates better communication among them, and that, in turn, fosters better playing.

I start by setting members of the rhythm section up as close to each other as possible. To get a tight sound on the drums and to ensure no leaking into the brass' or strings' mics, I'll set the drums up in the drum booth. Then, I'll set the upright bass, the keyboard, and the guitar near the drum booth so they all will be able to see and even talk easily to each other.

If there's a vocalist, 90 percent of the time I'll set them up in a booth. Very few choose to record in the open room with the orchestra, although Frank Sinatra and Natalie Cole come to mind.

On a large orchestral piece or a score for a motion picture, I set up the other instruments in the room as if I were setting up for a symphony orchestra. The violins are placed to the left, the violas in the center, and to the right will be the celli and the basses. Behind the violas will be the woodwinds, and behind them the percussion, with French horns to left of center in the room, and the other brass to the right of center.

If I am doing a big band setup, I'll put the saxophones to the left in the room and the trombones and trumpets to the right center. For a pop record, I will usually overdub these instruments.

Jazz setups generally involve small rhythm sections, so eye contact is critical. It's important that the bass player sees the piano player's left hand. Ideally, they should all be close enough to almost be able to reach out and touch each other.

If you had only one mic to use, what would it be?

A 67. That's my favorite mic of all. I think it works well on anything. You can put it on a voice or an acoustic bass or an electric guitar, an acoustic guitar, or a saxophone solo, and it will work well. It's the jack of all trades and the one that works for me all the time.

Glossary

ADC   Analog-to-digital converter. This device converts the analog waveform into the form of digital 1s and 0s.

AIFF   Audio Interchange File Format (also known as *Apple Interchange File Format*) is the most used audio file format in the Apple Macintosh operating system.

API   Automated Process Incorporated; an American console manufacturer noted for their sonic qualities.

attack   The first part of a sound. On a compressor/limiter, a control that affects how that device will respond to the attack of a sound.

attenuation   A decrease in level.

automation   A system that memorizes and then plays back the position of all faders, mutes, and sometimes panning and EQ on a console or in a DAW.

bandwidth   The number of frequencies that a device will pass before the signal degrades. A human being can supposedly hear from 20 Hz to 20 kHz, so the bandwidth of the human ear is 20 Hz to 20 kHz.

bass management   A circuit that utilizes the subwoofer in a 5.1 system to provide bass extension for the five main speakers. The bass manager steers all frequencies below 80 Hz into the subwoofer along with the LFE source signal. *See LFE.*

bidirectional   A microphone with a figure-8 pickup pattern. *See Chapter 1.*

binaural   A stereo recording technique using a model of a human head with microphones placed where the ears would be. This type of recording provides exceptional reproduction using headphones, but does not translate well to speakers.

Blumlein   A stereo miking configuration utilizing two figure-8 microphones. *See Chapter 5.*

buss   A signal pathway.

capsule   The part of a microphone that contains the primary electronic pickup element. *See Chapter 1.*

cardioid   A microphone that has a heart-shaped pickup pattern. *See Chapter 1.*

chamber (reverb)   A method of creating artificial reverberation by sending a signal to a speaker in a tiled room that is picked up by several microphones placed in the room.

chorus   A type of signal processor in which a detuned copy is mixed with the original signal, which creates a fatter sound.

click   A metronome feed to the headphones to help the musicians play at the right tempo.

clip   To overload and cause distortion.

close-miking   Placing a mic close to an instrument in order to decrease the pickup of room reflections or other sound sources.

coincident pair   A pair of the same model microphones placed with their capsules as close together as possible. *See Chapter 5.*

color   To affect the timbral qualities of a sound.

comb filter   A distortion produced by combining an electronic or acoustic signal with a delayed copy of itself. The result is peaks and dips introduced into the frequency response. This is what happens when a signal is flanged. *See flanging.*

condenser   A microphone that uses two electrically charged plates (thereby creating an electronic component known as a *condenser*) as its basis of operation. *See Chapter 1.*

contractor   The person who hires the musicians for a session. Mostly used for orchestral sessions.

cue mix   The headphone mix sent to the musicians that differs from the one that the producer and engineer are listening to. *See Chapter 9.*

cut   To decrease, attenuate, or make less.

DAC   Digital-to-analog converter. This device converts digital 1s and 0s back to an analog waveform.

DAW   Digital Audio Workstation. A computer with the appropriate hardware and software needed to digitize and edit audio.

decay The time it takes for a signal to fall below audibility.

Decca Tree A microphone arrangement used primarily for orchestral recording that uses a spaced pair with a center mic connected to a custom stand and suspended over the conductor. *See Chapter 5.*

delay A type of signal processor that produces distinct repeats (echoes) of a signal.

DI Direct Injection (also known as a direct box); an impedance-matching device that bypasses the use of a microphone and makes it possible to connect an electric instrument, such as an electric guitar, directly into a console, mixer, or recorder. *See Chapter 3.*

diaphragm The element of a microphone moved by sound pressure. *See Chapter 1.*

digital domain When a signal source is digitized, or converted into a series of electronic pulses represented by 1s and 0s, the signal is then in the digital domain.

digitize To record from the analog to the digital domain.

direct To "go direct" means to bypass a microphone and connect the guitar, bass, keyboard, and other electronic instruments directly into a recording device.

direct box *See DI.*

directional A microphone that has most of its pickup pattern in one direction. *See Chapter 1.*

Dolby SR Dolby Spectral Recording; a noise-reduction process used with analog tape.

double To play or sing a track a second time. The inconsistencies between both tracks make the part sound bigger.

dynamic A dynamic microphone changes acoustic energy into electrical energy by the motion of a diaphragm through a magnetic field. *See Chapter 1.*

echo For older engineers this is another word for reverb. For newer engineers this is another word for delay.

edgy A sound with an abundance of midrange frequencies.

EMT 250 A digital reverb (the very first digital reverb, in fact) noted for its smooth sound.

EQ Equalizer, or to adjust the equalizers (tone controls) to affect the timbral balance of a sound.

equalizer A tone control that can vary in sophistication from very simple to very complex. *See parametric equalizer.*

exciter An outboard effects device that uses phase manipulation and harmonic distortion to produce high-frequency enhancement of a signal.

FET Field Effect Transistor; a solid state electronic component that has many of the same electronic qualities as a vacuum tube. Meant as a replacement for the vacuum tube, the FET has a much longer useful lifetime but lacks the sonic qualities.

figure-8 A microphone with a pickup pattern primarily from the front and rear. *See Chapter 1.*

FireWire A fast computer interface that uses what's known as a *peer-to-peer* configuration, where each device has some built-in intelligence that can determine the best way for data to transfer. Usually used when more than just a few tracks are to be recorded at the same time.

5.1 A speaker system that uses three speakers across the front and two stereo speakers in the rear, along with a subwoofer.

flam A sound source played slightly off-time with another.

flanging The process of mixing a copy of the signal back with itself, but gradually and randomly slowing the copy down to cause the sound to "whoosh" as if it were in a wind tunnel. This was originally done by holding a finger against a tape flange (the metal part that holds the tape on the reel), hence the name.

Fletcher-Munson Curves A set of measurements that describe how the frequency response of the ear changes at different sound pressure levels. For instance, we generally hear very high and very low frequencies much better as the overall sound pressure level is increased.

gobo A portable wall used to isolate one sound source from another.

groove The pulse of the song and how the instruments dynamically breathe with it.

ground A switch on some audio devices (mostly guitar amps and direct boxes) used to decrease hum.

hi-pass filter An electronic device that allows the high frequencies to pass while attenuating the low frequencies. Used to eliminate low-frequency artifacts such as hum and rumble.

impedance   The electronic measurement of the total electronic resistance to an audio signal.

input buffer   A temporary memory location that collects the bursts of digital information and sends it smoothly to the CPU in the computer.

I/O   The input/output of a device.

latency   Latency is a measure of the time it takes (in milliseconds) for your audio signal to pass through your system during the recording process. This delay is caused by the time it takes for your computer to receive, understand, process, and send the signal back to your outputs.

lavaliere   A small microphone (sometimes called a *tie tac* or *lav*) favored by broadcasters because of its unobtrusiveness. *See Chapter 1.*

layer   To make a larger, more complex sound picture by adding additional tracks via overdubbing.

leakage   Acoustic spill from a sound source other than the one intended for pickup.

Leslie   A speaker cabinet, usually used with a Hammond organ, that features rotating high- and low-frequency speakers.

LFE   Low Frequency Effects channel. This is a special channel of 5- to 120-Hz information primarily intended for special effects, such as explosions in movies. The LFE has an additional 10 dB of headroom in order to accommodate the required level.

line level   The normal operating signal level of most professional audio gear. The output of a microphone is boosted to line level by a preamplifier.

makeup gain   A control on a compressor/limiter that applies additional gain to the signal. This is required since the signal is automatically decreased when the compressor is working. Makeup gain "makes up" the gain and brings it back to where it was prior to being compressed.

Marshall cabinet   The most widely used guitar speaker cabinet. It contains four 12-inch speakers and is manufactured by Jim Marshall Amplifiers.

modulate   The process of adding a control voltage to a signal source in order to change its character. For example, modulating a short slap delay with a 0.5-Hz signal will produce chorusing. *See chorus.*

M-S   Mid/Side; a stereo microphone technique utilizing a directional and a figure-8 microphone. *See Chapter 5.*

mute	An on/off switch. To mute something would mean to turn it off.
near-field	The listening area where there is more direct than reflected sound.
Neve	An English console manufacturer noted for its sonic qualities.
non-coincident pair	A stereo miking technique in which two microphones are placed apart from one another at the approximate distance of your ears. *See Chapter 5.*
null	The point on the microphone pickup pattern where the pickup sensitivity is at its lowest.
off-axis	A sound source away from the primary pickup point of a microphone.
omnidirectional	A microphone that picks up sound equally from any direction. *See Chapter 1.*
on-axis	A sound source aimed at the primary pickup point of a microphone.
ORTF	Office de Radiodiffusion Télévision Française; a stereo-miking technique developed by the Office of French Radio and Television Broadcasting using two cardioid mics angled 110 degrees apart and spaced 7 inches (17 cm) apart horizontally. *See Chapter 5.*
overalls	In orchestral recording, the primary microphone arrangement (such as a Decca Tree).
overheads	The microphones placed above the head of a drummer used to pick up either the entire kit or just the cymbals. *See Chapters 7 and 8.*
pad	An electronic circuit that attenuates the signal (usually either 10 or 20 dB) in order to avoid overload.
parametric equalizer	A tone control in which the gain, frequency, and bandwidth are all variable.
phantom image	In a stereo system, if the signal is of equal strength in the left and right channels, the resultant sound appears to come from in between them. This is a phantom image.
phase meter	A dedicated meter that displays the relative phase of a stereo signal. *See Chapter 6.*
phase shift	The process during which some frequencies (usually those below 100 Hz) are slowed down ever so slightly as they pass through a device. This is usually exaggerated by excessive use of equalization and is highly undesirable.

plate (reverb) A method to create artificial reverberation using a large steel plate with a speaker and several transducers connected to it.

plug-in An add-on to a computer application that adds functionality to it. EQ, modulation, and reverb are examples of DAW plug-ins.

pop filter A piece of acoustic foam, placed either internally near the diaphragm or externally over the mic, designed to reduce plosives, or "pops." *See Chapter 1.*

preamplifier An electronic circuit that boosts the tiny output of a microphone to a level more easily used by the other electronic devices in the studio.

predelay A variable length of time before the onset of reverberation. Predelay is often used to separate the source from the reverberation so the source can be heard more clearly.

presence Accentuated upper midrange frequencies (anywhere from 5 to 10 kHz).

proximity effect The inherent low-frequency boost that occurs with a directional microphone as the signal source gets closer to it. *See Chapter 1.*

Pultec An equalizer sold during the '50s and '60s by Western Electric that is highly prized today for its smooth sound.

pumping When the level of a mix increases and then decreases noticeably. Pumping is caused by the improper setting of the attack and release times on a compressor.

punchy A description for a quality of sound that infers good reproduction of dynamics with a strong impact. Sometimes means emphasis in the 200-Hz and 5-kHz areas.

PZM Pressure-zone microphone. *See Chapter 1.*

Q Bandwidth of a filter or equalizer.

range On a gate or expander, a control that adjusts the amount of attenuation that will occur to the signal when the gate is closed.

ratio A parameter control on a compressor/limiter that determines how much compression or limiting will occur when the signal exceeds threshold.

recall A system that memorizes the position of all pots and switches on a console. The engineer must still physically reset the pots and switches back to their previous positions as indicated on a video monitor.

reference level   This is the sound pressure level at which a sound system is aligned.

release   The last part of a sound. On a compressor/limiter, a control that affects how that device will respond to the release of a sound.

resonant frequency   A particular frequency or band of frequencies that are accentuated, usually due to some extraneous acoustic, electronic, or mechanical factor.

return   Inputs on a recording console especially dedicated for effects devices such as reverbs and delays. The return inputs are usually not as sophisticated as normal channel inputs on a console.

reverb   A type of signal processor that reproduces the spatial sound of an environment (such as the sound of a closet or a locker room or the inside of an oil tanker).

Rhodes   An electronic piano designed by Harold Rhodes and marketed by Fender in the '60s and '70s.

ribbon   A microphone that utilizes a thin aluminum ribbon as the main pickup element. *See Chapter 1.*

roll-off   Usually another word for hi-pass filter, although it can refer to a low-pass filter as well.

rotor   The high-frequency rotating speaker of a Leslie tone cabinet.

scope   Short for *oscilloscope*, an electronic measurement device that produces a picture of the audio waveform.

sibilance   A rise in the frequency response in a vocal where there's an excessive amount of 5 kHz, resulting in the "S" sounds being overemphasized.

soundfield   The direct listening area.

SoundField   A B-format microphone for recording stereo or 5.1. *See Chapter 11.*

spaced pair   A stereo-miking technique in which the microphones are placed several feet apart. *See Chapter 5.*

SPL   Sound pressure level.

spot mic   A microphone used during orchestral recording to boost the level of an instrument or soloist.

stems   Mixes that have their major elements broken out separately for individual adjustment at a later time.

sub   Short for *subwoofer*.

subwoofer   A low-frequency speaker with a frequency response from about 25 Hz to 120 Hz.

sweetener   Another name for a spot mic.

synchronization   When two devices—usually storage devices such as tape machines, DAWs, or sequencers—are locked together with respect to time.

talkback   The communication link between the control room and the cue mix in the musicians' headphones allowing the producer or engineer to speak with the musicians.

threshold   The point at which an effect takes place. On a compressor/limiter, for instance, the Threshold control adjusts the point at which compression will take place.

timbre   Tonal color.

transformer   An electronic component that either matches or changes the impedance. Transformers are large, heavy, and expensive but are in part responsible for the desirable sound in vintage audio gear. *See Chapter 3.*

trim   A control that sets the gain of a device, usually referred to on a microphone preamplifier. *See Chapter 3.*

tube   Short for vacuum tube; an electronic component used as the primary amplification device in most vintage audio gear. Equipment utilizing vacuum tubes runs hot, is heavy, and has a short life, but has a desirable sound.

tunnel   A makeshift extension mounted to a bass drum used to isolate a microphone placed away from the drum head. *See Chapter 8.*

USB 2.0   A computer interface used by many DAW I/O boxes that uses a *master-slave* configuration that adds system overhead, which results in slower data flow.

windscreen   A device placed over a microphone to attenuate the noise cause by wind interference.

X/Y   A stereo-miking technique in which the microphone capsules are mounted as closely as possible while crossing at 90 degrees. *See Chapter 5.*

Index

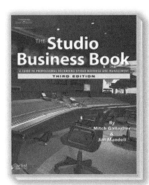
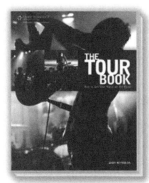

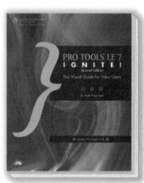

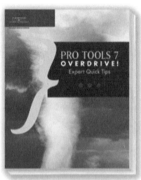